THE CRUSADES

THE CRUSADES

THE CRUSADES

Edited by RÉGINE PERNOUD

Translated by ENID McLEOD

CAPRICORN BOOKS

NEW YORK

CONTENTS

✤✤

PART THREE

CHRONOLOGICAL TABLE

✤✤

1095   Pope Urban II appeals at Clermont for First Crusade

1096   People's Crusade under Peter the Hermit begins and ends. Four expeditions of knights set out, under Godfrey of Bouillon; Raymond of Toulouse and Bishop Adhemar; Bohemond of Taranto and his nephew Tancred; Robert of Normandy, Robert of Flanders and Stephen of Blois

1097   They meet in Constantinople and cross the Bosphorus. Siege of Antioch begins

1098   Antioch taken

1099   Crusaders capture Jerusalem. Godfrey of Bouillon appointed "Advocate of Holy Sepulchre"

1100   On death of Godfrey, his brother Baldwin crowned King, thus creating Latin kingdom of Jerusalem

1118   Baldwin dies, succeeded by his brother, Baldwin II

1130   By this date, the three Frankish principalities: Antioch, founded by Bohemond of Taranto, Tripoli, by Raymond of Toulouse, and Edessa, by Baldwin I, are finally brought under suzerainty of Kingdom of Jerusalem to join in resisting attacks of Moslems under Zengi, atabeg of Mosul, lord of northern Syria

1144   Zengi captures Edessa. The kingdom in danger

1145   Pope Eugenius III launches appeal for Second Crusade. Saint Bernard preaches it. Louis VII of France takes the cross

1146   Conrad III, King of Germany, takes the cross. Zengi dies. His son, Nur ed-Din, Emir of Aleppo succeeds

1147   French and German armies set out independently. The Germans, fighting as they go, are heavily defeated at Dorylaeum, losing most of their troops. The French also lose many soldiers en route. Only small armies reach Jerusalem

1148   Louis VII, Conrad III and Baldwin III attack Damascus,
       their one useful ally against Nur ed-Din. Attack is
       routed and Conrad returns to Constantinople

1149   Louis VII returns to France and Crusade ends

1153   Franks and Nur ed-Din having become rivals for control
       of Egypt, Franks take Ascalon and block Nur ed-Din's
       passage thither

1154   Nur ed-Din conquers Damascus

1164   Nur ed-Din's armies, and Franks under King Amalric I,
       both fighting in Egypt in support of rival viziers, Dhirgam
       and Shawar

1169   Nur ed-Din's forces prevail. Saladin, nephew of his
       lieutenant Shirkuh, becomes vizier

1171   Saladin becomes Caliph and sole ruler of Egypt. His
       first aim, conquest of Nur ed-Din's Syrian possessions,
       leaving Frankish kingdom temporarily unmolested

1174   Nur ed-Din dies. Saladin conquers Damascus. Amalric I
       dies and is succeeded by Baldwin IV, aged 13 and a
       leper. Raymond of Tripoli acts as guardian of Latin
       kingdom

1184   Baldwin IV dies, leaving Raymond of Tripoli regent for
       Baldwin V, son of his sister Sybilla. Saladin conquers
       Aleppo, thus bringing Northern Syria and Egypt under
       one rule and imperilling Latin kingdom

1185   Raymond of Tripoli establishes four years' truce with
       Saladin

1186   Baldwin V dies. Sybilla's second husband, Guy of Lusig-
       nan, crowned King of Jerusalem. Reynald of Châtillon,
       lord of the Kerak of Moab, violates truce with Saladin,
       taking his sister prisoner. Saladin launches attack on
       Franks

1187   Saladin, victorious at Tiberias in May and Hattin in
       July, in October conquers Jerusalem which remains in
       Moslem hands for next forty years

1188   Conrad of Montferrat saves Tyre. He and Pope Innocent III
       appeal to West for Third Crusade to recover Jerusalem.
       Philip Augustus of France, Henry II of England and
       Emperor Frederick I (Barbarossa) of Germany all take
       the cross.

1189   Saladin besieges Acre. Henry II dies and Richard Cœur-de-Lion takes his place. Frederick I drowned on journey

1190 Philip Augustus and Richard meet at Vézelay and set out together

1191 Richard stops en route to conquer Cyprus, thus laying foundation of Latin kingdom of Cyprus. His arrival off Acre with reinforcements causes siege to be raised. Philip Augustus returns to France. Guy of Lusignan buys Cyprus from Richard and is crowned king of it. Richard's nephew, Henry of Champagne, succeeds as King of Jerusalem

1192 Richard leaves Holy Land, bringing Third Crusade to an end, with Jerusalem still in Saladin's hands. Latin kingdom now consists only of principalities of Antioch and Tripoli and some coastal towns

1193 Saladin dies and is ultimately succeeded by his brother, al-Adil

1200 Pope Innocent III launches Fourth Crusade

1202 Crusaders, led by Boniface of Montferrat, Baldwin IX of Flanders and other barons, gather in Venice to arrange transport by sea to Egypt, their first objective. There Alexius, son of deposed Byzantine Emperor Isaac Angelus, persuades them to help restore his father in Constantinople, on promise of help in crusade

1203 Isaac is restored to throne. While waiting for promised help, enmity arises between Franks and Greeks

1204 Crusaders take and sack Constantinople. Baldwin of Flanders is made first Latin Emperor of Constantinople and Fourth Crusade ends there

1212 The Children's Crusade

1215 Pope Innocent III, still desiring reconquest of Jerusalem, proclaims the Fifth Crusade, to begin in 1217 with Egypt as first objective

1218 Sultan al-Kamil succeeds al-Adil. Cardinal Pelagius, papal legate, replaces John of Brienne, King of Jerusalem, as leader of crusade

1219 Crusaders take Damietta

1220 Crusaders wait in Damietta for arrival of Emperor Frederick II (Hohenstaufen) who does not arrive

1221 Cardinal Pelagius decides to march on Cairo. Sultan al-Kamil offers generous peace terms, including surrender of most of kingdom of Jerusalem. Cardinal refuses terms.

battle is joined and Damietta lost again. The Crusaders
retreat and Fifth Crusade ends

1225   Emperor Frederick II, who had taken the cross in 1215
but never gone on crusade, marries Isabella, daughter of
John of Brienne and heiress of Jerusalem, and takes title
of King of Jerusalem

1227   Pope Gregory IX, doubting Emperor's intention to go on
crusade, excommunicates him

1228   Frederick II at last sets out for Holy Land (Sixth Crusade)

1229   By negotiations with Sultan he obtains treaty giving
Christians possession of Jerusalem for next fifteen years.
Frederick then enters Jerusalem and crowns himself.
Spends next fifteen years in strife with Frankish barons
in Cyprus and Holy Land and quarrels with papacy

1244   The truce having expired the Christians are defeated
at Gaza by the Mameluk Baibars, and forced to surrender
Jerusalem

1245   Pope Innocent IV preaches Seventh Crusade at Lyons,
and Saint Louis (Louis IX of France) takes the cross. The
Pope sends a mission to the Mongols of South Russia
and another to Persia, hoping to convert the khans of the
great Mongol Empire to Christianity and persuade them
to help in reconquest of Jerusalem from Islam

1248   Saint Louis leaves for the Crusade

1249   The Crusaders take Damietta, march on Cairo, but are
halted and forced to retreat. Saint Louis is captured, but
released on surrendering Damietta, and leaves Egypt

1250   Saint Louis arrives in Acre and spends next four years
striving to strengthen Frankish position in Holy Land.
Turanshah, the last of Saladin's line (the Ayubites) is
killed and succeeded by the first Mameluk (Turkish)
sultan

1253   Saint Louis sends a mission to the Mongols

1254   Saint Louis returns to France on the death of his mother
Blanche, the regent

1260   The Mameluk Baibars becomes Sultan of Egypt. The
Mongol Khan of Persia invades Syria and captures
Damascus. His army attacks the Mameluks of Egypt,
but is beaten by Baibars, who now resolves to drive the
Christians from Syria

1267   Saint Louis takes the cross a second time, to oppose Baibars
1268   Baibars captures Antioch
1270   Saint Louis begins Eighth Crusade by going to Tunis to try to convert the Emir, but falls ill and dies there
1274   Pope Gregory X preaches another crusade, without result
1277   Death of Baibars
1289   His successor, Qalawun, captures Tripoli
1291   Qalawun's son, al-Ashraf Khalil, captures Acre, the last Frankish possession, the Kingdom of Jerusalem comes to and end and the Franks leave Syria for good

Note.—The customary numbering of the Crusades has been followed in the above chronology, but it must be remembered that the Crusades were one continuous process, with fresh recruits setting out for the Holy Land all the time. There were many smaller expeditions which are not reckoned in the usual numbering.

THE NEAR EAST
AT THE TIME OF THE CRUSADES

INTRODUCTION

++

ANY ATTEMPT to understand the Crusades in the light of
such modern concepts as migrations or colonisations
is doomed to failure. They cannot even be entirely
explained by certain notions which belong to their own time,
such as the "holy war", the Moslem *jihâd*, which lies at the root
of the conquests of Islam. On the other hand, a study of them
brings out certain characteristics of feudal life, and makes it
easier to understand. For in this tremendous adventure, which
even in its own day was unique, the men of that epoch appear
in stronger relief, with their habits and their preoccupations,
than anywhere else, seen through the magnifying glass which the
"Way of the Cross", as they called it, was for them.

For it is to be noted that even the word "crusade" was never
used in the Middle Ages. It is a modern term. People at that time
spoke of the road to Jerusalem, the voyage, the journey, the
pilgrimage. This last term, the one most frequently used, is
extremely significant, for the crusades can only be explained if one
imagines a society in which practically everyone had faith. That
Christian faith which held sway both in the West and in the
Byzantine East was not imposed by any outside authority,
whether Pope or Emperor; it sprang from a conviction anchored
in the hearts of men: the faith was, in their view, the reason
which made life worth living. One can no more understand the
cathedrals than the crusades unless one first grasps this fact.

Pilgrimages were one of the manifestations of that ardent
faith. A pilgrimage was not for the Christians, as it was for the
Moslems, an act of ritual piety; nothing, either in the Scriptures
or the Liturgy, expressly recommends it. But it so profoundly
expresses what, to a Christian, is the meaning of life, the journeying towards another life; it realises in so concrete a way the first

duty imposed by the Gospels, the duty of casting off self to submit to something greater than self, that in the ages of faith it developed spontaneously. In addition there was the desire to see for oneself, to touch, to find oneself body and soul in the very place where Christ and, after Him, the saints, lived. And here we touch on a notion that was implanted very deep in the medieval Christian. Hardly had the right of the Church to declare herself in broad day been recognised, in the fourth century, than, according to a very probable tradition, the Empress Helena, mother of Constantine, set off for Palestine to institute a search there for all possible evidence of the life, death and resurrection of Christ. After her, the great initiator of pilgrimages to the Holy Land was Saint Jerome, who devoted his erudition as much to searching for the authentic text of the Bible as to establishing monasteries and hospitals in the Holy Land itself.

Later on, the impulse towards pilgrimages became less frequent, but did not die out completely; it was so rooted in custom that even the medieval serf, the pre-eminently static man whose whole existence was bound up with the land that could not be taken from him and that he could not leave, yet had the right to leave it to go on pilgrimage, without anyone's being able to oppose him. In England, as we know, a pilgrimage to Canterbury was still a normal event in Chaucer's day. And in France, as late as the time of Joan of Arc, it was still customary to take the pilgrim's staff, especially to go to Notre Dame at Le Puy which was then the most important sanctuary dedicated to the Virgin in the land of France.

It was in fact by a pilgrimage to Notre Dame at Le Puy that the epic of the Crusades began. An illustrious pilgrim was concerned: Pope Urban II, head of the Christian world. On August 15th, 1095, the Pontiff was celebrating a solemn Mass in the sanctuary that still exists in the ancient city of Auvergne, where he had been received by its Bishop, Adhemar of Monteil. There he launched his appeal not only to the pilgrims gathered there but to the whole Christian world, to go on a still greater pilgrimage, to drive the infidel from the Holy Land.

A glance at the map of the world as it was then known shows that it comprised two parts: much the larger part was Moslem; the smaller, Christian. Four hundred years earlier the Arabs, in the course of a crushing conquest, had annihilated the Christian parts of Syria, Egypt and North Africa, which had had such a prosperous past. In less than a century cities such as Alexandria, the seat since the beginning of the third century of one of the most brilliant schools of Christian thought, Hippo, which had had Saint Augustine as its bishop, and above all Antioch and Jerusalem, cradles of Christendom, were partly or utterly destroyed. The dates of the destruction of the great Christian basilicas exactly coincide with the stages of the Arab conquest; the assault of Islam was only checked under the walls of Constantinople in 718 and as far north as Poitiers in 732.

What had been the lot meanwhile of the Christians who had remained where they were, and of the pilgrims who persisted in visiting the holy places? It had varied in different places and times; sometimes agreements had been concluded, such as that between Charlemagne and the Caliph Harun al-Rashid, which made it easier and more pleasant, at other times these agreements were flouted in the cruellest and most deplorable way, as when the Caliph Hakim, at the beginning of the eleventh century (1009), for no apparent reason ordered the destruction of the Holy Sepulchre (rebuilt after the successive destructions of the Persians and the Arabs) and began to harry and massacre Christians and Jews everywhere.

Some idea of the stories circulating on the subject at that time, and of what the average Christian knew of the condition of the Holy Land then, can be obtained from the following account taken from a twelfth-century historian, William of Tyre:

"It happened that the people of Egypt left their own lands and conquered all the countries as far as Antioch. Among the other cities that were taken, the Holy City of Jerusalem fell into their power. Life continued there as well as it can in captivity until it happened, with Our Lord's approval and in order to test his people, that a false and cruel man became lord and Caliph of Egypt; he was called Hakim and his desire was to surpass all his ancestors in malice and cruelty. Such he was that even the people of his own law considered him mad with pride, rage and treachery. Among other perfidies he ordered the destruction of the holy Church of the Sepulchre of Jesus Christ, which had originally been built, at the command of the Emperor Constantine, by the Patriarch of Jerusalem called Maximus, and rebuilt by Modestus, another patriarch in the time of Heraclius.*

"From that time the situation of our people in Jerusalem began to be much more difficult and painful than it had been, for their hearts were full of sorrow at seeing the Church of the Resurrection of Our Lord thus destroyed. Then again they were grievously burdened with taxes, tolls and forced labour, in defiance of the customs and privileges they had obtained from the miscreant princes; and one thing that had never been interfered with, the celebration of their festivals, was now forbidden them. On the day known to be the most solemn feast of the Christians, they were made to work harder still and put to forced labour. They were forbidden to leave the doors of their houses, where they were kept shut up to prevent them from making any celebration. Even inside their houses they were neither in peace nor safety, for great stones were thrown at them, and dung, mud and all kinds of filth was thrown through the windows. If one of the Christians chanced to say a single word which displeased those unbelievers, he was immediately dragged off to prison and there lost a foot or a hand; or else he was led to a gibbet and all his goods were seized by the Caliph. Often, the miscreants took the sons and daughters of the Christians into their houses, and did their will with them; several young people were forced to deny their faith by means of blows or flattery. . . . The greater the injuries inflicted on them, the more firmly did the good Christians strive to keep their faith."

Throughout the whole of the eleventh century, pilgrimages were only carried out with the greatest possible difficulty. There are many stories of pilgrims being ransomed, imprisoned or tortured on their way to the Holy Land. One of the best known of these, no doubt because it concerned many thousands of pilgrims, is the story of the pilgrimage of Gunther, Bishop of Bamberg, in the course of which, when they were not far from Jerusalem, the pilgrims suffered a regular attack, which lasted for three days, from the Bedouins of the region.

Towards the middle of the century, the Turkish invasion suddenly occurred and strengthened still further the Moslem

* The Byzantine Emperor Heraclius, who had the Holy Sepulchre rebuilt after the destruction of Jerusalem by the Persians in 614.

power. The Turkish Seldjuks, who had adopted Islam, after they had imposed their authority on the Arab Caliph of Baghdad, started the holy war against the Christians again on their own account. At the battle of Manzikert, in 1071, they wiped out the Byzantine forces and seized Armenia. Their settling in Syria and Asia Minor once again affected the fate of the Christians in the East, and the safety of pilgrimage.

In view of such things the Crusaders can certainly not be considered merely as "aggressors" of the eastern Moslem world. The Christians of the time certainly had no feeling that they were indulging in an aggression. They believed that they were repairing an injustice, using violence only to reconquer what had been torn from them by violence, and bringing to an end the oppression endured by those populations which had remained Christian: above all, those Armenians who, in their capital of Ani where the population had been savagely massacred, had seen the great silver cross, which surmounted the cupola of their cathedral, torn off and melted down to serve as a doorstep for a mosque. If in our day the Moslem world nurses a grudge against the Crusades and still celebrates, after seven centuries, the anniversary of the capitivity of Saint Louis, one can understand that the Christians should have felt a similar grievance against the Moslems because of a conquest which had taken place four centuries earlier, but which recent events had just then aggravated. It must be remembered that as late as the tenth century, the Saracens were constantly pillaging the Mediterranean coasts where they possessed settled bases of which the last, La Garde-Freinet, only fell in 975. It was not until the beginning of the eleventh century that the monks of Saint-Victor in Marseilles were able to rebuild the walls of their monastery, and that life began again on the shores of the Mediterranean where, as an Arab historian put it, the Christians had not previously been able "to float a plank". Even at the close of the twelfth century, the threat of a Saracen invasion there was still feared. As for the holy cities of Palestine, it will be remembered that it was in 1009 that the Caliph Hakim caused the Holy Sepulchre to be destroyed, together with a great number of Christian churches. In the meantime Rome itself had not been safe from the Arab menace, and we know how the city was taken and its churches destroyed and profaned in 846. Finally, in a still more recent past, the city of Antioch, which had returned to the hands of the Byzantines, had been conquered by the Seldjuk Turks in 1084.

Then again, for a true understanding of what the reconquest of the Holy Land meant to an eleventh-century Christian, we have to recall everything that was contained at that time in the idea of a fief, meaning the piece of land to which you belong, which nourishes you, and over which you possess certain rights: this was the very nub of feudal society. For every Christian at that time, the Holy Land was the common fief of all Christendom; for that reason the Emperor Charlemagne, as the highest temporal authority, as soon as he had re-established the Empire, began to concern himself with its fate. No Christian could have resigned himself to thinking of it as definitely lost; and that was why, when pilgrimages thither had become difficult, the Pope, as the highest spiritual authority, urged the whole of Christendom to reconquer its fief, its Land. This was the impulse which gave birth to the First Crusade, and caused such a tremendous repercussion throughout the feudal world.

Later on, other interests and other motives, born partly of the desire to keep Palestine once it had been reconquered, caused this original impulse to be deflected, and turned the crusade into a struggle against the Islamic world. But in the eyes of the Pope and of such a man as Godfrey of Bouillon, the first aim was quite clear: Jerusalem must once again become a Christian fief. Certain historians have tried to define the "idea" behind the crusades, and to discover the origins of it. But before being an "idea", they were the outcome of an actual situation, and nothing could have been simpler or more concrete than the motive which gave rise to them. A Christian could no more disregard the fate of Jerusalem than a Moslem could the fate of Mecca.

Another cause for a change of impulse was that in the course of the thirteenth century the crusades became an institution and, like many other aspects of medieval civilisation, they assumed an almost juridical character, as recent research has underlined. For certain crusaders, the taking of the cross necessitated a legally authenticated deed, and their situation, both as regards their person and their possessions, was regularised by the civil and religious authorities. No doubt such an evolution was natural; but it made the Council of Clermont seem a long way off.

On the other hand, is it not a lesson for the modern world to notice, in the chronicles that follow, the reciprocal esteem between those adversaries who knew how to appreciate bravery wherever it was found, and were innocent of race prejudice?

"Who can be wise enough and learned enough," writes an anonymous chronicler* as early as the First crusade, "to make bold to describe the sagacity, the warlike gifts and the valiance of the Turks? The truth is that if they had always firmly kept the faith of Christ and of holy Christendom, without doubt none could be found to equal them in power, in courage and in the science of war.

"In truth, they themselves say they belong to the race of the Franks, and claim that none, save the Franks and themselves, has the right to call himself knight."

This is proof enough that the Westerner of that time considered the Arab his equal, that there was in his hostility no trace of contempt, and that he was able in perfect fairness to pay homage to the nobility of soul of such a man as Saladin.

One more remark: the narratives which follow are above all narratives of wars. Inevitably wars occupy more space in the chronicles than do periods of peace; and this is true in all epochs, since everyone knows that happy people have no history. But that must not lead to false conclusions concerning the respective lengths of the periods of war and peace. The historian Jean Richard, one of the greatest living specialists on the history of the Crusades, has reckoned that during the second, and most troubled, period of the existence of the Latin Kingdoms, there were eighty years of peace in the century 1192–1291. That compares very favourably with the seventeenth century in France, where there were only twenty-one years without important military operations, and seven years of complete peace.

Finally, it is often said that the Crusades were a failure. But were they entirely so? After the Crusades, exchanges between the East and West gradually diminished. From then on each part of the world lived its own life, Europe developing an original civilisation, while the East fed on its own substance, in a reciprocal ignorance that a few travellers and a few merchants' warehouses were not enough to dissipate: it was a far cry to the time when

* The author of the *Gesta Francorum*.

every preacher of the Crusade was bound to read the Koran. It is difficult not to feel that, at the time of the Crusades, even the struggles, however bloody and however appalling they may have been, nevertheless bore some fruit because they were waged between equals.

NOTE ON ORTHOGRAPHY OF NAMES

In this translation the version adopted for all proper names, whether of persons or places, is wherever possible that used by Steven Runciman in his *History of the Crusades*, as being the latest and best authority. The titles of the different works quoted in the list of chroniclers, etc., at the end of the book also follow his versions.

PART ONE

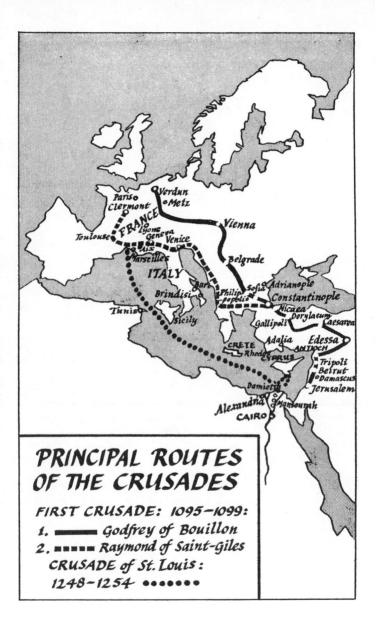

PRINCIPAL ROUTES
OF THE CRUSADES

FIRST CRUSADE: 1095–1099:
1. ━━━━━ Godfrey of Bouillon
2. ▪▪▪▪▪ Raymond of Saint-Giles
CRUSADE of St. Louis:
1248–1254 ••••••

THE COUNCIL OF CLERMONT

✠✠✠

*I*T WAS *at Clermont in Auvergne that Pope Urban II issued the appeal that was to shake the Christian West. A council had been convoked there, and according to custom, a certain number of barons were invited with the prelates to its last session, held on November 27th, 1095.*

We have taken from the account of one who was present at this ceremony, the chronicler Fulcher of Chartres, the text of the discourse which the Pope pronounced on that occasion, and which was to have such widespread and lasting repercussions.

Beloved Brethren,

Impelled by the exigencies of the time I, Urban, wearer by God's leave of the triple crown, pontiff of the whole world, have come here to you, servants of God, as a messenger to reveal to you the divine command.... You must with all speed take to your brethren in the East the help so often promised and so urgently needed. The Turks and the Arabs have attacked them and advanced into the territory of Romania [Byzantium] as far as that part of the Mediterranean known as the Sound of Saint-George [the Bosphorus]. And now, penetrating ever further into the land of those Christians, they have vanquished them seven times in battle, killing and taking captive a great number; they have destroyed the churches and ravaged the kingdom. If you do not now resist them they will extend their sway still further over the faithful servants of God.

For this reason I beseech and exhort you—and it is not I but God who beseeches and exhorts you as heralds of Christ—both poor and rich, to make haste to drive that vile breed from the regions inhabited by our bethren, and to bring timely aid to the worshippers of Christ. I speak to those here present, I will proclaim it to the absent, but it is Christ who commands. . . .

If those who go thither lose their lives on land or sea during the journey, or in battle against the pagans, their sins will at once be forgiven; I grant this through the power of God conferred on me. . . .

Let those who have hitherto been accustomed to fight wrongfully in private strife against the faithful, now combat the infidel and bring to a victorious end the war which should have been begun long since; let those who until now have been brigands become soldiers; . . . let those who once were mercenaries for sordid hire now win eternal rewards; let those who toiled to the detriment of both body and soul now strive for a double recompense. What can I say more? On one side there will be poor wretches, on the other the truly rich; there the enemies of God, here his friends. Pledge yourselves without delay; let the warriors put their affairs in order and collect what is needful for their expenditure; when the winter is over and spring come, let them set out with cheerful hearts to take the road under the guidance of the Lord.

Thus spoke the Pope,* and immediately all who heard him, feeling themselves inspired with holy zeal for this great enterprise, thought that nothing could be more glorious. A great number of those present forthwith declared that they would go, and promised to do their utmost to persuade those who were not at the assembly to follow them.

Baudri of Dol:

We saw the Bishop of Le Puy draw near to the Pope with a radiant face and, bending his knee, ask the Pope's leave to go, and his blessing. The Pope granted more; he ordained that all should obey the Bishop and that he should rule over the whole army. . . . While all this was happening there arrived unexpectedly messengers sent by Raymond of Saint-Giles, Count of Toulouse, to tell the Pope that the Count himself was coming and had decided to take the cross.

* Other chroniclers, who were not present, give different versions of the Pope's speech, but Fulcher of Chartres heard it himself.

Fulcher of Chartres:

What a sweet and wonderful sight it was for us to see all those shining crosses, whether of silk or gold or other stuff, that at the Pope's order the pilgrims, as soon as they had sworn to go, sewed on the shoulders of their cloaks, their cassocks or their tunics!

The news spread throughout Christendom. On the orders of Urban II messengers carried the decision he had taken at Clermont to the barons of the most distant domains and to the inhabitants of what he called his "good towns". Here for example is the letter which he sent in February 1096 to the rulers of Flanders and their subjects:*

Urban, Bishop, servant of the servants of God. . . .

We believe that you and your brethren have already heard from many sources that the fury of the barbarians has grievously laid waste and destroyed the churches of God in the East; what is more, that the Holy City of Christ, made illustrious by his Death and Resurrection, has been brought into intolerable bondage. . . . We have therefore visited the land of France . . . and urged the princes and subjects of that country to undertake the liberation of the churches of the East. . . . And at the Council of Auvergne we laid down that the sins of those who went should be remitted, and appointed our very dear son Adhemar, Bishop of Le Puy, as leader of this expedition and enterprise. . . . If God should inspire some among you to take this vow, let them know that they may with their followers join the departure that is to take place, with God's help, on the day of the Assumption of the Blessed Virgin. . . .

Other letters set out in detail the conditions necessary for taking the cross. In that which the Pope sent to the inhabitants of Bologna on September 19th, 1096, he wrote: "Clerks and monks may only take the cross if authorised by the bishop or the abbot to whom they are subordinate." *And here is a remark that illustrates medieval morality:* "Newly married men may not take the cross without their wives' consent."

* For the full text of this letter see *Archives de l'Orient Latin.* Paris 1881. Vol. I, p. 220.

PETER THE HERMIT AND THE
PEOPLE'S CRUSADE

✛✛✛

*T*HE POPE'S *appeal was transmitted not so much by letters and
writings as by word of mouth, for at that time this was the usual
way in which laws and ordinances were made known. For us a
law is first and foremost a written text, officially published; in feudal
times laws and rulings were at first "cried": the town-crier still occasionally found in our countryside is the humble descendant of the
public herald. In the same way a literary work was at that time not
meant to be written down but rather to be sung or declaimed—which
explains, it may be remarked in passing, why certain very important
works, above all the* Chanson de Roland, *have only come down
to us in a single manuscript. They were only written down as a reminder,
and the more widely a work was known, and consequently present
in everyone's memory, the less was the need felt to write it.*

*That is why wandering preachers played the chief part in making
the Crusade known. These preachers were to be met everywhere, not
only in churches and at Mass, but on the highway, at fairgrounds, at
cross-roads, in market-places, everywhere where people could gather
together. The most stirring and gifted of them nearly always found
enthusiastic listeners who followed them, forming round each of them
more or less compact groups which would grow larger as they went from
hamlet to hamlet, and village to village. One of these was Peter the
Hermit. Here he is, described by a witness, Guibert of Nogent:*

While the princes, who needed the services of all their retainers,
were slowly and tediously making their preparations for departure, the humble folk with no possessions, of whom there were a
great many, attached themselves to one called Peter the Hermit,
and obeyed him as a master, at least while they were in our

country. I have discovered that this man, who came, if I am not mistaken, from the town of Amiens, had at first lived a solitary life in the habit of a monk in some part or other of Northern Gaul. I do not know for what reason he left it, but thereafter he was to be seen wandering through large and small towns, preaching everywhere; the people crowded about him, overwhelming him with gifts and extolling his saintliness with such praises that I cannot remember similar honours ever having been paid to any other person. He showed great generosity in giving away everything that was given him. He brought back to their husbands women who had turned prostitute, adding gifts from himself at the same time, and with wonderful authority he restored peace and good understanding between those who had become estranged. In all that he did or said it seemed that there was something divine in him, so that people even went so far as to pull out hairs from his mule to keep them as relics; this I report not as having a basis of truth, but to satisfy the taste of the vulgar who like any extraordinary thing. Out of doors he wore a woollen tunic and over it a homespun cloak which came down to his heels. His arms and feet were bare, he ate no bread or hardly any, and lived on wine and fish.

To the general surprise a certain number of these humble folk, especially those who had attached themselves to Peter the Hermit, decided to go on the Crusade. To realise how unusual this was we have to remember that in the Middle Ages war was the affair of the nobles: the barons, the knights and those who had means enough to arm themselves, equip a horse, and engage squires and men. The peasant, the man of the people, did not fight. But now—and this was the singular thing about the First Crusade—suddenly the humble people turned out in force, so that they too could go and deliver Jerusalem and win back the tomb of Christ.

Guibert of Nogent:

The poor themselves were soon inflamed with so burning a zeal that none stopped to consider the slenderness of his means, nor whether it was wise for him to leave his house, his vines and his fields; and each set about selling the best things he had for a price much less than if he had found himself cast into the most cruel captivity, shut up in prison and forced to ransom himself as speedily as possible. At that time a general dearth prevailed, the rich themselves suffered from a shortage of grain and some of them had nothing, or almost nothing, with which to buy the many things they needed. . . .

But when Christ inspired those countless masses of men to go voluntarily into exile, the wealth of a great many of them was at once revealed, and what seemed very dear when everyone was at peace, was suddenly sold very cheap when all were preparing to undertake this journey. And since a great number of men were in a hurry to wind up their affairs, you saw such things as seven sheep being sold for five deniers,* an astonishing thing to hear, and one which may serve as a single example of the sudden and unexpected drop in all values. The scarcity of grain likewise became a source of wealth. . . .

Truly astonishing things were to be seen then, things which could not but provoke laughter; poor people shoeing their oxen as though they were horses, harnessing them to two-wheeled wagons on which they piled their scanty provisions and their small children, and which they led along behind them. And as soon as these little children saw a castle or a town they eagerly asked if that was the Jerusalem towards which they were journeying.

Whereas the appeals of the Apostolic See seemed to be particularly addressed to the French nation, there was hardly a people living according to the law of Christ that did not at once come out in force and, thinking they owed God the same allegiance as did the French, make every effort to join them and share in their perils. One saw the Scots, savages at home and unversed in the art of war, bare-legged, wearing cloaks of shaggy skins and carrying their sacks of provisions hanging from their shoulders, hastening in crowds from their mist-shrouded lands, and those whose arms would have been ridiculous, at least in comparison with ours, coming to offer us the help of their faith and their vows. I call God to witness that I have heard tell that in one of our seaports there arrived men from I know not what barbarian nation, who spoke a language so unknown that, unable to make themselves understood, they laid their fingers on one another in the form of a cross, to show by signs, in default of words, that they wanted to set out for the cause of the faith.

* The average price of a sheep varied from six deniers to twelve in the twelfth and thirteenth centuries.

*Nothing could curb the impatience of this crusade of the people.
The departure of the barons had been fixed for the month of August,
but as early as April 1096 a whole troop of humble folk took the road
in the wake of Peter the Hermit, or of little local leaders like the one
significantly called Walter Sans-Avoir. They were well received in
Germany, especially by the Jews, as Salomon Bar Simeon a contemporary Jewish chronicler relates.*

I have been told what happened at Trèves. . . . On the first day of
Easter [April 10th, 1096], a messenger from France came to our
friends. It was a Christian preacher called Petron who was a
monk, known as the prelate Peter. When he reached Trèves, on
his way to Jerusalem, accompanied by a great number of people,
he brought with him a letter from the Jews of France requesting
the Jews of all the places through which he should pass to supply
him with victuals because, being a monk and enjoying great
popularity, he would benefit Israel. The Jews therefore gave gifts
to Peter, who continued on his way with his companions.

*But as soon as it reached Germany the Crusade began to get slightly
out of hand:*

Orderic Vitalis:

On Easter Saturday Peter reached Cologne and spent the whole
week resting there, though at the same time he continued to
preach. . . . While he was staying in Cologne and increasing his
army by his preaching, the French, not willing to wait for him,
set off for Hungary under the leadership of Walter Sans-Avoir.

*But after both Peter and Walter had left, bloody scenes took place
which filled their contemporaries with horror. They were the work of
local Germans who, under the command of Emich de Leisinger, a
petty baron, half-brigand and half-nobleman, took advantage of the
Crusade to recruit gangs and commit misdeeds, particularly indulging in
horrible massacres of the Jews. Those brigands were in no way con-
nected with the Crusaders. The Jewish chroniclers of the time relate
these events.*

Salomon Bar Simeon:

On the Sabbath Day [May 3rd] enemies attacked the community in Speyer and killed eleven saintly persons.

Anonymous of Mainz-Darmstadt:

When Bishop Jean learnt of this he had the Jews [of Mainz] all brought to his house and saved them from the hands of their enemies. Thereafter he caused some of the murderers to be seized and by his order their hands were cut off.

Similar scenes took place later at Worms, always at the instigation of Emich and his followers, who took the Bishop's palace by storm.

Salomon Bar Simeon:

During the Whitsuntide feast [May 29th, 1096] terrible news reached Cologne. When the Jews learnt that the communities [of Speyer, Worms and Mainz] had been decimated, each Israelite took refuge with some Christian of his acquaintance and remained there during the two days of the Whitsuntide Feast. . . . On the third day a rumour spread that their enemies had attacked the Jews and that they were destroying their houses and stealing and pillaging their goods. They demolished the synagogue, dragging out the rolls of the Thora which they made mock of, scattering them about the streets. That same day, June 1st, they laid hold of Mose Isak just when he was leaving his house, and took him to a church. But he spat upon them and reviled them, so they put him to death. . . . A respected woman called Rebecca was also killed by them. . . . The other members of the community had taken refuge in the houses of the Christians, and remained there until the Bishop had them transported to his villages on June 3rd. He distributed them among seven localities belonging to him, in order to save their lives.

But though the Crusaders had had no share in these acts of brigandage, in the end a similar spirit of violence unfortunately seized them too. As they continued on their wearisome way across Europe, disorder and indiscipline began to invade that huge throng of men, women and children from every province, and soon from every country, that followed in the wake of Peter and his fellows. When they reached Hungary disaster threatened the enterprise, for the Crusaders began to pillage.

Guibert of Nogent:

When Peter the Hermit had gathered together an immense army, as much by the force of public opinion as by his preaching, he resolved to march across the land of the Hungarians. His un-ruly followers, finding all the necessities of life in great abundance in that country, soon began to commit outrageous excesses against the very gentle inhabitants of it. The custom in that land was for the grain harvest of several years to be piled up in the middle of the fields in heaps (which we at home call ricks), which rose up like towers. There were also to be found in that most fertile land meats of all sorts and many kinds of other foodstuffs; but not content with the kindness with which they were received, and urged on by unbelievable fury, it was not long before the foreigners began to trample underfoot the very inhabitants of the country; and while they, who were Christians, were kindly offering their fellow Christians all that they had to sell, the others, unable to restrain their unbridled passions, and forgetting the hospitality and benevolence of the Hungarians, made war on them without any kind of motive, hoping that they would not dare to attempt anything against them, or that it would be quite beyond their power to keep up any resistance. Impelled by a detestable rage they set fire to those public granaries of which I have spoken; they carried off the young girls and subjected them to every sort of violence; they dishonoured marriage by tearing wives from their husbands; they plucked out or singed the beards of their hosts; none thought any longer of buying the things he might need, but each lived by his wits, murdering and plundering, and all boasted with inconceivable effrontery that they would behave in the same way with the Turks. As they continued on their way they came to a certain castle, which they could not avoid since they were entering the country, where it stood, through a pass from which there was no escape either to right or left. They prepared to attack this castle with their customary arrogance, but at the moment when they were about to take possession of it they found themselves suddenly overwhelmed, although I am unable to say how this came about. Some perished by the sword, others were drowned in the waters of a river, others returned to France worn out with fatigue, penniless, in the most terrible state of want and, worse still, overcome with shame. . . .

Peter, in the meantime, finding himself unable either to restrain this unruly mob by his exhortations or to govern them as one would govern prisoners or slaves, escaped as best he could with a company of Germans and a few of our countrymen who remained with him, and arrived in the city of Constantinople towards the calends of August. He had been preceded by a considerable body of Italians, Ligurians, Lombards and other peoples from the lands beyond the Alps, who had resolved to await in that city the arrival of Peter and of the other leaders from France, since they did not feel themselves strong enough to be able to proceed beyond the provinces of Greece and venture against the Turks.

THE END OF THE PEOPLE'S CRUSADE

✤✤✤✤✤✤✤✤✤✤✤✤✤✤✤✤✤✤✤✤✤✤✤✤✤✤✤✤✤✤✤✤✤✤✤✤✤✤

*O*N AUGUST 1ST, *1096, Peter the Hermit reached the walls of Constantinople. The Emperor Alexius Comnenus and the whole population awaited with some apprehension the arrival of this mob whose unfortunate reputation had preceded it. When the Emperor's daughter Anna Comnena came later to write her memoirs, she referred to the impression made in the territory of Byzantium by that crowd of "Celts" following in the footsteps of the man she calls Little Peter as his contemporaries did.*

Anna Comnena:

These people, as though aflame with divine fire, flocked in crowds about Little Peter with their horses, their arms and their provisions. Every street swarmed with men whose faces were full of good humour and zeal for their righteous cause. Behind the Celtic warriors could be seen a countless throng of ordinary people with their wives and children, all with the red cross on their shoulders. They outnumbered the grains of sand on the sea-shore and the stars in the sky. They had rushed headlong like torrents from every country and invaded the Greek Empire through Dacia. . . . They made up a throng of men and women such as had never before been seen in the memory of man.

The Emperor had ordered certain generals to go and meet the crusaders peacefully and help them in every way to obtain supplies, but at the same time to keep a close eye on them as they went along and, if they should stray at all, to bring them back into line, by force if necessary but without definitely coming to blows.

Guibert of Nogent:

The Emperor issued an edict granting them all power to buy anything they liked that was on sale in the city. At the same time

he advised them not to cross that arm of the sea known as the
Sound of Saint-George [the Bosphorus] which separated them
from the lands inhabited by the Turks, saying that because of their
inferior numbers it would be dangerous for them to expose
themselves to meeting the numberless forces of the Turks.
However, neither the hospitality of the inhabitants of the Greek
provinces, nor even the affability of the Emperor, was able to
mollify the pilgrims; they behaved with the utmost insolence,
pulling down the palaces in the town, setting fire to public
buildings, removing the lead from the roofs of churches and
selling it afterwards to the Greeks. Alarmed by this excess of
effrontery the Emperor ordered them to cross the Sound of Saint
George without further delay.

*Nicomedia, on the shores of Asia Minor, was the most distant point
of the territories controlled by the Greeks. Beyond lay the domain of the
Turks, the "land of the pagans" as the chroniclers call it. It would
obviously have been prudent to await the arrival of the barons and not
to become involved in any warlike actions. But it was hardly to be
expected that this badly led rabble should listen to the voice of prudence.
The castle of Xerigordon, a small fortified place on the frontier, had
been abandoned by the Turks. The Christians occupied it.*

The anonymous author of "Gesta Francorum":

The Turks, learning that the Christians were occupying this
castle [Xerigordon] went to besiege it. There was a well before
the gate of the castle, and at the foot of its walls a spring of
water close to which Reynald [a section leader] had stationed
himself to lay an ambush for the Turks. They arrived on the day
of the Feast of Saint Michael, found Reynald and his companions
and massacred a great number of them, while the others took
refuge in the castle. The Turks straightway besieged it and cut off
its water supply. Our men suffered so much from thirst that they
opened the veins of their horses and donkeys to drink their blood;
others threw belts and rags into the latrines and squeezed the
liquid into their mouths; some urinated into the hand of a
companion and then drank; others dug up the damp earth and
then lay down and spread it over their chests, so great was their
burning thirst. The bishops and priests comforted our people
and urged them not to give up.

This adventure of the humble folk ended abruptly there. Soon after they had established themselves in the neighbourhood of Civetot, they were attacked by the Turks, who had no difficulty in massacring them to the last man. Peter the Hermit, feeling that matters had got beyond him, had returned to Constantinople, no doubt to ask for supplies or perhaps, as some have suggested, to beg the Emperor to send troops which might have helped to stiffen his followers. While he was gone the greater part of the troops who were entrenched in Civetot were foolish enough to make a sortie, leaving their wives and children behind. On October 21st the combatants were ambushed by the Turks, who thereafter had merely to massacre indiscriminately the women, old people and children who had remained in Civetot.

The year after this the chronicler Fulcher of Chartres, taking the road from Constantinople to Nicaea with the regular army, saw piles of bones, whitened by the sun, all along the gulf of Nicomedia, the only witness of that unfortunate popular adventure:

We crossed the sea known as the Sound of Saint George and hastened towards the town of Nicaea. Ever since the middle of May, Bohemond, Duke Godfrey, Count Raymond and the Count of Flanders had been besieging this town, which was occupied by the Turks, who are eastern pagans of great courage, and skilled archers. These barbarians came from Persia fifty years ago and, after crossing the Euphrates, they conquered the whole of Romania [Byzantium] as far as the town of Nicomedia. Scattered in the fields beyond that city we found a mass of severed heads and bones of slaughtered men. They were our countrymen who, being new to the art of using the cross-bow, or rather quite ignorant of it, had been massacred that same year by the Turks.

Anna Comnena:

These bones made up a huge pile, or rather mound or, better still, a hill or a high mountain of considerable size. Later on, when men of the same race as the massacred barbarians came to build walls of the sort that are used for a city, they put the bones of the dead in the interstices instead of mortar and thus made of that city as it were their tomb. This fortified place still exists in our day, surrounded by a rampart made of both stones and bones.

THE LEGEND OF PETER THE HERMIT

✤✤

*S*O ENDED *the People's Crusade. But the memory of it lived on with surprising vigour in the folklore and poetry of the time. Peter the Hermit, who had escaped from the disaster and later joined the regular armies, became, less than fifty years after his own unfortunate story, an epic hero. Furthermore, as the result of an extraordinary poetic transference, he came to be universally considered as the great hero of the First Crusade: and it was not long before the initiative of the movement that was to shape Europe and change the destinies of the Near East was attributed to him. Not only the* Chansons de Geste—Chanson de Jerusalem, Chanson d'Antioch, Chanson des Chétifs—*but even otherwise serious and well-documented historians like William of Tyre regarded him as the man responsible for the First Crusade. The figure of the Pope was completely obliterated by that of the humble, obscure hermit, the wandering preacher who personified the glorious rank and file that had got itself massacred to no purpose, but not without honour, and the tale of whose adventures seems to have moved their contemporaries more than the exploits of a Raymond of Saint-Giles or a Godfrey of Bouillon were to do thereafter.*

Here is an example of the kind of story that was told later on as being that of a first pilgrimage of Peter the Hermit to the Holy Land (this pilgrimage seems to have been entirely legendary) and of a vision which Our Lord granted him in the course of this pilgrimage:

William of Tyre:

It is related that pilgrims from many lands came to Jerusalem. Among others there was one called Peter, born in the diocese of Amiens in the kingdom of France. He had been a hermit in a wood and for that reason he was called Peterkin the Hermit. He was a little man and rather sickly, but he had a great heart, a clear mind and a good understanding, and he spoke very well.

When he reached the gate of Jerusalem he paid the tax and entered the city, where a wise and experienced Christian gave him lodging. . . . Peter questioned his host about the city and about the manner of life of the Christians subject to the unbelievers. His host, who had lived long in the city, told him tales that were grievous to hear, of former wanderings and how Christendom had for long been crushed and the Holy Places dishonoured. Peter himself, after living some time in the city to complete his pilgrimage, understood in what captivity the Christians were. He learnt that the patriarch of the city, who was called Simeon, was a very wise man, and most religious. Peter thought that he would go and talk with him and question him about the state of the Church, the clergy and the people. So he went to him. . . . The patriarch saw well from his words and countenance that he was a man who feared the Lord God, and he began at leisure to tell him of all the sufferings of Christendom. When Peter heard these words from the mouth of the prelate, he could not refrain from sighing deeply, and he wept great tears for pity, often asking the patriarch if, and how, a council could be held on this matter. The wise man answered him: "Brother Peter, if Our Lord wanted our sighs and tears and prayers He has had them in plenty. But we see clearly that our sins are not yet forgiven; we know well that we are still at fault when Our Lord, who is so just, keeps us in affliction still. But it is widely known in this country that the people beyond the mountains, known as the Franks of France, are very good Christians, and for that reason Our Lord keeps them to this day in great peace and power.

"If they would take pity on us, if they were to pray to Our Lord or take counsel to succour us, we have a sure hope that God would help us through them and send them His grace to end our difficulties; for you well see that we can have neither help nor counsel from the Greeks and from the Empire of Constantinople, who are our neighbours and like kinsmen to us, for they are all destroyed and have no power to defend their lands."

When Peter heard this he replied to him in this manner:

"What you have said of the land from which I come is true, for by the mercy of Jesus Christ faith in Our Lord is better preserved and kept there than in those other lands that I have traversed since I left my own country; and I am sure that if my countrymen knew the distress and servitude in which these unbelievers keep you, I could trust in our God and their good will to give advice and aid in this matter of yours. For this reason I will propose to you, if you think well of my plan, that you should without delay send to our lord the Apostle [the Pope] and to the Church of Rome, to the kings and princes and their kinsmen of the West, letters telling them that you are crying quarter, and that for the sake of God and the faith of Jesus Christ they should succour you in such a way as will honour God and profit their own souls. And since you are poor folk and cannot afford heavy expenses, if you think that I am worthy to bear so great a message for the love of Jesus Christ and the remission of my sins, I am willing to undertake this journey and carry out this task. I promise you that I will loyally make them understand how the matter stands, if Our Lord God leads me that far."

When the patriarch heard this he was full of joy and sent word to the greatest men of Christendom, both clerks and laymen, telling them of the kindness and the services that this wise man was offering them. They were glad of it and thanked him. And without delay they wrote the letter and gave it to Peter, sealed with their seal. . . .

At that time there occurred a thing which lifted up his heart and gave him courage to pursue his undertaking; for after he had been charged with their message, this good man went more often than hitherto to the Church of the Sepulchre. One evening after he had been to pray there he fell asleep on the paved floor of the church; and it seemed to him that Our Lord Jesus Christ appeared before him and gave him this message, saying to him: "Peter, make haste and rise and go without fear where you have decided, for I will be with you; for the time has come for my holy City to be cleansed and my people succoured."

Peter awoke and from thenceforth was more decided, and assured of his mission as though his task were already accomplished. He took the road, with the benediction of the patriarch. He went down to the sea and found a merchant ship; he went on board, had good wind and weather and soon arrived at Bari. Then he went overland to Rome where he found Pope Urban. He gave him greeting from the patriarch and the Christians of Syria, showed him their letter and told him loyally and wisely of the sorrows and suffering of Christendom in the Holy Land, speaking as one certain of the truth and knowing well how to tell it.

In these ways the adventure of the humble folk became magnified in the person of Peter the Hermit.

THE ARMY OF CHRISTENDOM

✤✤✤

WHILE THE people's expedition of Peter the Hermit was being massacred, what one might call the "regular army" of Christendom was making its preparations:

William of Tyre:

When winter with its frosts was over, as soon as the first signs of spring and of softer weather appeared, everyone made ready his horses, arms and baggage and all sent messages inviting each other to set forth. The time of departure of each one was carefully agreed in advance, as were also the meeting-places, and the routes which it would be both safest and easiest for them to take. It would in fact have been impossible for these thousands of travellers to find in every country all that was needful for them; it was therefore carefully arranged that the most notable princes should each separately lead the legions belonging to their suite and take different roads. So it was that their armies were not united until they were in the neighbourhood of Nicaea. It will be seen later that the chief commander with his troops passed through Hungary; that the Count of Toulouse and the Bishop of Le Puy took the route through Dalmatia, and the other princes that through Apulia; and that they all arrived in Constantinople by different roads and in different seasons.

Meanwhile, all made ready what they judged sufficient for so long a journey; they strove, as far as possible, to proportion their supplies to the length of the road, unaware that the ways of God do not lie in men's hands; for frail mortality knows not even what the next day has in store for it. In all the countless provinces of the West one saw not a single house idle. Whatever his domestic affairs, each one everywhere, according to his condition—here the father of the family, there the son, in some places even the whole household—was preparing to undertake the journey. Everywhere those who were to leave together kept sending letters urging each other to make haste, exhorting each other to admit of no delay, or reproaching each other sharply for the slightest tardiness. Those who had been appointed leaders of groups called together all the others: they tore themselves from the arms of their friends in the midst of sobs and sighs and, bidding each other an eternal farewell, after tender embraces, they separated at last.

There were in fact four principal expeditionary corps, each of which went its way separately. The Crusaders from the north, Lorrainers, Walloons, and those from Brabant, were grouped under a leader called Godfrey of Bouillon, of whom much was to be heard. They went by way of Hungary and followed, more or less closely, the route that the People's Crusade had taken. After crossing the Hungarian frontiers, they traversed Bulgaria and finally reached Constantinople towards Christmas 1096. The Crusaders from the south were led by Raymond of Saint-Giles, Count of Toulouse; they crossed Northern Italy, followed the coast of Dalmatia, crossed Albania and then took the antique Via Egnatia, through Salonika, Roussa [Keshan], and Rodosto, arriving in Constantinople on April 27th, 1097. Another group was that of the Normans of Sicily led by Bohemond of Taranto and his nephew Tancred, of whom we shall have occasion to speak later. They crossed the Adriatic, passed through Castoria and reached Constantinople on April 16th, 1097. Finally, a group of Frenchmen from the north and centre of France came in the train of Robert of Normandy, Robert of Flanders, and Stephen of Blois. This group crossed the Alps and passed through Italy.

But Christendom was at that time enduring a severe trial: a false pope, an antipope called Guibert, a creature of the Emperor, had risen against Pope Urban II. Guibert installed himself in the Vatican, while Urban took refuge in Lucca. The antipope was of course hostile to the Crusaders who had answered the call of the true Pope.

Fulcher of Chartres, who was one of those who went through Italy, tells us of the affronts put upon them by Guibert:

So we Western Franks traversed the whole of Gaul and took our way through Italy. When we reached Lucca we met, near that city, Urban, the successor of the apostles; and Robert the Norman, Count Stephen, and any others of us who wished to, conferred with him. After receiving his blessing we went on our way towards Rome, full of joy. On our entry into the basilica of the blessed Peter we found, standing in front of the altar, the followers of that rash pope, Guibert. Sword in hand, they were unlawfully carrying away the offerings that the faithful had laid on the altar. Others, climbing along the beams that formed the roof of the monastery, threw stones down on the place where we were humbly bowed in prayer. Indeed the moment they saw anyone devoted to Urban, they were consumed with a desire to cut his throat immediately. But there were some of Urban's men in a tower of this same monastery and out of faithfulness to this pontiff they guarded it vigilantly and resisted the opposing party as well as they could. We were pierced with sadness at seeing such great wickedness committed in such a place; but we could do no more than hope that the Lord would avenge it. From Rome, many of those who had come with us thus far, returned home in a cowardly manner, without waiting any longer. As for us, after crossing Campania and Apulia, we reached Bari, a sizeable town situated beside the sea. There, after praying to God in the church of Saint Nicholas, we went to the port, hoping to embark at once to cross the sea; but we lacked sailors, and luck was against us. The fact was that winter was now beginning and we were told that it would be a very dangerous time for us at sea. So Robert, Count of Normandy, found himself forced to retire into Calabria and spend the whole winter there. Nevertheless, Robert, Count of Flanders, embarked then with all his troops. But at that time, too, many of the poorest and least brave, fearing that misery awaited them, sold their bows, took up their staffs and returned to their homes. This desertion demeaned them in the eyes of God and in those of men, and covered them with lasting shame.

. . . In the year of Our Lord 1097, as soon as the month of March had brought back the spring, the Count of Normandy and Stephen Count of Blois, who had waited for favourable weather before embarking, went down to the sea-shore again. As soon as the fleet was ready, and the nones of April had come, on which date the holy feast of Easter fell that year, these two counts with all their men went on board their vessels in the port of Brindisi. How mysterious and incomprehensible are the judgments of God! Among all those vessels we saw one which, though not threatened by any unusual danger, was suddenly thrown up out of the high sea and shattered near the shore. Some four hundred people of both sexes perished by drowning; but very soon we had to sing to the Lord sweet praises because of them: for when those who had witnessed this shipwreck had picked up as many as they could of the corpses of those men, they found, on the shoulder-blades of some of them, marks in the form of a cross, stamped into their flesh. So it was the Lord's wish that these people, who had died beforehand in His service, should keep on their bodies, as a witness to their faith, the victorious sign that they had in life worn on their clothes.

Not everyone was so prompt to proclaim a miracle. When Fulcher's story reached the West, Guibert of Nogent, part of whose own story we have already quoted, protested vigorously:

Just as we were about to bring to an end this work which we had undertaken under the protection of the Creator of the world, we learnt that a certain Fulcher, a priest of Chartres, who had long been chaplain to Duke Baldwin at Edessa, had reported certain matters which had remained unknown to us, and others, though very few, in a different way from ours, these last always erroneously and in a coarse style like that of common writers. Although we had no wish to go over all he said, we have nevertheless felt obliged to challenge some of his stories and insert these corrections in our work. Since this man always writes in turgid language, using only words a foot and a half long, and watering down the feeble images of his style with colourless words, I resolved to take the events he reports just as they are and to set them down in the words that come naturally to my pen, instead of clothing them in pompous terms.

It is said, if I am not mistaken, that he reports, in the beginning of his little work, that some of those who undertook the journey to Jerusalem, hired ships and embarked on the sea which separates the inhabitants of Apulia from those of Epirus; and whether it was that they had entrusted themselves to a sea that they did not know, or whether they were too crowded in their ships, I know not, but whatever it was, it is certain that about six hundred men were lost on those ships, and that after they were drowned in the midst of the tempest and thrown up immediately on land by the rolling of the waves, the same sign of the cross was found on their shoulders as all of them had been accustomed to wear on their homespun cloaks or on their tunics. That this sacred seal could have been stamped on their skin by the power of God, to make their faith manifest, none of the faithful doubts for an instant; all the same anyone who writes these things should carefully examine whether they really happened as he reports. We know that, when the news of this expedition had gone abroad throughout all the Christian nations, and while it was being proclaimed in the whole Roman Empire that such an enterprise could only be accomplished by the will of Heaven, certain very obscure men and the least worthy of women too, made use of this pretended miracle for all sorts of tricks. One such, drawing a little of his blood, traced on his body lines in the shape of a cross and then showed them to all comers. Another pointed to a blemish in the pupil of his eye, that obscured his sight, as a divine oracle that had warned him to undertake this journey. Another used the juice of fresh fruit or any other kind of colouring matter to trace on some part of his body the shape of a cross; and just as people often paint the lower lids of their eyes, so they painted themselves green or red in order to exhibit themselves, as a result of this trick, as living witnesses of heavenly miracles. In this connection let the reader recall that abbot of whom I have already spoken, who made an incision in his fore-head with the help of a piece of iron, and who later, as I have said, became bishop of Caesarea in Palestine. I call God to witness that in Beauvais, where I was living at that time, I once saw, in the middle of the day, some clouds placed one in front of the other, slightly obliquely, in such a way that one might just have thought they looked like a crane or a stork, when suddenly thousands of voices were raised on all sides proclaiming that a cross had just appeared in the sky.

What I am going to say is very ridiculous, and yet the thing is based on evidence that one cannot scoff at. A little woman had undertaken the journey to Jerusalem; waddling along behind her, taught in I know not what new school, and acting in a way far beyond what her nature, deprived of reason, could admit, came a goose. Immediately the report spread with lightning speed through castles and cities that geese had been sent by God to conquer Jerusalem; and people would not even admit that it was this wretched woman who was leading the goose, insisting on the contrary that it was the goose who was leading her. This whole story was well put to the test at Cambrai where, hedged about with people on all sides, the woman walked into the church right up to the altar and the goose, always following in her footsteps, went in after her, without anyone driving it. Soon afterwards, so we heard, this goose died in Lorraine. She would have been much more sure of getting to Jerusalem if, on the eve of her departure, she had been given to her mistress to be eaten as a feast. My only reason for reporting all this detail, in this history whose object is to establish the truth, is to warn everyone to be careful not to lower the dignity of their quality as Christians by lightly adopting fables current among the people.

CONSTANTINOPLE: THE CLASH OF
THE TWO CHRISTIAN WORLDS

✛✛✛✛✛✛✛✛✛✛✛✛✛✛✛✛✛✛✛✛✛✛✛✛✛✛✛✛✛✛✛✛✛✛✛✛✛

*I*N CONSTANTINOPLE *meanwhile, things were on a war foot-
ing. The old Byzantine city had been designated as a general meeting place for all the crusaders. But the Emperor Alexius Comnenus
must have felt some anxiety on seeing the arrival of such an expedition.*

Anna Comnena:

The rumour that innumerable Frankish armies were approaching came to the Emperor's ears. He dreaded their arrival, for he
knew their impetuosity, their unstable and fickle character, and
indeed everything about the Celtic temperament and its inevitable
consequences. He knew how grasping the sight of riches made
them and that at the first opportunity they would violate their
treaties without scruple. That was something he had always
heard, and thoroughly proved. Yet far from being discouraged he
made all arrangements to be ready to fight if the need arose. The
reality proved to be much more serious and more terrible than
the rumour reported, for it was the entire Western world, all the
foreign nations inhabiting the land lying between the far shores of
the Adriatic and the pillars of Hercules—the whole lot was
emigrating en masse, complete families marching together and
crossing Europe from one end to the other on their way to Asia.

*To the Byzantines, who had behind them centuries of refined culture
and considered themselves the descendants and heirs of the Roman
Empire, these people from the barbarous regions whom Anna vaguely
calls Celts—rather as we are tempted to call Slavs all peoples east of the
Teutonic countries—could be nothing but simple brutes. In her chronicle
the Emperor's daughter exactly expresses the disdain that the Greeks*

felt for the Franks: a disdain mingled with a certain fear for, as she writes: "The Celtic people are very ardent and very fiery: once they rush headlong there is no stopping them." *Well may the inhabitants of Constantinople have dreaded being overrun by these hordes that they saw pouring over the shores of the Bosphorus.*

Anna Comnena:

The Celts arrived on the heels of each other with arms, horses and full military equipment. These men were so full of ardour and impetuosity that they swarmed over all the roads. The Celtic soldiers were accompanied by a multitude of unarmed people carrying palms and with crosses on their shoulders: they were women and children who had left their country. The sight of them was like waves flowing together from all directions. . . . They were as numerous as leaves and flowers in spring. . . . Willing though I am, I prefer not to give the names of the chiefs: I can no longer find the words, partly because I am incapable of articulating those barbarous sounds that are unpronounceable, and partly because I shrink before the number of them.

Now, these Franks who were arriving already had a bone to pick with the Byzantines. As they saw it, they were coming to the help of the whole of Christendom, in the East as well as in the West, and were going to reconquer the lands that the Emperor of Byzantium had been incapable of defending. One can judge their feelings then, on seeing themselves treated like common adventurers. This feeling was described by Raymond of Aguilers, a clerk in the train of the Count of Toulouse, Raymond of Saint-Giles:

We had reached Durazzo [February 1097] and found there letters from the Emperor speaking of peace, friendship and filial alliance. All that was mere words, for before and after that, to the right and left of us, the Turks, the Cumans, the Petchenegs* and the Bulgarians (all peoples more or less subject to Byzantium, and some in its pay) had not ceased to lay ambushes for us. . . . One day, when we were in the valley of Pelagonia [towards Ochrida], the Bishop of Le Puy [Adhemar of Monteil], had gone a little distance away from the camp to install his tent in comfort. He was attacked by some Petchenegs who pulled him off his mule,

* Turkish tribes.

stripped him and wounded him grievously in the head. . . . Having got through all these ambushes at last, we reached a castle called Bucinat [Vodena]. There, the Count learnt that in the passes of the mountain the Petchenegs were getting ready to attack our army; so he secretly went into ambush close by, and they fell upon them, killed a good number and put the rest to flight. All this time messages of peace were reaching us from the Emperor, but by his wiles, enemies were surrounding us on all sides. . . .

The Petcheneg horsemen were in fact squadrons equipped and maintained at the expense of the Emperor.

. . . We arrived next at a city called Roussa and here, as it was obvious that the inhabitants were preparing to overwhelm us with injuries, in the end our accustomed patience gave way, so much so that, having taken the men prisoner, we began to demolish the ramparts. We took much booty, the city surrendered to us and we entered it with our standards flying to the cry of "Toulouse!". This was the war-cry of the Count. . . . We reached another city, called Rodosto, where soldiers paid by the Emperor sought to take vengeance upon us, but we slew many of them and took a little booty. The legates whom we had sent before us to the Emperor arrived there. . . . On their word, and that of the Emperor's messengers, the Count left the army and going quickly ahead with a small escort went, unarmed, to see the Emperor. . . .

While he was gone, about April 20th, Raymond's army was attacked by the imperial troops.

. . . When the Count learnt of the death or the flight of his people, he thought himself betrayed and sent warning of an act of treason to the Emperor Alexius by the intermediary of some of the leaders of our army. . . .

Yet when Raymond of Saint-Giles arrived towards April 22nd in the suburbs of Constantinople he was received by Alexius Comnenus.

. . . The Count was received with many honours by the Emperor and his suite. The Emperor asked him to take the oath and swear homage as the other princes had done. The Count replied that he had not come so far to recognise another lord or to fight for anyone other than Him for Whom he had left his country and his possessions.

Indeed the only concern of Emperor Alexius Comnenus in the meantime had been to make each of the leaders who arrived in his territory swear fealty to him. A fine opportunity lay open to him which his Greek subtlety would not allow him to neglect: the lands that the Crusaders were going off to reconquer had formerly belonged to the Byzantine Empire; if they were reconquered, would they be given back to him? The surest means of obtaining them was to make the leaders of the expedition his vassals in advance. The Crusaders reacted in different ways to this pretension. The first of them to arrive, Hugh of Vermandois, made no difficulty about taking the oath. The others protested: did the Emperor think he was going to turn into mere mercenaries Crusaders who had risen up at the Pope's call to go and win back the Holy Sepulchre? But whether they liked it or not, they had to accept: Alexius, the "Basileus", had at his disposal the simplest and most efficacious means of bending the Crusaders to his will: to cut off their supplies. In the event it was Raymond of Saint-Giles who showed the greatest independence. The Emperor was never able to obtain from him any other oath than that he would "respect the life and honour of the Emperor". The others, on the advice of Bohemond of Taranto, ended by taking the oath of allegiance. This Bohemond, who had arrived at the last moment to join the Frankish Crusaders, had had long years of experience of Byzantine diplomacy and had already tried conclusions with the imperial armies. He was one of those Normans of Sicily, a mere handful of whom had been able to win Sicily, and Southern Italy too, from the Moslems, and had established themselves there, half condottieri and half feudal lords, feared as much for their guile as for their power. Anna Comnena, who spent no time on the description of the other Crusader chiefs, devoted herself with a combination of pleasure and retrospective fear to painting for us a portrait of Bohemond, who had clearly made a strong impression on her youth:

Never before had any man like him, either barbarian or Greek, been seen in the land of the Byzantines, for the sight of him created admiration, and his reputation, fear. To describe the appearance of this barbarian in detail, he was so tall that he overtopped the tallest by a cubit, and he was slender, not at all stout, with wide shoulders, a well-developed chest and strong arms. His person as a whole was neither gaunt nor corpulent, but in conformity, one might say, with the canon of Polycletus. He had strong hands and a firm stance, with a robust neck and build. . . . His skin was very white, but on his face the white was mingled with red. His hair was white and did not fall about his shoulders, like that of the other barbarians; this man in fact did not follow the craze for long hair, but wore his cut short at the ear. Was his beard red or some other colour? I could not say, for the razor had passed over it, leaving a surface as smooth as marble; yet it certainly seemed to be red. His blue eyes expressed both courage and dignity. He breathed freely through his nose and his nostrils, his chest was in keeping with his nostrils and his nostrils with his wide chest.

There was about this warrior a certain charm, though partly spoilt by something frightening that emanated from him. For the whole man, in every part of his person, alike in his stature and his glance, was hard and wild, and even his laugh made those about him shiver. Body and soul, he was so made that in him courage and love were barbed and both were turned towards war. His mind was supple, full of guile, and rich in subterfuge on all occasions. His words were always calculated and his replies ambiguous. Where fortune, eloquence and the other gifts of nature were concerned, this man, superior to such a degree, was surpassed only by my father.

Another of Anna Comnena's descriptions is that of a very significant scene which shows how opposed the Franks and Greeks were in everything, to begin with in education and culture:

When they were all gathered together, including Godfrey himself, and the oath had been taken by each Count, one noble had the audacity to sit in the chair of the Basileus himself. The Basileus suffered this without saying a word, for he had long known the arrogant nature of the Latins; but Count Baldwin intervened and, taking the other by the hand, made him get up, rebuking him sharply. "You should not act in this way," he said, "particularly because you have just promised vassalage to the Basileus. The Basileis are not in the habit of letting their subjects sit where they sit themselves; those who have become vassals of

His Majesty must also observe the customs of the country."
The man did not answer Baldwin but shot a furious look at the
Basileus and muttered a few words to himself in his own language:
"See what a boor he is! He alone sits when such valorous captains
remain standing near him." The movement of the lips of this
Latin did not escape the Basileus, who called one of his interpreters of the Latin tongue and asked him the meaning of the
words. When he learnt what the Latin had said, he made no
remark to him for the time being. . . .

When they were all taking leave of him, the Basileus called
the arrogant and impudent Latin and asked him who he was, from
what country and of what lineage: "I am a pure Frank," answered
the other, "and I belong to the nobility. And one thing I know is
that, at a cross-roads in the country where I was born, there is a
sanctuary founded long ago, where anyone who wishes to fight a
duel takes up his position for that purpose and there asks God to
help him while he is waiting for the man who will dare to
challenge him. I stayed for a long time at this cross-roads doing
nothing and waiting for an antagonist; but a bold enough man
never came." At these words the Basileus replied: "If you have
been looking for an occasion to fight without finding one, you
are now going to have your fill."

THE WAY OF THE CROSS

✠✠✠✠✠✠✠✠✠✠✠✠✠✠✠✠✠✠✠✠✠✠✠✠✠✠✠✠✠✠✠✠✠✠✠✠✠✠✠

*T*HERE WAS indeed to be no shortage of combats. But their outcome was not exactly what the Emperor hoped; he had, after all, from the military point of view, made only a trifling effort. It is true that a corps of Greek soldiers had joined the expedition, commanded by the general Taticius, who was known as "the man with the gold nose" because, his nose having been cut off in an earlier fight, some plastic surgeon of the time had, it was said, replaced it by a nose made of gold. But Anna Comnena herself says that this army joined the Crusaders as much to assist them in any emergency and forewarn them of dangers as "to take possession of any towns they might seize". Besides, Taticius and his troop soon deserted, before Antioch, when the position of the Crusaders began to be untenable.

One wonders, on the other hand, what the feelings of the Turks can have been when they learnt of the approach of the Frankish armies? The ordinary Moslem people must certainly have experienced some fear; but what of their chiefs, especially those Turkish Seldjuks who not long before had made the world tremble? In their eyes the issue of the adventure could hardly have been in doubt. How could this expeditionary corps, entering an unknown land with reduced forces brought from such a distance, resist very long against forces solidly established in the country, renowned for their courage and possessing all the strategic advantages? According to William of Tyre the sultan Suleiman had heartened his subjects, the inhabitants of Nicaea, by sending them the following letter, which clearly expressed the general feeling:

Have no fear of this great host. They have come from far distant lands where the sun sets, they are worn out by the length of the road and the labours they have endured, and have not even got horses able to bear the brunt of war; they cannot then, either in forces or in ardour, equal us who have but recently arrived here. Besides, you will remember how easily we have already triumphed over their numerous swarms, when in a single day we exterminated more than fifty thousand of them. Take heart then and fear nothing; tomorrow, before the seventh hour of the day, you will be completely consoled by seeing yourselves delivered from your enemies.

But the exploits of this multitude were to surprise the whole world. In the first place, in addition to their valiance and physical courage, the barons had a quality which we too may find surprising and which was called into play to the full on those foreign shores: the spirit of invention, the practical sense which enabled them to find the best possible solution for every difficulty: in other words the barons, as their skill in building confirmed later on, immediately showed themselves to be technicians. Evidence of this is the way in which, from the moment of their arrival in "pagan" lands, as soon as they had crossed the uncertain frontier of the Byzantine Empire, they planned and marked out roads.

"*Gesta Francorum*":

Duke Godfrey first reach Nicomedia with Tancred and all the others; they remained there three days.

When the Duke saw that there existed no road by which he could lead his troops as far as Nicaea, for the path that the first Crusaders had originally followed was insufficient for such a number of people, he sent on as an advance guard three thousand men, armed with hatchets and swords, whom he ordered to clear and widen this path to make it usable for our pilgrims as far as Nicaea. They opened a road through the passes of an immense mountain and as they went along they constructed crosses of iron and wood, which they placed on plinths, to guide our pilgrims. In this way we arrived close to Nicaea, which is the capital of all Romania [Byzantium], on the fourth day before the nones of May, and there set up camp.

Before the arrival of the Lord Bohemond there was such a shortage of bread amongst us that a single loaf sold for as much as 20 or 30 deniers.* But when the wise Bohemond arrived he had

* It is always difficult to establish equivalences of prices in the Middle Ages, but in comparison with the normal price of a sheep (six deniers) we can see that this sum is exorbitant. In Marseilles, at a time when the cost of living had risen appreciably (thirteenth century), a pound and a half of white bread could be bought for one denier.

an abundance of victuals sent by sea. Indeed it came by both land and sea at the same time, and great prosperity reigned in the army of Christ.

They needed all the wisdom at their command in Nicaea, the first town they reached. Nicaea stands on the shore of the Ascanian lake and as this connects with the Sea of Marmara the Turks were easily able to obtain supplies from that direction. They had conquered the city, which lay about 65 miles from Constantinople, in 1081, and it had constituted a permanent threat to the Byzantine Empire. It was powerfully fortified by an enclosing wall with 240 towers, dating from the fourth century. It was May 14th when the Crusaders came in sight of these walls; and it was June 19th before they took possession of them, after a brilliant display of their pioneering skill. They used all possible means to mine and sap the walls; and in addition to this, since the town, because of its situation, could only be blocked on one side, the other being open to the lake, the Crusaders thought out a strategem which their enemies could never have foreseen: they begged the Byzantine Emperor to give them a fleet and they brought this fleet overland right into the lake.

"*Gesta Francorum*":

On that very day, the Saturday after the Ascension of our Lord, one gate [of Nicaea] was occupied by the Count of Saint-Giles and the Bishop of Le Puy [the first to arrive within sight of the town]. The Count, at the head of his brave army, ran straight into the Turks, who were advancing towards us. Armed on every side with the sign of the cross, he charged them vigorously and vanquished them, and they took flight, leaving behind many dead. But new Turks came to the help of the first, in high spirits, and counting joyfully on certain victory, dragging with them ropes to send us bound into the Khorassan. Full of joy, they began to climb slowly down from the summit of a hill; but as they came, they remained where they were, their heads cut off by our men. And with the help of a catapult our soldiers hurled into the town the heads of the slain, so as to strike terror into the Turks.

Then the Count of Saint-Giles and the Bishop of Le Puy considered how best to mine a tower that stood in front of their tents. They chose some men to mine it, with crossbowmen and archers to protect them. They dug down to the very foundations of the wall, and then piled up the beams and the wood and set fire to them. That evening the tower collapsed, when night had already come; and because of the darkness there could be no fighting. During the course of the night the Turks rose hastily and repaired the wall so solidly that, when day came, it was impossible to do them any damage on that side.

Soon there arrived Robert, Count of Normandy, Count Stephen and many others, and then Roger of Barneville. Bohemond attacked the town on the nearest front; beside him was Tancred, then came Duke Godfrey, the Count of Flanders, supported by Robert of Normandy, then the Count of Saint-Giles and, near him, the Bishop of Le Puy. The blockade by land was such that none dared leave the town nor enter it: and on this occasion the whole army formed but a single corps. Who could enumerate this formidable army of Christ? No one, I think, had ever seen or could ever see a like number of such brilliant knights.

Fulcher of Chartres:

Then our leaders ordered the concentration of war-machines, such as battering rams, machines for sapping walls, wooden towers and perriers.* Arrows flew from the stretched bows, and stones were rained upon the enemy. They returned the attack with all their might, and we replied with all ours, combat for combat. With the help of the machines, and covered by our arms, we launched frequent assaults on the town; but the resistance of the wall was so strong that we were forced to stop. Many Turks and many Franks perished, pierced by the arrows or crushed by the stones.

It was grief enough to make one sigh with compassion to see the Turks, when they had succeeded by some means or other in slaughtering one of our men at the foot of the walls, throw down iron hooks from the heights to the wretched man while he was still alive, and then haul up his now lifeless body in its cuirass and drag it towards them while none of us dared or could tear their prey from them, and then strip the corpse and throw it over their wall.

"Gesta Francorum":

But on one side of the town there was an immense lake on which the Turks launched their ships and they could thus go out and return bringing fodder, wood and other commodities.

* A ballistic engine or cannon for discharging stones. (*O.E.D.*)

Albert of Aix:

It was decided in common council to send as far as the port of Civetot large troops of knights and foot-soldiers whose task would be to bring from the sea, overland on wagons, as far as the lake of Nicaea, the ships given in reply to our requests to the Lord Emperor. This they did in silence, at night, dragging those ships, of a weight and size to carry a hundred men, over seven miles of road, so as to set them in the water close to the shore by sunrise.

William of Tyre:

They pulled them up on to the shore. Then, having lashed three or four wagons together one after the other, according to the length of the ships, they placed these on top and in the space of one night dragged them as far as the lake, a distance of seven miles and more, with the help of cables and the combined efforts of men and horses. When they had arrived and been floated on the lake the Christian army felt inexpressible rapture; all the leaders hastened to the shores of the lake and sent for rowers skilled in the art of navigation; then they embarked men who were mighty in the exercise of arms and commendable for their courage, and all with complete confidence indulged in the hope that with God's help the town would soon fall into the power of the besiegers.

The enemy, meanwhile, seeing on the lake a greater number of ships than usual, were much astonished and at first wondered whether it was a convoy of provisions coming to their aid, or whether our men were taking up new positions. When they learnt that our soldiers had gone to seek these ships on the sea and had with much toil transported them overland, in order to launch them thence on the lake, they admired the skill and the strength which had conceived and carried out so extraordinary an undertaking.

Now that the town was surrounded on all sides, the princes resolved to send to the neighbouring forest in search of all the necessary material, and to construct as speedily as possible machines popularly called *scrophae*, used for the demolition of walls, ballistas, commonly called mangonels and other machines for hurling stones. At the same time they called the workmen together and urged on the completion of these labours to the limit of their power, so as to be able to attack the place with more success.

The fortress of Nicaea would certainly have been captured. But at the moment when the Crusaders were going to launch the decisive assault, to their astonishment they saw the imperial Byzantine standard floating from the tops of the towers. What had happened was that, unbeknown to the Crusaders, an agreement had been reached with the Turks, (Anna Comnena, the Emperor's daughter, admits it) whereby they would hand back the town to the Emperor without further combat in return for which the lives of the inhabitants of Nicaea would be saved. This agreement obviously baulked the Crusaders of their victory; having vanquished by their arms, they were vanquished by the imperial diplomacy. It is understandable that as a result of this they felt a certain rancour against the Byzantines. Thanks to this event, the Emperor reconquered the coastal provinces, Mysia, Ionia and Lydia, while the Frankish barons continued on their way.

It was not long before they met the Turkish squadrons in open country. On June 29th, 1097, they noticed some patrols on the outskirts of their camp, and the next day the battle took place: the first pitched battle against an enemy of whose tactics they were ignorant, and of greatly superior strength. After weakening for a time, disconcerted in particular by the mounted archers who surrounded their ranks, the Crusaders re-formed and finally obtained the victory, but not without heavy losses. This was the battle of Dorylaeum, which marked a decisive step in that, for the first time, the Turks were vanquished on their own territory.

Fulcher of Chartres:

We had barely been marching for two days when we learnt that the Turks were laying ambushes and preparing to fight us in the plains that they thought we should have to cross. This news in no way lessened our boldness.

At the second hour of the day, our scouts saw the advance-guard of the Turks approaching. As soon as we learnt this we immediately set up our tents near a certain place filled with reeds so that, quickly dropping our packs, saddles and baggage there, we could the sooner be ready to come to grips with them. We had hardly completed these preparations when the Turks appeared, at their head their prince and emir Suleiman, who wielded power over the town of Nicaea as well as Romania.

Around him were gathered Turks from the most eastern countries, who at his orders had marched for thirty days and even more, in order to bring him help. With him there were also many emirs, such as Amurath, Miriath, Omar, Amirai, Lachin, Caradig, Boldagis and others. All these men together formed a mass of three hundred and sixty thousand combatants, all on horseback and armed with bows, as their custom is. On our side there were both foot-soldiers and mounted men; but for two days Duke Godfrey, Count Raymond and Hugh the Great had not been with us; misled by a road which branched in two, they had without knowing it got separated, with a very large body of troops, from the main army. For us this was an irreparable misfortune, both because it brought about the death of a large number of our people, and because it prevented us from taking prisoner or killing many Turks; but as our leaders were late in receiving the messengers we sent them, neither could they come to our aid until it was too late. Meanwhile the Turks, full of daring, and uttering frightful cries, began to loose a shower of arrows violently upon us. Taken by surprise at finding ourselves struck by such a swift succession of blows, which killed or wounded a mass of our men, we fled, not surprisingly considering that that kind of fighting was unknown to us.

William of Tyre:

The moment they arrived the Turks let fly their arrows at us so thickly that they darkened the air more than rain or hail, and many of our men were wounded by them. And when the first rank had quite emptied their quivers and shot all their arrows, the second, in which there were still more horsemen, came on and began to shoot more densely than one could believe.

The Turkish squadrons at once flung themselves upon our army, and loosed such a quantity of arrows that you would have thought hail was falling from the air; hardly had a first cloud of them fallen, describing an arc, than it was followed by a second, not less dense; and those who had not been wounded the first time could hardly escape being so a moment after. This kind of fighting was completely unknown to our soldiers; and being quite unused to it, and seeing their horses fall without being able to save themselves, they were unable to sustain it calmly. Struck unawares by wounds that were often mortal, and which they could not escape, they strove to repel their enemies by hurling themselves upon them and smiting them with sword or lance. But they, unable in their turn to bear this sort of attack, at once split up to avoid the first shock and so, finding no one in front of them, and cheated of their hopes, our soldiers were forced to fall back on the main body of the army. While they were thus withdrawing without having succeeded in their attempt, the Turks promptly rallied and began once more to shoot their arrows, which fell among our ranks like rain, leaving hardly anyone without a mortal wound. Our men resisted as best they could, protected by their helmets. . . .

Fulcher of Chartres:

Already from the other side of the reed-covered marsh, dense squadrons of Turks, swooping down at full speed on our tents, pillaged our baggage and massacred our people. But all of a sudden, and thanks to the will of God, the advance-guard of Hugh the Great, Count Raymond and Duke Godfrey arrived from the rear on the scene of this appalling disaster. As we for our part were, in our flight, falling back on our tents, those of the enemy who had penetrated in among our baggage retired in haste, believing that we were returning to attack them; but what they took for boldness and valour in us, they would have been only too justified in attributing to the effect of fear. What more can I add? Huddled against each other like sheep shut into a pen, in the grip of fear, and trembling, we were surrounded by the Turks on all sides, and dared by no means advance in any direction at all. . . .

The air resounded on the one hand with the piercing cries of our men, women and children, and on the other side with those of the pagans rushing upon us. Already, having lost all hope of saving our lives, we were proclaiming ourselves sinners and criminals and piously imploring the divine pity. Among the pilgrims was our lord the Bishop of Le Puy and four other prelates, as well as many priests, all clothed in white, humbly begging the Lord to weaken the strength of our enemies and to shed upon us the gifts of his mercy; all sang and prayed with tears, and a crowd of our people, fearing to die soon, threw themselves down at their feet and confessed their sins. Meanwhile our leaders, Robert, Count of Normandy, Stephen of Blois and

Bohemond Count of Flanders, were striving with all their might to repel and often even to attack the Turks, who on their side were boldly swooping down on our men. But fortunately the Lord, appeased by our supplications . . . little by little restored our courage and more and more weakened that of the Turks. And indeed, seeing our companions hastening from the rear to our aid, we praised God, plucked up our former courage and, forming ourselves again into troops and cohorts, tried to hold our own against the enemy.

As I have said, the Turks kept us herded closely together from the first hour of the day until the sixth; but little by little we revived and our ranks were reinforced by the arrival of our companions; the heavenly grace miraculously revealed itself in our favour and we saw all the infidels turn their backs and take flight, as though carried away by a sudden movement. Then, yelling war-cries behind them, we pursued them across mountains and valleys and did not stop chasing them before us until our advance-guard had reached their camp. There, part of our men loaded the baggage and even the tents of the enemy on a throng of horses and camels that they had abandoned in their fear, while the remainder continued in hot pursuit of the Turks until nightfall. As our horses were worn out with hunger and fatigue we could take but few prisoners; but what was a great miracle of God was that these pagans did not stop in their flight either on the next day nor even on the third day, although the Lord alone pursued them.

ACROSS THE DESERTS

✝✝✝

O N J U L Y 14T H, 1097, *the Crusaders took the road again, a painful road, during which it proved difficult to obtain supplies.*

Anonymi Gesta Francorum:

And we pursued them across deserts and an uninhabitable land without water which we had difficulty in coming through alive. Hunger and thirst beset us everywhere and we had hardly anything left to eat except thorns, which we pulled up and rubbed in our hands: such was the food on which we wretchedly lived. Most of our horses died there, so that many of our knights had to go on foot; because of our lack of mounts we used oxen as battle-steeds and, in our extreme need, goats, sheep and dogs to carry our baggage.

The Crusaders discover a manna in this desert: sugar cane.

Fulcher of Chartres:

When they reached the interior of the land of the Saracens, they could obtain neither bread nor any kind of food from the odious inhabitants of this country; no one offered to sell or give them any; and so after they had gradually consumed all their provisions, many of them were cruelly tortured by hunger. As for the horses and beasts of burden, they suffered dumbly for lack of nourishment, for they were marching without eating. But in the land under cultivation there were to be found certain ripe plants like reeds which were called canna mellis [sugar canes], a name composed of two words, canna [cane] and mel [*miel,* honey]. I believe that is the reason why what is skilfully extracted from these plants is called wild honey. We devoured them ravenously because of their sweet taste; but they were only a feeble resource for us: hunger, cold, torrents of rain—all these evils and many others we had to bear for the love of God. For want of bread a great many of our men ate the horses, donkeys and camels. The crowning misery was that we often had to endure biting cold and incessant rain, without even being able to dry ourselves in the rays of the sun after having been soaked by the rain, which fell continuously from the skies for four or five days. I saw many of our people perish from these cold showers, for lack of tents where they could shelter. Yes, I, Fulcher, who was with this army, saw in a single day many individuals of both sexes and a great number of animals die benumbed by these rains.

However, one circumstance aided the advance of the Crusaders; the existence ready to hand of a "fifth column" among the population. The Armenians and Christians of Asia Minor and Syria were naturally only too glad to welcome the Christians. They were thus able to advance into the region of Iconium [Konya], and penetrate into Heraclea. They then split into two groups, one of which headed south in the direction of Cilicia and took Tarsus, while the other pursued its way towards Caesarea of Cappadocia.

Fulcher of Chartres:

By good fortune we reached Caesarea of Cappadocia. Leaving Cappadocia, we arrived at a magnificent and very rich city which, shortly before our arrival, the Turks had besieged for three weeks [Placentia]. But they had not gained their end and, on our arrival, the city immediately surrendered to us with great joy. A knight named Peter of Aulps begged all our lords to hand it over to him so that, in all faithfulness to God and the Holy Sepulchre, he might defend it from the Emperor and his lords. They granted it to him with a very good grace. The following night Bohemond learnt that the Turks, who had besieged that city, were often to be found in front of us. So, with the help of his knights alone, he made ready to drive them completely away. But he could not encounter them.

Next we reached a city called Coxon [Güksün, on the southern slopes of the Taurus] which possessed the abundant resources we needed. The Christians inhabiting this town [probably Armenians] surrendered immediately. We stayed there for three days in good conditions and our men were able to recuperate completely.

After Caesarea the main army travelled south-east and found itself up against the difficulties of the terrain when it came to crossing the passes of the Anti-Taurus.

"*Gesta Francorum*":

We penetrated into the diabolic mountain [Ouzoun-Tozair-Dagh], that was so lofty and narrow that none dared go before the others on the path along its flank. The horses fell headlong into the ravines and each pack animal dragged another down. On every side the knights gave way to despair and beat their breasts for sorrow and sadness, wondering what to do with themselves and their arms. They sold their shields and their good coats of mail with their helmets for a sum of three to five deniers, or for no matter what. Those who had not been able to sell them cast them away for nothing and continued on their road.

When we had left this accursed mountain behind we reached a town called Marash. The inhabitants came out joyfully to meet us, bringing us copious provisions, and we stayed in the midst of that abundance waiting for the arrival of the Lord Bohemond. At last our knights reached the valley where lies the royal city of Antioch, capital of all Syria.

THE SIEGE OF ANTIOCH

✚✚✚

*O*N OCTOBER 21ST, *1097, the first corps of Crusaders arrived before Antioch. The chronicler Albert of Aix describes them thus:* "The Crusaders, in all the splendour of their shields of gold, green, red and other colours, unfurling banners of gold and purple, marched towards Antioch. They were mounted on war-horses and wore glittering helmets and bucklers."

The passage might be taken from a medieval romance, but it is the work of a chronicler, generally reliable, who is merely recording the effect created by that army in the gleaming colours beloved of the time. The city it was attacking was itself worthy of a medieval romance. Backed by Mount Silpius and watered by the Orontes, which afforded it an outlet to the sea, Antioch was practically impregnable, with its enclosing wall, some eight miles long, bristling with three hundred and sixty towers. When the Crusaders arrived they certainly never imagined that they would be held up there for nearly a year. While they were still below the walls, Count Stephen of Blois, one of the principal barons, sent news* of himself to his wife, Adela of Normandy—daughter of William the Conqueror:

Count Stephen to Adela, his most sweet and amiable wife, to his dear children and all the vassals of his line, greeting and blessing.

You may rest assured, my dearest, that the messenger I am sending to give you comfort has left me safe and sound before Antioch and, by the grace of God, in the greatest prosperity. At this moment, with the whole army chosen by Christ and endowed by Him with great worth, we have for the past twenty-three weeks continually been drawing nearer to the House of Our Lord Jesus.

* Letter published in *Recueil des Historians des Crusades, Historiens Occidentaux*. T. III, p. 887.

And you must know for a certainty too, my well-beloved, that I have doubled the gold, silver and all the other riches that in your love you handed me when I left you; for all our princes, with the common consent of the whole army, against my own desire, have made me up till now the chief, the head and the leader of their expedition.

You must have heard how, after we had taken the city of Nicaea, we fought a great battle against the perfidious Turks and, with the help of God, vanquished them. After that we conquered for the Lord the whole of Romania and thereafter Cappadocia. On learning that a certain Turkish prince, Assam, lived in Cappadocia, we marched in his direction. We took all his castles by force and made him flee to another castle, a very strong one, situated on a high rock. We gave the land of this Assam to one of our chiefs, leaving many soldiers of Christ with him so that he might hold his own against him. From there, always on the track of the accursed Turks, we thrust them back towards the middle of Armenia, near the great river Euphrates. Leaving their baggage and their pack animals on the bank, they fled across the river towards Arabia.

Nevertheless, the boldest of the Turkish soldiers, entering Syria, hurried on by forced marches day and night so as to enter the royal city of Antioch before we arrived. When they heard this the whole army of God gave thanks and praise to almighty God. Joyfully hastening ourselves towards the city of Antioch, we laid siege to it. Many a clash did we have there with the Turks and seven times, with the fiercest courage, and under the leadership of Christ, we fought the inhabitants of Antioch and the countless troops who came to their aid. In all those seven battles with the help of the Lord God we were the victors and killed a large number of enemies. But in those same battles, to speak truth, and in the many other attacks launched against the city, many of our brethren were killed and their souls born away to Paradise. . . .

In front of that city, throughout the whole winter, we suffered for the sake of Christ Our Lord from excessive cold and tremendous torrents of rain. People said that it would be impossible to bear the heat of the sun in Syria, but this is not true, for the winter here is just like ours in the West. . . . While my chaplain Alexander was writing this letter in great haste on Easter Day,

some of our men, on the look-out for the Turks, fought a victorious battle against them and seized sixty horsemen, whose heads
they brought back to the army.

I am only telling you, dearest, a few of the many things we have
done; and because I cannot tell what is in my thoughts, I will
merely counsel you to act well, to watch carefully over my lands
and do your duty rightly to your children and vassals. You will see
me again as soon as I can return to you. Farewell.

*The alliances that they were able to establish with the populations
of the interior, the Armenians in particular, were of great assistance to
the Crusaders.*

William of Tyre:

The moment our armies arrived below the walls of Antioch
and had started to beleaguer them, the inhabitants of that town
began to look with suspicion on the Greeks, Syrians and Armenians and all those of their fellow citizens, no matter what nation
they belonged to, who professed the Christian faith. Following on
this they had driven out from their midst, as mere encumberers,
all the weak and all who had to struggle to get enough to eat and
could not provide for their families as well as themselves, thus
keeping in the town only the rich, those who had great patri-
monies and found it easy to stock their houses with all sorts of
goods. Nevertheless these were weighed down with so many
ordinary and extraordinary burdens that you might have thought
it better to be one of those who had been expelled than of those of
whom it was claimed that they had as a special favour been
granted permission to remain. Very often, heavy money fines
were imposed on them; all they possessed was violently extorted
from them, and in addition they were taken from their houses
and forced to perform the basest of services and to shoulder the
heaviest burdens. If there were machines to be set up, or beams of
enormous size to transport, they were immediately ordered to
set about it. Some were obliged to carry stones, cement and all
the materials necessary for building, others were ordered to
feed the machines with the stones and slabs of rock which it
was their task to hurl over the walls; others again helped with the
cables which flung all kinds of projectiles for great distances, and
all were obliged to follow blindly the whims of their leaders,

without being able to obtain the slightest remission or a few moments of rest. . . .

Meanwhile, anxiety crept into the camp of the Crusaders established before Antioch. They were beginning to suffer from hunger.

. . . The siege was already in its third month: supplies had begun to run short in the camp and our troops were suffering greatly from the scarcity. At first there had been great abundance of everything we needed: the horses had more fodder than they could eat, and the soldiers, believing like the improvident that this state of prosperity would last for ever, hardly ever restrained themselves on any occasion; in other words they had so misused their wealth that in a few days they squandered stocks that, carefully used, would have lasted very much longer. No rule was observed in the camp, nor did they follow any principle of economy, that counsellor of prudent men; everywhere there was abundance and unexampled profusion, and this prodigality reigned not only in all that concerned the nourishment of the men; no care was taken over the fodder for the pack animals either. Little by little the army reached such a state of destitution that it was not long before famine broke out and all the people found themselves threatened with death for want of provisions. The soldiers banded themselves together in detachments and bound themselves on oath to share between them, in equal portions and fairly, everything that they could pick up on their expeditions; then they set off in bands of three or four hundred men and scoured the whole country in the attempt to procure victuals for themselves. . . .

This was not the only cause for anxiety. Established in a country where both customs and the people were unknown to them, the Crusaders had their work cut out to guard against the spies who insinuated themselves into their camp:

. . . Some said they were Greeks, others Syrians, others Armenians, and each was careful to assume exactly the language, manners and customs of the part he was playing. . . . It was no easy task to expel from our camp men whom no difference of customs or language distinguished from the rest of the people. . . .

Finally Bohemond proposed to the other leaders that he would rid them once for all of this danger, by an expedient which gives the measure of the man:

. . . Towards nightfall, while everyone was as usual occupied with preparations for dinner, he gave orders that certain Turks whom he was holding captive should be brought out of prison; and handing them over to the executioner, he had them killed on the spot. Then, having had a great fire lit, as though to prepare the repast, he ordered that they should be roasted, and very carefully prepared as though they were to be eaten. Finally he commanded his people, if anyone came to ask them what such preparations portended, to reply that "the princes had decided in council that in future all enemies or spies who were taken prisoner should be treated in this way, and used for the nourishment of the princes and the people". . . . These stories spread throughout the whole Orient and reached the most distant lands. And all that heard them were alike seized with terror.

It was Bohemond again who, by one of those tricks of which he had the secret, put an end to an exhausting siege which had lasted many months. This is how he did it:

"*Gesta Francorum*":

A Turkish captain, called Firouz, had become greatly attached to Bohemond. Often, in the messages they mutually exchanged, Bohemond begged him to admit him to his friendship; in return he promised to receive him into the Christian faith and led him to hope for riches and great honours. Firouz agreed to all his words and promises saying: "There are three towers under my protection; I promise them to him gladly and, at whatever hour he wishes, I will receive him there."

Being thus assured of entering the town, Bohemond rejoiced: with his mind at rest, he approached the other lords with a calm face and said to them joyfully: "Most prudent knights, consider our poverty, in what a wretched state we all are, both great and small, and that we know not whence any improvement in our affairs may come. Therefore, if it seems to you good and honourable, let one among you be chosen from among the others and if, by some means or other, by his efforts, he manages to seize the city, or carry it by assault, either by himself or with the help of others, grant him with one voice the possession of it." But they refused and opposed him saying: "None shall receive the possession of this city, but we will all share it equally among us; we have borne the same labours, we will all receive the same honour." At these words Bohemond smiled slightly and at once withdrew.

Not long afterwards we received news of the army of our enemies—Turks, Publicans, Azymites and other nations. Our leaders immediately met and held a council, saying: "If Bohemond can take the city by himself or with the help of others, we will willingly give it to him on condition that, if the Emperor comes to our help and is ready to observe the agreement that he promised and swore to us, we will hand over the town to him as of right, even if Bohemond has it in his possession."

Soon Bohemond began humbly pressing his friend Firouz with daily requests, promising him all kinds of considerations and advantages in these terms: "The right moment for performing the good deed we have resolved upon is at hand; let my friend Firouz now grant me his aid." Firouz was delighted and declared that he would help him as he had promised. The following night he sent Bohemond his own son as a hostage, to confirm that he would surrender to him the entrance to the town, and he sent him this message: "Tomorrow you must convoke the whole Frankish army, as though to go off and devastate the land of the Saracens; then you must dissimulate and return rapidly by the mountain on the right. As for me, I will keep a careful watch on those troops and will wait for them and receive them in the towers that are under my control and in my custody."

Bohemond immediately sent for one of his sergeants, called Male Couronne, and ordered him, as he would a herald, to summon the great army of the Franks to make ready in all loyalty to march into the land of the Saracens; and so it was done. Bohemond confided his plan to Duke Godfrey, to the Count of Flanders and also to the Count of Saint-Giles and the Bishop of Le Puy, saying: "If God's grace favour us, this night Antioch will be surrendered to us."

William of Tyre:

Meanwhile, Bohemond, with bated breath and full of anxiety, lest at the moment of achieving his plans the slightest delay should prevent their execution, visited all the princes one after the other, and begged them with the most earnest solicitations to hold themselves in readiness. He himself carried in his hand a ladder cunningly made of hempen rope, whose lower end was provided with iron hooks, while the upper part was to be strongly attached to the outer walls of the ramparts. It was the middle of the night; a profound calm reigned in the town; the citizens were drawing new strength from sleep and finding in it relief from their watches and their long fatigues. Then Bohemond sent his friend a faithful interpreter, completely devoted to him, whom he had ordered to go with all speed to ask if it was desired that his master should advance at the head of his troops. The messenger arrived at the foot of the ramparts and found Firouz on the look-out in the shelter of one of the openings; he repeated to him the words of his lord, and the other at once replied: "Sit down and keep silent until the officer in charge of the watch, who is approaching with a large escort and bright lights, has passed beyond this post." When the man in charge of this watch had passed the tower of Firouz and had seen him keeping watch, he praised his conduct and continued on his way. Then Firouz, thinking that the right moment had arrived, called the interpreter, who was at the foot of the ramparts, and said to him: "Run quickly and tell your master to hasten here with a troop of chosen men." The messenger returned at once to Bohemond, who was all ready; he sent warning to all the other princes who had made their dispositions and, each one taking his place at the head of his followers, in the twinkling of an eye they all arrived together, as it were a single man, at the foot of the tower decided upon, marching in the greatest silence and making not the slightest noise.

He [Firouz] gave them the signal of recognition, received the same from them, and at once let down a cord to be tied to the ladder to draw it up. When it had reached him and been firmly fixed at both ends, no one could be found who, either at the command of his chief or on the invitation of Bohemond, would dare to climb up and risk himself as the first in this new trial. So Bohemond advanced intrepidly and climbed up himself. He swarmed rapidly up all the rungs until his hand reached the revetment of the rampart. Firouz, posted behind the wall, grasped it strongly, and, as he knew it was Bohemond who had climbed up, it is reported that he said to him at that moment: "Long live this hand!"

Bohemond embraced him, praising his constancy and the sincerity of his faith; then returning to the rampart and thrusting his head through the opening, in a muffled voice he invited his companions to mount. Nevertheless they continued to hesitate; everything that was said to them from the top of the ramparts seemed to them suspect and ambiguous, and still none dared venture. When Bohemond realised their doubts, he came down the ladder again and reassured all his people by this clear proof that nothing had happened to him. So then they climbed up, each emulating the other.

"*Gesta Francorum*":

About sixty of our men mounted and were distributed among the towers under his charge.

. . . When they saw this, those who were already in the towers began to cry with a joyful voice: "It is the will of God!" We ourselves gave the same cry. Then the marvellous ascent began; at last they reached the top and ran quickly to the other towers; they massacred all those they found there and the brother of Firouz perished in this way. Then the ladder we had climbed up broke, plunging us in great anguish and sadness. However, although the ladder was broken, there was on our left a closed door, which some knew not of. It was still night, but by feeling and groping we ended by finding it: we all ran to it and, having smashed it, thanks to it we entered.

At that moment an immense clamour resounded throughout the town. Bohemond had lost no time in ordering that his glorious banner should be hoisted on a high place facing the castle. At daybreak those who were still in their tents heard the terrific noise which rang through the town. Hurrying out they saw Bohemond's banner floating on a height; then rushing along at a great pace they passed through the gates into the town, massacred all the Turks and Saracens they met, except those who managed to flee into the citadel above: other Turks got out by the gates and escaped.

Cassian, their lord, fled also, with many others who were in his suite, and in their flight they came to the land of Tancred, not far from the city. As their horses were tired, they penetrated into a village and took refuge in a house. But they were recognised by the Syrian and Armenian inhabitants who at once seized Cassian and cut off his head, which they took to Bohemond so as to obtain their freedom. The sword-belt and the sheath of his scimitar were sold for sixty bezants.

These events took place . . . three days before the nones of June. Every open space in the town was littered with corpses, so that none could stay there because of the stench. It was not possible to walk in the roads without walking on the corpses of the dead.

THE HOLY LANCE

✠✠✠✠✠✠✠✠✠✠✠✠✠✠✠✠✠✠✠✠✠✠✠✠✠✠✠✠✠✠✠✠✠✠✠✠✠✠✠

*T*HEY WERE *hardly established in the town before new difficulties arose. A citizen of Lucca, called Bruno, described them to his compatriots:*

The next day there arrived countless troops of Turks, who immediately attacked the gates of the city and completely prevented our men from entering or leaving; those of them who had remained near the sea, they either put to death by the sword or they burnt them. So what with the difficulty of living there and the ordeal of getting away, a terrible famine began to afflict us. Count Stephen, William, a relation of Bohemond, and some others, had arrived full of fear at Constantintople. There, when it was heard that they were about to leave, people dissuaded them from continuing on their way, thinking that the whole army had perished. As for those in the city, who were gnawed by famine, they lacked everything, including bread and even the meat of donkeys and horses.

The Crusaders had been turned from besiegers into besieged, and the Turkish army which encircled them—that of Sultan Kerbogha, the Corboran of the Chansons de Geste—*was numerous enough to undertake a full-scale attack. The Crusaders had to endure terrible sufferings and their adventure very nearly ended at Antioch.*

"Gesta Francorum":

These sacrilegious enemies of God kept us so closely blockaded in Antioch that many died of hunger. A little roll of bread was sold for a bezant—no need to speak of wine! The flesh of horses and donkeys was sold and eaten; a hen cost fifteen sous, an egg two sous, a nut one denier. All prices were prohibitive; the famine was so great that the leaves of fig-trees, vines and thistles were cooked for food. Others cooked and ate the dried skins of horses, camels, oxen and buffalo. We endured this anxiety, and torments so varied that I cannot recall them, for the sake of Christ, and to open the route to the Holy Sepulchre. We were a prey to that famine, with all its tribulations and terrors, for twenty-six days. . . .

One Crusader who escaped these miseries was the leader, Count Stephen of Blois, who had written so optimistically to his wife a short while before.

. . . Before Antioch was taken, Stephen, Count of Chartres [and Blois], whom our great ones had elected as supreme leader, misguidedly pretended to be taken ill and shamefully retired to another fortified town called Alexandretta, while every day we were expecting that he was going to bring us aid, shut up as we were in the town without any useful help. But when he heard that the Turkish army had surrounded us and was besieging us, he secretly climbed a neighbouring mountain not far from Antioch and saw the countless tents. Seized with great terror, he descended and fled in haste with his troops. As soon as he got back to his camp, he struck it and retreated rapidly.

Fulcher of Chartres:
We were all greatly grieved at this, for he was truly a noble man and of eminent virtue. At the very moment when he was leaving, and on the day after his departure, the town of Antioch fell into our hands; so if he had had more perseverance, he could have greatly rejoiced with the rest at this success. But as it was, his retreat became a disgrace to him.

There appeared to be no way out of the situation. Then Saint Andrew intervened, as a Crusader who was there relates:

Raymond of Aguilers:
God in his goodness chose a poor churl, a Provençal, to bring comfort to us all. He came to find the Count [Raymond of Saint-Giles] and the Bishop of Le Puy and addressed them thus: "Andrew, the Apostle of our God and Lord Jesus Christ, has warned me four times and ordered me to go to you and give you

the Lance which opened our Saviour's side in the city. It so happened that today, when I left Antioch to go into battle with the others, I was pursued by two horsemen. I withdrew, out of breath and half-fainting, and sat sadly on a stone. It was then, when I was overcome with sadness and weighed down by grief and fear, that Saint Andrew appeared before me with a companion. He threatened me greatly if I did not quickly hand the Lance over to you." The Count and the Bishop then ordered him to tell them in what circumstances the revelation of the apostle had first been made to him. And he replied: "During the first earthquake which took place in Antioch when the Frankish army was besieging it, I was so afraid that I could say nothing but: Lord, come to my help. It was night, I was in bed and there was no one under the roof which sheltered me whose company could afford me any comfort. This earthquake, then, had been going on a long time and my terror was growing greater and greater when two men in gleaming garments appeared before me; one, the elder, had fair, reddish hair, black eyes, a pleasant face, a white beard, long and full, and was of middle height; the other, younger and more attractive, was the most beautiful of the children of men. And the older one said to me: What are you doing? I was greatly afraid, for I knew there was no one there, and I answered: Who are you? He said to me: Arise, and do not be afraid, but listen to what I have to say to you. I am the apostle Andrew. Go and find the Bishop of Le Puy, the Count of Saint-Giles and Peter-Raymond of Hautpoul and say to them: Why does the bishop not preach and exhort and bless the people every day with the cross he carries? It would do them great good. . . .

So I rose and followed him into the city, wearing nothing but my shirt. He led me into the church of the Apostle Saint Paul, by the north door that the Saracens once held. In the church there were two lamps, which gave light as though it had been the blaze of day. He said to me: Wait here. And he made me sit down against the pillar nearest the steps leading to the altar from the south side. His companion was standing not far away in front of the altar steps. Saint Andrew disappeared below the ground, brought out a Lance and put it in my hands and said to me: Here is the Lance that opened the side whence came the salvation of the whole world. While I was holding it and weeping for joy, I said to him: Lord, if thou wilt, I will take it and give it to the

Count. He said to me: Act quickly, for the town is about to be taken. So you must come with twelve men and seek in the place whence I took it and where I am hiding it again. And he put it back in the same place. When he had done this, he led me over the wall of the city to my dwelling, and they then departed. Then I, seeing my poverty and your magnificence, was afraid to draw near to you. Some time afterwards, when I had gone as far as a place close to Rois [Edessa] on the first day of Lent [February 10th, 1098], at cock-crow Saint Andrew appeared to me in the same garment and with the same companion who had come the first time, and a great light filled the house. And Saint Andrew said to me: Have you reported what I ordered you to say? I answered: Lord, did I not pray thee to send them someone else? I was afraid because of my poverty; I did not dare approach them. . . . Thereupon I departed towards the port of Mamistra; my intention was to reach Cyprus by sea in search of victuals, but Saint Andrew threatened me again very sternly if I did not return and carry out his orders. As I was wondering how to get back to the camp (for this port is about three days' march from the city) I began to weep very bitterly. . . . Urged on by those who were travelling with me, we boarded the ship and began to row towards Cyprus. All day long, with the help both of the oars and of favourable winds, we sailed on until sunset, when such a tempest arose that, in the space of an hour or two, we had been driven back to the port we had left. A second and a third time the passage proved impossible for us, so that we returned to the port of Saint Symeon. There I was very ill. Then it was that the city was taken and now I am come to find you and beg you to make the attempt I have asked of you." The Bishop thought that all this was nothing but words; but the Count believed it at once and gave the man who had thus spoken into the charge of his chaplain Raymond [*the actual author of this account*].

. . . Then the princes swore not to flee from Antioch nor to leave the town except by the common consent of all. At that moment the people did in fact believe that the princes wanted to flee towards the port, so this promise fortified many of them. The night before there had been very few who had remained confident and had not sought to flee. If Bohemond had not shut the gates of the city, very few would have stayed. Even William of

Grant-Mesnil, his brother and many others, both clerks and laymen, fled. And more than one, having escaped with great peril from the city, fell into still greater peril at the hands of the Turks. At that time, many revelations were made to us by our brothers and we saw a wonderful sign in the sky. A very large star appeared during the night above the city; after a moment it split in three and fell on the camp of the Turks. Then our men, somewhat reassured, awaited the fifth day that the priest had announced. On that day, when the necessary preparations had been made, twelve of us joined the man who had spoken of the Lance and, when all the others had been sent out of the church of Saint Peter, we began to dig. Among us was the Bishop of Orange, and Raymond, the Count's chaplain. . . . We dug from morning to evening; by evening we began to despair of finding the Lance. The Count had left to look after the guard of his camp, but we took his place and that of others who had grown tired of digging, and bravely went on with the task. The young man who had spoken of the Lance, seeing that we were getting tired, took off his belt and shoes and, barefoot and in his shirt, descended into the ditch we had dug, exhorting us to pray God to give us His Lance for the consolation and victory of His people. At last in His goodness, God showed us His Lance, and I who write this, when only the point appeared above the earth, I kissed it; the joy and exultation that then filled the city are beyond my power to describe. It was on June the 14th that this Lance was found. . . .

In the interval there had been such a famine in the city that the head of a horse without the tongue sold for two or three sous; the guts of goats for five sous; a hen for eight or nine sous. And as for bread! one man by himself could not manage to appease his hunger for five sous. This was not surprising and did not seem excessive to those who bought so dear, for gold, silver and precious stuffs abounded. . . . Unripe figs were plucked from the trees and sold very dear once they were cooked. The hides of oxen and horses, after they had been cooked so long that they could be eaten, were sold for two sous. The greater part of the knights lived on the blood of their horses. Hoping for the mercy of God, they did not want to kill them yet. All these ills and many more that it would be difficult to enumerate, we suffered, besieged as we were, and there was another thing more serious still: this was that many of our people fled to the Turks and told them of the misery that reigned in the city, so that the Turks became bolder and threatened us more violently every day.

However, consoled by the unexpected discovery, the Crusaders took heart again and began by sending on an embassy to Kerbogha a crusader who was already well known: Peter the Hermit. As a matter of fact, he had recently deserted and Bohemond had literally seized him by the scruff of the neck and brought him back to the camp. This had obviously in no way lessened his prestige, since it was he who was chosen for the embassy as a result of which it was hoped that they would be able to leave Antioch on honourable conditions. But the Sultan Kerbogha rejected all their proposals, thinking that the city could not fail to fall into his hands. So after having resolved on three days of fasting and praying, the Crusaders prepared to deliver an assault which would decide matters one way or the other.

Raymond of Aguilers:

Our men advanced like clerks in a procession, and in truth it was a procession, for priests and many monks wearing white robes led the army of our soldiers, singing and calling on the help of God and the support of the saints. The enemy fell on us and rained arrows on us. . . . Kerbogha informed our princes that he was now ready to do what he had formerly refused: he proposed that five or ten Turks should fight against an equal number of Franks, and that those whose soldiers were vanquished should surrender peacefully to the others. To this our side replied: "You would not have this when we wanted it; now that we have joined battle, let each one fight as best he can."

When we had filled the whole plain, a section of the Turks remained in our rear and attacked some of our foot-soldiers. These, wheeling about, courageously sustained the assault of the enemy. Then the Turks, seeing that they were not getting the better of them, lit a fire all round them so as to subdue by fire those who did not fear the sword. In this way they forced them to yield, because it happened there was in that place much dry hay. The priests left the ranks and stood on the city walls, bare-foot and wearing their priestly vestments, beseeching God to defend His people and to bear witness in this fight, by the victory of the Franks, to the alliance that He had sealed with His blood. While we were covering the ground between the bridge and the mountain we suffered greatly because the enemy tried to encircle us. During this attempt, although strong enemy ranks were directed against those of us who belonged to the troop of the Bishop, yet, because of the Holy Lance that we were carrying, they wounded no one; not a single arrow touched us. I who speak saw it. It was I who carried the Lance in this fight. And if anyone says that the Viscount Heraclius, who was the Bishop's standard-bearer, was wounded in this battle, let it be known that the Bishop had entrusted his standard to someone else and that Heraclius had gone a great distance away from our ranks. When all the combatants had left the city, it seemed to us that there were among us five extra ranks of soldiers. In fact, as we have said, our princes had only been able to make up eight battle corps; and as soon as we were outside the city we found we had thirteen.

So this siege of Antioch ended in victory for the Crusaders. Peter Bartholomew, the Provençal priest to whom the discovery of the Lance was due, was not to survive it for long. As a matter of fact, more than one Crusader felt sceptical about this discovery, for they did not all share the enthusiasm of the narrator, Raymond of Aguilers; as he himself tells us, the Bishop of Le Puy, Adhemar of Monteil, always refused to believe in the truth of it. Bartholemew offered to prove his good faith by the ordeal of fire. He came out of it alive but died a few days later.

William of Tyre:

Bartholomew died a few days afterwards and some declare that, as he had previously seemed perfectly well and full of life, so sudden a death could only have been caused by the ordeal that he wished to undertake, and that the fire caused his death because he had been defending a fraud. On the contrary, others said that he had emerged safe and sound from the pyre, and that, after he had escaped from the fire, the crowd, rushing at him in its transport of devotion, had so pressed and crushed him on all sides that that was the true and sole cause of his death. This question was thus left completely unsettled and even became wrapt in a still greater obscurity.

The path of the Crusaders was thenceforth open and, as Bruno of Lucca wrote, from then on they were in control of the whole region from Nicaea as far as Antioch, which was the most important citadel of Northern Syria. The riches contained in the Turkish camp, and in particular the tent of Sultan Kerbogha, seem to have struck them very forcibly.

William of Tyre:

Among those rich spoils was a tent, a wonderful piece of work, which belonged to the Prince Kerbogha. It was constructed like a town, adorned with towers, walls and ramparts, and covered with sumptuous hangings of silks of many colours. From the centre of the tent, which formed a sort of principal lodging, one could see numerous compartments opening out on all sides and forming as it were roads, in which again were many other dwellings, like inns. It was said that two thousand men could easily be housed in this vast edifice. . . .

JERUSALEM

✠✠

*A*FTER THE *taking of Antioch, a series of attacks was launched during the summer of 1098 against the small fortified places of the region. In this way the Crusaders seized Marra [Maarat-al-Numan] after a siege in which they once again revealed their skill as engineers and technicians.*

"Gesta Francorum":

When our lords saw that there was nothing to be done and that all their efforts were in vain, Raymond, Count of Saint-Giles, had a tall, strong wooden castle built, standing on four wheels which were part of the structure. In the upper storey there were several knights, including Everard the Huntsman who sounded the trumpet very loudly. On the ground below there were knights clad in armour, who pushed the castle near the walls, against a tower. When they saw this the pagans at once built a machine which hurled great stones at the castle, so that nearly all our knights were killed. They also threw Greek fire upon the castle in the hope of burning and destroying it, but almighty God willed that the castle should not burn this time, for it overtopped the walls of the city.

Our knights who were in the upper storey, among them William of Montpellier and many others, cast huge stones at the defenders of the wall. They fell with such force on their shields that both shield and man, the latter mortally wounded, fell down inside the town. These fought in this way; others carried lances adorned with pennants and, with the help of these lances and of iron hooks, they tried to pull the enemy towards them. And so they fought until evening.

Behind the castle were the priests and clerks in their sacred vestments, praying and beseeching God to defend His people, to exalt Christendom and confound paganism. On another side, our knights fought the enemy daily, erecting ladders against the walls of the town. But the pagans resisted so strongly that our men could make no progress. Meanwhile, Goufier of Lastours was the first to reach the top of the wall by a ladder; but immediately the ladder broke under the weight of his too numerous companions. However, he and a few others managed to get on to the wall. Others, having found another ladder, quickly propped it against the wall. But the Saracens attacked them with such force, both on the wall and on the ground, shooting their arrows and pointing their lances at them at close range, that many of our men, struck with terror, threw themselves from the top of the wall.

While those valiant men who remained on the crest of the wall were enduring these attacks, those who were below the castle were sapping the walls of the town. When the Saracens saw that we had sapped their wall, they were seized with terror and fled into the city. All this took place on Saturday, December 11th, at sunset, the hour of vespers. Through an interpreter, Bohemond told the Saracen chiefs, their wives and children, to take refuge with their baggage, in a palace situated above the gate, and promised to preserve them from death.

It was from that city of Marra that a penitent was seen to go one day, barefoot and in his shirt, in a southerly direction: it was Raymond of Saint-Giles who, on January 13th, 1099, set off again on the interrupted pilgrimage. By this he showed both his repentance for the quarrels which had been disorganising the army and his intention of listening to the humble folk who, a few days previously, had indulged in a demonstration to show their indignation with the laziness and quarrels of their barons.

The main body of the army at first followed the valley of the Orontes as far as Shaizar [Caesarea]. Several sultans in the coastal regions towards the south-west chose to enter into negotiations with them rather than expose themselves to a fight.

Fulcher of Chartres:

After spending four days in this town [Lydda], establishing a bishop in the basilica of Saint George and putting some men in the forts to guard the place, our troops continued their march towards Jerusalem. On the first day they got as far as a little castle called

Emmaus. That night a hundred of our knights, tempted by the idea of a bold plan and prompted by their own courage, dashed off on their coursers, passed close to Jerusalem just when the dawn was beginning to pale the sky, and rode at top speed as far as Bethlehem. Among them were Tancred and Baldwin of Le Bourg. When the Christians, that is to say the Greeks and Syrians who lived there, realised that it was Franks who were arriving, they were transported with great joy. All the same, at first, not knowing what people were coming towards them, they took them for Turks or Arabs; but as soon as they saw them distinctly and closer to, and could no longer doubt that they were Franks, they joyfully took their crosses and banners and came to meet our men, weeping and singing pious hymns. They wept because they feared that so small a handful of men would easily be slaughtered by the vast hordes of pagans whom they knew were in the country; they sang because they were glad at the arrival of those whose coming they had so long desired, and who they felt were destined to re-establish in its ancient glory the Christian faith shamefully trampled on by the wicked during so many centuries. Our men lost no time in addressing pious supplications to the Lord in the basilica of the Blessed Mary, and visiting the place where Christ was born; after which they cheerfully gave the kiss of peace to the Syrians and precipitately took again the road to the Holy City. Meanwhile, at that very time the rest of our army was approaching the great city, leaving on their left Gabaon, fifty stades [a little over five miles] distant from Jerusalem. Just as our advance guard raised their standards and showed them to the inhabitants, the enemy suddenly came out of the town; but those men, so quick to show themselves outside their walls, were pushed back inside more quickly still and forced to retreat.

It was on June 7th, 1099, that the Crusaders arrived within sight of Jerusalem. They had been on their way for three years.

"*Gesta Francorum*":

Mad with joy, we reached the city of Jerusalem on the Tuesday, eight days before the ides of June, and laid siege to it in a remarkable manner. Robert of Normandy besieged it from the north, near the church of Saint Stephen, the first martyr, at the place where he was stoned in the name of Christ. With him was Robert,

Count of Flanders. The besiegers on the west were Duke Godfrey and Tancred. The Count of Saint-Giles attacked it from the south, on Mount Sion, near the church of Saint Mary, the mother of God, where the Lord celebrated the Last Supper with His disciples.

On the third day Raymond Pilet, Raymond of Turenne, and many others who were eager to fight, separated themselves from the army. They encountered two hundred Arabs, and the knights of Christ fought those unbelievers; with God's help, they got the upper hand, killed a great number and took thirty horses.

Certain curious stories were afterwards circulated of events that took place during the siege of Jerusalem. They perhaps belong only to legend; but because of the taste for the romantic, they were frequently reported in the Chansons de Geste. *Guibert of Nogent quotes one as something he has heard:*

Those who were there relate that, during the siege of the town, when besiegers and besieged, in their frequent encounters, intermingled promiscuously, it very often happened that, when the men on both sides retreated, wisely restraining their impetuosity, battalions of children were to be seen advancing, some coming from the town, others from the midst of our army and the camp of their parents, and then attacking each other and fighting just as the men had, and equally well worth watching. For, as we said at the beginning of this history, when the news of the expedition to Jerusalem had spread through all the countries of the West, fathers undertook the journey, taking with them their sons while they were still children. The result of this was that, even when the parents of some of them were dead, the children nevertheless continued on their way. They got used to the fatigue and, as for the miseries and privations of all kinds that had to be endured, they showed themselves in no way inferior to grown men. So these children, having formed a battalion, gave themselves princes chosen from among them; one took the name of Hugh the Great, one of Bohemond, another of the Count of Flanders, and still another that of the Count of Normandy, impersonating in this way those illustrious persons and others too. Whenever those young princes saw that some of their subjects lacked food or other things, they would go and find the princes whom we have named, to ask them for supplies, and these they gave them in abundance, so that the children should be honourably provided for in their weakness. This youthful and singular militia often went to harry the children of the town, each armed with long reeds instead of lances, each having woven for his use a shield of osier, and each carrying, according to his strength, little bows and arrows. These children, then, as well as those of the town, advanced and met in the middle of the plain, while their parents on both sides watched them, the inhabitants of the town betaking themselves to the ramparts and our men coming out of their tents to be present at the fight. The children urged each other on, uttering cries as they charged, and inflicting on each other blows that were often bloody, although there was never any danger of death. These preludes often stimulated the courage of the grown men and provoked new combats when they saw the unavailing ardour that animated all those delicate limbs and those feeble arms, joyfully brandishing weapons of every kind; and after both sides had inflicted and received wounds, as a rule the older spectators went up and sent the children back from the middle of the plain, and started a new combat among themselves. So the army of the Lord was rarely at rest, some practising for fights and others taking part in them every day.

There was besides in the army another kind of men, who always went barefoot, carried no arms and were not allowed to have any money at all. They were filthy with poverty and want, and marched in front of everyone, eating only roots, plants and the coarsest products of the earth. A Norman, who was said not to be of obscure birth, but who, from being a knight, had turned foot-soldier, and possessed no land, saw these men wandering every-where like vagabonds, and thereupon put off the arms and garments that he usually wore and desired to be their king. He began by taking a name from the barbarian language of the country, and had himself called the "King of the Tafurs": the Gentiles give the name Tafurs to those whom we Franks might call vagabonds. . . . Whenever the men marching under his orders arrived at a bridge, or at the entry of a narrow pass, this man used to go and occupy the approaches to it, and severely search his men one by one. If one of them happened to have on him only the worth of two sous, he immediately dismissed him from his troop, ordered him to buy arms, and forced him to go and join the corps

of armed men. Those on the contrary who he realised had an in-
born liking for poverty, and who he saw had not put any money
aside or had not sought any, he made particular efforts to win
over, so as to incorporate them in his troop. One might perhaps
have thought that those people were harmful to the general
interest and that, when the others might have had a superfluity,
these absorbed it without any corresponding advantage. But it
would hardly be believed how useful they made themselves by
carrying burdens, marching always in front of the donkeys and
pack animals, and finally overturning the ballistas and machines of
the enemy, by heaving stones at them.

According to the Gentiles of antiquity, the Turks grieve as
keenly over a corpse that remains unburied as any Christian may
at the thought of a soul condemned to damnation. So, to excite
their rage to the utmost, the Bishop of Le Puy gave orders, by an
edict proclaimed throughout the army during the siege of
Antioch, that a reward of twelve deniers should be given and paid
immediately, to whomever would bring the head of a Turk;
and when the prelate had in this way received some heads, he
ordered that they should be set on the ends of very long poles
before the walls of the town and before the very eyes of the
enemy. This always caused them the most violent grief and froze
them with terror.

This same bishop, with the agreement of our princes, did
another thing here that I must not omit to mention. When the
besieged were beginning to notice that we were suffering from a
scarcity of provisions, the bishop proposed that our people for
their part should harness oxen to wagons and set to work to
plough and sow the fields, under the very eyes of the inhabitants,
so as to make them understand that nothing would induce the
besiegers to abandon their enterprise, since they were already
engaged in making sure of crops for the following year.

*The besieging army was in fact suffering acutely from hunger and
thirst:*

William of Tyre:

Meanwhile, the army began to suffer horribly from thirst. As I
have already said, the surroundings of Jerusalem are waterless and
arid and it is only at a considerable distance that a few streams,

fountains or wells of fresh water are to be found. Even those springs the enemy had dammed up not long before the arrival of our troops, to shorten the time when they would be able to lay siege to the place; they had thrown earth into them or blocked them up by various other means; they had also opened the cisterns and other reservoirs of rain water, so that they could no longer hold it; or else, again, they had maliciously hidden them so that the poor wretches, tormented by thirst, could not go and seek some relief there. The inhabitants of Bethlehem and the faithful who lived in Thecus, the town of the prophets, frequently visited the army and then led the Crusaders to the springs situated four or five miles from their camp. There new difficulties arose: on arriving there they pushed each other in their mutual eagerness to draw water; often they fell into sharp altercations and only at last, after long delays, they filled the water-skins with water that was all muddy, which they afterwards sold at a high price, distributing it nevertheless in such small quantities that a thirsty man hardly got enough to satisfy his barest need.

The burning heat of the month of June further increased their pangs of thirst, and made the incessant feeling of suffocation still more painful for everyone, quite apart from the excess of work, and the abundance of dust which continually dried up their palates and throats. The Crusaders left the camp in secret and scattered throughout the neighbourhood, seeking everywhere with the utmost care for water. They marched in small detachments and the moment they thought they had found some hidden trickle, they immediately found themselves surrounded by a huge throng of people engaged in the same search; sometimes, when they had discovered some spring, fierce quarrels broke out among them; all strove to push the others away and often they fell to fighting.

"Gesta Francorum":

On the Monday [June 13th] we attacked the town with such force and speed that, if the ladders had been ready, it would have fallen into our hands. Nevertheless, we destroyed the little wall and placed a ladder against the principal wall; our knights climbed up and struck the Saracens and defenders of the town at close range with their swords and spears. Many of our men, but still more of theirs, found death there. During this siege we could get no bread to eat for the space of ten days, until the arrival of a messenger from our ships, and we were a prey to so burning a thirst that we tramped as much as six miles in desperate fear, to water our horses and our other animals. The pool of Siloam, at the foot of Mount Sion, was a comfort to us, but the water was sold among us much too dear.

After the arrival of the messenger from our ships, our lords held a council and decided to send knights who would faithfully guard the men and ships in the port of Jaffa. At daybreak a hundred knights were detached from the army of Raymond, Count of Saint-Giles, among them Raymond Pilet, Achard of Montmerle and William of Sabran, and set off in all confidence towards the port. Then thirty of our knights separated themselves from the others, and encountered seven hundred Arabs, Turks and Saracens from the admiral's army. The knights of Christ attacked them vigorously, but the enemy so greatly outnumbered our men that they surrounded them on all sides and killed Achard of Montmerle as well as some poor foot-soldiers.

Our men were already surrounded and expecting death when another messenger came and said to Raymond Pilet: "What are you doing there with these knights? At this very moment some of our men are at grips with Arabs, Turks and Saracens; perhaps by now they are all killed; help them, help them!" At this news our men hurried off with all speed and very quickly reached them, fighting as they went. When the pagans perceived the knights of Christ they divided and formed two columns. But our men, after invoking the name of Christ, charged those unbelievers with such force that each knight slew his enemy. When the pagans realised that they could not withstand the valour of the Franks, they were seized with great terror and turned their backs; our men pursued them for about four miles, killed a great number, took one alive so as to obtain information from him, and captured a hundred and three horses.

During this siege we suffered the torment of thirst to such a degree that we sewed together skins of oxen and buffalo in which we carried water for six miles. These containers infected the water, and its fetid condition, as well as the bread made of barley, daily caused us discomfort and distress. The Saracens were in fact secretly laying traps for our people by infecting the fountains and springs; they killed and cut in pieces all those they found and hid their animals in caves and grottoes.

Our lords then began to study methods of attacking the town with the help of machines, so that we could enter it to worship the sepulchre of our Saviour. They built two wooden castles and a good many other contrivances. Duke Godfrey set up a castle provided with machines and Count Raymond did the same. They had the wood brought from distant lands. When the Saracens saw our people building these machines, they fortified the town marvellously and reinforced the defences of the towers during the night.

Then our lords, having discovered the weakest side of the city, had our machines and our wooden castle transported there during the night of Saturday [the 9th, to Sunday, July 10th] : this was on the east. (The eastern wall had not yet been attacked. The rolling tower was transported between the Church of Saint Stephen and the valley of Kedron.) They set them up at daybreak, then on the Sunday, Monday and Tuesday they made the castle ready and manned it. In the southern sector the Count of Saint-Giles was having his machine repaired. At that time we were suffering so much from thirst that even for a denier a man could not get enough water to quench his thirst.

On the Wednesday and Thursday we attacked the town with great vigour from all sides, but before we took it by assault, the bishops and priests made it known by their sermons and exhortations that in honour of God there was to be a procession round the ramparts of Jerusalem and that it would be accompanied by prayers, alms and fasts.

On the Friday, early in the morning, we launched a general attack on the town but were not able to harm it; and this astonished us and filled us with fear. Then, at the approach of the hour when our Lord Jesus Christ consented to suffer for us the agony of the Cross, our knights who were posted on the castle, among others Duke Godfrey and his brother Count Eustace, fought zealously. At that moment one of our knights, by name Litold, scaled the wall of the town. As soon as he reached the top, all the defenders of the town fled from the walls through the city and our men followed them and harried them, killing and felling them right up to the Temple of Solomon, where there was such a carnage that our men were wading in their blood up to their ankles.

Count Raymond on his side, to the south, led his army and the wooden castle near to the wall. But between the castle and the wall there stretched a ditch and it was given out that any who carried three stones into the ditch should have a denier. It took three days and three nights to fill it. When at last the ditch was filled, the castle was brought close to the wall. The defenders within the wall fought vigorously against our men, using [Greek] fire and stones. The Count, learning that the Franks were inside the town, said to his men: "What are you waiting for? All the French are already in the town!"

The governor commanding the Tower of David surrendered to the Count and opened to him the gates where the pilgrims were accustomed to pay tribute [the Jaffa Gate]. Once in the town, our pilgrims pursued the Saracens, massacring them as they went, right up to the Temple of Solomon, where they mustered their forces and fought a most furious battle with our people throughout the whole day, so that the whole Temple ran with their blood. After our men had at last routed the pagans, they seized the Temple and a great number of men and women, whom they killed or left alive as they thought fit. On the roof of the Temple of Solomon a large group of pagans of both sexes had taken refuge, and Tancred and Gaston of Bearn gave them their banners. Soon the crusaders were running all over the town, carrying off gold, silver, horses and mules, and plundering the houses, which were crammed with riches.

Then, full of happiness and weeping for joy, our people went to worship the Sepulchre of our Saviour Jesus and to discharge their debt to Him. The next morning, they climbed up to the roof of the Temple, attacked the Saracens, both men and women, and drawing their swords, cut off their heads. Some threw themselves from the top of the Temple. When he saw this, Tancred was filled with indignation.

Then our people decided in council that each one would give alms and say prayers, that God might choose whom He wanted to rule over the others and govern the city. Orders were also given that all the dead Saracens should be thrown out of the city because of the terrible stench, for the whole town was almost entirely filled with their corpses. The living Saracens dragged the dead out of the town and made piles of them almost as high as the houses before the gates. No one had ever seen, no one had even heard tell of, such a carnage of the pagan race: funeral pyres were set up like milestones, and none but God knows their number.

Thus it was that, on Friday, July 15th, 1099, Jerusalem, the holy city of Christendom, was taken, or rather retaken, from the Saracens, a victory stained by the appalling massacre which marked it. ("It was impossible to see without horror that mass of dead," *writes William of Tyre,* "and even the sight of the victors covered with blood from head to foot was also a ghastly sight.") *For all that, the exploit filled the known world, Christian as well as Saracen, with amazement: no one had expected that the city would be so quickly conquered. Guibert of Nogent, who collected all the testimonies available at the time, recalls for us the echoes of what the West was able to learn about it. And the first thing that strikes one in reading his narrative is the glory that resulted from it for the Franks, who formed by far the larger part of the expedition:*

When I was talking last year with an archdeacon of Mainz I heard him abuse our King and people, solely because the King had received the Lord Pope Paschal and his princes in a friendly way and treated them well: he mocked at the French on that occasion, going as far as to call them, contemptuously, Francons. So I said to him: "If you consider the French so weak and cowardly that you think you can insult by your jibes a name whose fame stretches as far as the Indian Ocean, tell me then who it was to whom Pope Urban turned to ask for help against the Turks? Was it not to the French? If they had not been pre-eminent, if they had not, by their mental activity and the firmness of their courage, put up barriers against the ever-increasing advance of the barbarian nations, would all your Teutons, whose very name is quite unknown, have been of any use in such circumstances?" With these words I left him.

PART TWO

THE CRUSADERS DISCOVER THEIR KINGDOM

✤✤✤✤✤✤✤✤✤✤✤✤✤✤✤✤✤✤✤✤✤✤✤✤✤✤✤✤✤✤✤✤✤✤✤✤✤

*T*HE CHRISTIANS *were masters of the Holy City. Their task thenceforward was to hold this possession so dearly won. So on July 17th, 1099, two days after the conquest of the town, the barons called a solemn council to decide who among them should be empowered to defend and rule the city. After several days they chose the Duke of Lower Lorraine, Godfrey of Bouillon. According to Guibert of Nogent, he refused to wear a crown of gold in the place where our Saviour wore a crown of thorns. Whether or no that was the reason, Godfrey modestly took the title of "Advocate of the Holy-Sepulchre".*

It was not long before he had to exercise his authority. No one had expected Jerusalem to be taken so soon, and only a few days after the election of Godfrey came the news that the Egyptian relief-troops, who thought they were going to take the besiegers in the rear, had arrived on July 22nd in sight of Jerusalem. Godfrey now found himself in a dangerous situation, for the greater part of the Frankish barons, together with their troops, had already set off on the return journey. It must of course not be forgotten that, for the greater number of them, the crusade was the result of a temporary vow and that, as soon as the vow was fulfilled, their one idea was to return to their own country. The first thing Godfrey had to do then was to send messengers after his former companions to ask them to return. Having joined forces once more, they gave battle in the neighbourhood of Ascalon and this fight (August 12th, 1099) ended in victory.

"*Gesta Francorum*":
   On the Wednesday those princes set out and marched towards the battle. The Bishop of Marturana returned to bring messages to the Patriarch and the Duke. The Saracens went to intercept

him, captured him and carried him off. Peter the Hermit remained in Jerusalem to make arrangements and he ordered the Greeks, Latins and clerks to hold a procession in honour of God and to say prayers and give alms, that God might give the victory to His people. The clerks and priests, wearing their sacred vestments, led the procession to the temple of the Lord and sang masses and orisons, that God might defend His people.

Finally, the Patriarch, the bishops and the other lords met together on the bank of the river which is on this side of Ascalon. There, they carried off a great number of animals—oxen, camels, sheep—and all kinds of booty. The Arabs arrived, about three hundred in number: our men threw themselves upon them, captured two and pursued the others as far as their army. When evening came, the Patriarch had it proclaimed throughout the army that, first thing the next day, they must all be equipped for the battle, and that any man who should think of taking booty before the battle was ended would be excommunicated; but as soon as it was over, they might return joyfully to seize everything that the Lord had predestined for them.

At daybreak they made their way into a magnificent valley, close to the sea-shore, where they set out their battle array. The Duke drew up his troops in battle order, the Count of Normandy his, the Count of Saint-Giles his, the Count of Flanders his, Count Eustace his, Tancred and Gaston theirs. And besides these, archers and foot-soldiers were ranged in front of the knights. When all was then in place, they began to fight in the name of the Lord Jesus Christ.

Duke Godfrey with his troop was on the left flank and the Count of Saint-Giles was riding close to the sea, on the right flank; the Count of Normandy, the Count of Flanders, Tancred and all the others rode in the centre. In this formation our army gradually moved forward. The pagans, on their side, were ready for the fight. Each had his water bottle slung from his neck, so that they could all drink even while they were pursuing us, but, thanks be to God, they had no time to do so.

The Count of Normandy, seeing the Emir's standard adorned with a gold apple at the tip of a silvery lance, rushed violently at the bearer of it and mortally wounded him. The Count of Flanders was attacking vigorously in another quarter. Tancred, from his side, burst into their camp and at sight of him the pagans immediately took flight. There were vast numbers of them, God alone knows how many. The battle was desperate, but a divine force accompanied us, so great and so powerful that in almost no time we conquered them.

The enemies of God were blind and stupefied: their eyes could plainly see the knights of Christ, but it was as if they saw nothing, and they no longer dared to rise against the Christians, for the divine power terrified them. In their fright they climbed into the trees to hide themselves there, but our men, striking them with arrows, spears and swords, dashed them to the ground and massacred them. Others lay down on the earth, no longer daring to stand up against us, and our men beheaded them as one cuts up animals in the market. Near the sea, the Count of Saint-Giles killed an incalculable number of them; some threw themselves into the sea, others fled in all directions.

After that Godfrey remained in Jerusalem with about three hundred knights. But his reign did not last long, for he died on July 18th, 1100. He was succeeded by his brother, Baldwin of Boulogne, who had become Count of Edessa, and who did consent to take the title of King of Jerusalem.

Fulcher of Chartres:

On the day of the Nativity of Our Lord in the year 1101, Baldwin was consecrated with all pomp by the holy anointing, and crowned king in the basilica of the Blessed Mary, at Bethlehem, by the hands of that same Patriarch, in the presence of the Bishop, the clergy and the people: this had not been done for Godfrey, brother and predecessor of Baldwin, both because some people did not approve of it, and because he himself did not wish it; but after they had considered the question more deeply, all agreed that it should be done for Baldwin.

Fulcher of Chartres, who was a member of Baldwin's suite, had remained in the Holy Land. He shows the precarious state of the kingdom:

At that time the land route was still forbidden to our pilgrims; but the French, as well as the Italians and Venetians, setting sail in one or two, or even three and four ships, managed to make their way by sea through the midst of enemy pirates, and passing close by the walls of infidel cities. And when God deigned to lead them they managed by this means, although mortally afraid, to reach

Jaffa, the only port which at that time was in our hands. As soon as we learned of their arrival from the regions of the west, we at once went with joyful hearts to meet them, and congratulate ourselves mutually. We received them like brothers on the sea-shore and each one of us enquired anxiously for news of his country and his family. They on their side told all they knew of them; and then, according to what we learnt, we either rejoiced at the prosperity or were saddened by the misfortune of all those dear to us. These newcomers went on to Jerusalem and visited the Holy Places; then some of them settled in the Holy Land while others returned to their homeland and even as far as France. As a result the holy land of Jerusalem always remained under-populated and had not enough men to defend it against the Saracens, if ever they had dared to attack us. . . .

In fact we had at that time no more than three hundred knights and as many foot-soldiers to guard Jerusalem, Jaffa, and Ramleh.

In addition to the Kingdom of Jerusalem, which was very small in extent and so poorly defended, Frankish Syria comprised the principality of Edessa, on the north-east (which, after Baldwin, went to one of his cousins, Baldwin of Le Bourg), and the principality of Antioch in Northern Syria, which fell into Bohemond's hands. When Tripoli had been conquered, in 1109, after the death of Raymond of Saint-Giles, by his bastard son Bertrand, it also included the principality of Tripoli, on the coast, between Antioch and Jerusalem.

The chroniclers who remained on the spot, Fulcher of Chartres among others, have left us some glimpses of the characteristics of the country and also of the way in which the barons administered it. It is evident that, in the circumstances, they all showed astonishing powers of adaptation, in spite of a climate to which they were not accustomed and a population which for the most part remained strange to them, with an undercurrent of hostility.

Here is Baldwin I discovering his kingdom:

Fulcher of Chartres:

When Baldwin was settled in his tent, the king of this last town [Cayphas] sent him bread, wine, wild honey and sheep; and he informed him by a written message that Duqaq, king of the people of Damascus, and a certain emir of Ginahaldole, prince of Aleppo, were waiting for us with the Turks, Saracens and Arabs on the road which they knew we had to take, and were getting ready to fall upon us. At first we did not at all believe this news, but afterwards we realised the truth of it. About five miles away and not far from the town of Berytus [Beirut] there was a road along the sea-shore that not only we but everyone going in that direction had to take, and that was much too narrow for the passage of an army. If any enemies had entrenched themselves in advance in this defile, a hundred thousand men at arms could by no means have got through it, unless they had arranged that a hundred or seventy well-armed soldiers should hold the narrow entrance to it. It was there that the infidels imagined they would stop us and slay us all. And indeed when the runners who preceded us approached the said passage, they saw several of those Turks, isolated from their companions, advancing against us and awaiting our arrival. When they saw this our scouts, feeling sure that far larger troops were hiding behind these pagans, sent a courier to tell the Lord Baldwin what they had discovered. At this news he immediately set out his army in battle array, divided into several lines, according to the rules of the art of warfare, and we advanced against the enemy, banners unfurled, but marching slowly. As we knew that the fight would soon begin, with true contrition we piously besought the help of the Most High, even as we were marching towards the enemy. The advance-guards of the infidels promptly came to grips with our first lines; many of their men were killed in this skirmish, and four of ours also lost their lives. Both sides soon ended this fight, whereupon we held a council at which it was decided that we would pitch our camp in a place nearer to the enemy, lest, if we abandoned our present place, they should think we were terror-stricken, or about to flee. We were pretending one thing but thinking another; we feigned boldness, but we were dreading death. To retrace our steps was difficult; to go forward more difficult still; on all sides the enemy were besieging us, those at sea from the decks of their ships, while those on the crest of the mountains harried us without respite. That day our men and our pack animals enjoyed neither food nor rest. For my part I would rather have been at Chartres or Orleans than in that place. We spent the whole of that night, then, outside our tents, overwhelmed with sadness and without closing an eye. At the first light of day, when dawn was beginning to chase away the darkness over the earth, we held another council to decide whether we should still strive to live, or if we must die.

The course we chose was to strike camp and retrace our route, sending in the van the pack animals laden with our baggage, herded along by the servants of the army; the men at arms were to follow, vigilantly defending them against the attacks of the Saracens. When it was broad daylight the infidels, seeing us turning back, did in fact descend with all speed to pursue us like fugitives. . . .

All at once God, in His mercy, gave our men at arms such bold courage that, suddenly facing about, they put to flight, along a road which split into three, those who a moment before were pursuing them, not even giving them time to think of defending themselves. Some of these barbarians cast themselves from the top of steep rocks, others ran with all speed to places which seemed to offer some chance of safety; but others were caught and perished at the point of the sword. . . .

The next day we made for a wider country where we and our beasts of burden were able to live in rich places, and ravage the lands of the enemy. On our way we came across many hamlets; at our approach the Saracens who inhabited this country had hidden themselves in caves with their flocks and belongings. As we only succeeded with difficulty in killing a few of them, we lit great fires at the mouths of these lairs; soon an unbearable heat and smoke forced them to come out and surrender to us. Among them were several brigands whose sole task was to waylay our Christians between Ramleh and Jerusalem, and slay them. Some Syrians, Christians like ourselves, who lived in the same hamlets and had hidden themselves in the same caves underground, told us of their crimes; as they really were guilty of them we cut off their heads as they set foot outside the caves. As for the Syrians and their wives, we spared them; but of the Saracens we killed there about a hundred. Then King Baldwin gave orders that all those Syrians should be sent to Ascalon, lest one day or other they should be massacred where they were. When we had eaten and consumed everything that was to be found in those parts, grain as well as animals, and could no longer hope to get anything useful out of those places that had been laid waste in times long past, we held a council with certain Saracens who had been born and bred in that country, but recently converted to the Christian faith, and who knew what there was in the way of both cultivated and uncultivated lands on all sides and far off; and it was decided that the army should go to Arabia. So we crossed the mountains near the place, some forty miles from Jerusalem where, in the tombs of the patriarchs, lie, buried in glory, the bodies of Abraham, Isaac, Jacob, and of their righteous son Joseph, as well as of Sarah and Rebecca; and we reached the valley where the criminal cities of Sodom and Gomorrha, destroyed and swallowed up by the just judgment of God, have given place to the great lake Asphaltite, that is called the Dead Sea. The length of this lake, from the places near Sodom as far as Zoaras in Arabia, is five hundred and eighty stades,* and its width a hundred and fifty; its water is so salt that neither quadrupeds nor birds can drink of it; I myself, Fulcher of Chartres, made trial of it, for, getting down from my mule on the edge of the lake, I tasted its water and found it more bitter than hellebore. It is because nothing can live in this lake, and no fish can be kept there, that it is called the Dead Sea. The river Jordan flows into it at the northern end, but neither river nor lake flows out at the south. Near this lake or Dead Sea is a mountain equally salt, not the whole of it, but in certain parts, where it is as solid as the hardest stone, and as white as snow; the salt it is made of is called rock-salt and one often sees splinters of it falling from the top of the mountain to the bottom. My conjecture is that this lake becomes salt in two ways; first by ceaselessly absorbing some of the salt of the mountain whose foot the waters at the edge of the lake constantly bathe; and secondly by receiving into itself all the rain which falls on the mountain and runs down it. It is also possible that the abyss formed by this lake is so deep that, as a result of an invisible reflux, the great sea, which is salt, infiltrates into it below the earth. Furthermore, it would not be easy to sink and drown oneself in this lake, even on purpose. We walked round the north side of it and found a little town said to be Segor, pleasantly situated and very rich in those fruits of the palm-tree called dates, very sweet to the taste, and which we lived on, for we could get nothing else. Indeed at the first rumour of our march the Arabs who lived in that land had all fled, with the exception of a few wretches blacker than soot, whom we left there like the most worthless seaweed. I saw on several trees in that place a kind of fruit whose outer covering I broke, and found nothing inside but black dust. From there we began to enter the mountainous part of Arabia and spent the night in the caves of which it is full. The next morning, when we had climbed

* A stade was approximately 180 yards.

the mountains, we came across several hamlets where there were no provisions of any kind and whose inhabitants, learning of our arrival, had fled and hidden themselves with all their belongings in the underground caverns. Since there was therefore nothing to be gained by staying there, we bent our steps in another direction, led always by the guides who preceded us. Then we found a valley abounding in fruits of all kinds, the very valley where Moses, instructed by God, struck a rock twice with his rod and made gush out of it, as we read in the scriptures, a spring of living water which was enough to supply all the people of Israel and their beasts of burden. This spring still flows today no less abundantly than then, and forms a little stream which runs so swiftly that it works machines to grind grain. I myself, Fulcher of Chartres, made my horses drink from it. On the summit of a mountain there is a monastery, known as the monastery of Saint Aaron, built on the spot where Moses and Aaron himself usually talked with God. It was therefore a great joy for us to see so holy a place of which we had not known. Since beyond this valley the whole land as far as Babylon is empty and uncultivated, we decided to go no further. It is true that this valley abounded in produce of all kinds; but during our first stay in some hamlets there, the inhabitants, taking their chattels with them and leading their flocks, fled and hid themselves in the most secret places of the mountains, as well as in the caves of the rocks, and boldly defended themselves every time we tried to approach them. So after we had rested there for three days, and sufficiently refreshed ourselves and our beasts of burden with good food, we loaded our animals with all the provisions we needed and then, on a favourable day, at the second hour of the day, and at the signal given by the royal trumpet, we judged the time ripe to take the road again and return. So going once more by the aforementioned sea and the tombs of the patriarchs, of which I have spoken above, we passed through Bethlehem, as well as the place where the tomb of Rachel lies, and happily arrived at Jerusalem on the very day of the winter solstice.

We can get an impression of what the Moslem towns of that time looked like from contemporary writings, such as this description of the city of Aleppo by Ibn Jubayr, a Spanish Moslem who made the pilgrimage to Mecca in the twelfth century (1184):

Aleppo covers an immense surface. It is admirably planned and extraordinarily beautiful, with monumental bazaars regularly set out in long adjacent rows. One goes from one row, reserved for one trade, to another, until one has been through all the trades of the city. All these bazaars are covered with wooden roofs so that inside there is a great deal of shade, and they are so beautiful that everyone looks at them; even people in a hurry stop short in admiration. The principal bazaar looks like an enclosed garden, so gracious and beautiful it is; it surrounds the chief mosque and its stalls are principally shops made of wood, of an original style.

That is a description of a big town, but here, seen by the same traveller, is a little rural market in Dunaysar, a small place in Northern Syria:

Dunaysar lies in a vast plain surrounded by sweet-smelling plants and well-watered market gardens. It has a rural look and is not walled; it attracts the crowds with its well-frequented and well-stocked bazaars; it is the supply centre for the peoples of Syria. It has huge fields and produces many kinds of food. We camped outside the city with the caravan, and on the Thursday morning we went in and stayed there until after the hour of prayer on Friday. The caravan put off its departure so as to be there for the market, for on consecutive Thursdays, Fridays, Saturdays and Sundays a much frequented market is held there. The people come from all the neighbouring places, for the whole road, both to right and left of the town, is an uninterrupted series of villages and inns. This market, to which the people come from all parts, is called the Bazaar.

We can compare two descriptions of the same city, Tripoli, made at an interval of a hundred years. The first description is by a Persian who visited the town in the middle of the eleventh century, that is to say fifty years before the First Crusade.

This city is a thousand cubits long and as many wide. Its hostelries are four or five storeys high and there are even some which are six. The private houses and the bazaars are well built and so clean that each one, as far as cleanness is concerned, might pass for a palace. Every kind of meat, fruit and edible thing that is to be seen in the land of Persia can be found here, and a hundred times better in quality. It is said that there are 20,000 men in this city and many territories and villages belong to it. Very good paper is made there, like that of Samarkand, and of better quality.

The other description was made in the middle of the twelfth century, when the city had been in the hands of the Christians for about fifty years;

It is a big city protected by a stone wall and impregnable: it possesses villages, territories, beautiful domains, many trees such as olives, vines, sugar canes, fruit trees of all kinds, and every sort of crop in countless variety. There is a constant coming and going here. The sea surrounds the town on three sides and it is one of the greatest fortresses of Syria. All kinds of merchandise are brought there and there is a great quantity of foodstuffs.

A new town had been built at Tripoli round the castle of Raymond, the successor of Raymond of Saint-Giles. When the Christian occupation ended it was reputed to have 4,000 silk looms. The Franks had transported to the Orient a custom that had brought great prosperity in their own country, and created a number of towns which enjoyed tax exemptions, as did the new towns of France at the same period. It was by this means that King Baldwin, from the beginning of the twelfth century, attracted the Christians of Transjordan to the neighbourhood of Jerusalem.

He gave the citizens of Jerusalem a great franchise and confirmed it to them by a charter sealed with his seal. It was customary in the city to levy very heavy duties and tolls on the merchandise and people who came to the town; and he granted them such freedom that no Latin and no merchandise of whatever kind paid on entering Jerusalem, nor on leaving, and that everyone bought and sold quite freely what he wanted in the city; and he likewise allowed the Syrians, Greeks and Armenians, and even the Saracens, to bring into the city wheat, barley and all kinds of vegetables without paying any duty.

There was thus freedom of trade, as practised in the West, for Moslems as well as Christians. After Baldwin, Queen Melisande had a bazaar built in Jerusalem where, in the twelfth century, there were twenty-seven bakeries. The chronicles tell us of certain useful public works which were often instituted by private individuals:

"Estoire d'Eracles":

In the first year after the death of Baldwin the Leper it so happened that it rained neither in Jerusalem nor in the territory around, so that there was nothing to drink, or very little. Now in Jerusalem there was a citizen called Germain who was always very ready to do good for the love of God. Because of this dearth of water he had had made, in three different places in Jerusalem, marble tanks.

In each of the three tanks there were two chained bowls, and he had them always kept full of water. Everyone who wanted to, both men and women, went to drink there. When this Germain saw that there was hardly any water left in his cisterns, and that it was not raining, he was much distressed and feared that the good work he had begun would be wasted. Then he remembered how he had heard that men who dwelt there in former days said that close to the pool of Siloam there was an ancient well, the well of Jacob, which had been filled in and covered over; so that now one walked over it and it would be extremely difficult to find. So this prudent man went and prayed to Our Lord that He would give him the grace to find this well and help him to continue the good he had begun, and that by His grace the poor people might enjoy the blessing of water. When the next morning came, he arose and went to the monastery and prayed God to counsel him. After that he immediately went and got workmen and went to the place where he had been told the well had been. He had so much tapping and boring done that the well was found. When he had found it he had it emptied and walled anew, all at his expense. Then he had a wheel made above it, with a bar which an animal turned. And stone tanks were put in place where the water drawn from the well poured out. And everyone in the region who wanted water had it and carried it into the city; the citizen used his own horses day and night to draw up water, and filled the cistern for all those who wanted to take it, and all at his expense, until such time as God gave them rain and they had water in their own cisterns. Even then this prudent man did not stop and he had three beasts of burden and three servitors who did nothing but carry water to the cisterns which he had in the city to supply the poor people. This well from which he had the water drawn was a good fifty fathoms or more in depth. Later, when the Christians saw that the Saracens were going to besiege the city, they destroyed it and filled it in. [*This text was in fact written after the fall of Jerusalem in 1187.*]

A frequently quoted text of Fulcher of Chartres excellently sums up the way in which the Franks of the Holy Land adapted themselves to their new conditions:

We who had been Occidentals have become Orientals; the man who had been a Roman or a Frank has here become a Galilean or an inhabitant of Palestine; and the man who used to live in Rheims or Chartres now finds himself a citizen of Tyre or Antioch. We have already forgotten the places where we were born; already many of us know them not, or at any rate no longer hear them spoken of. Some among us already possess, in this country, houses and servants which belong to them as of hereditary right. Another has married a wife who is not his compatriot, a Syrian or Armenian woman, or even a Saracen who has received the grace of baptism; another has in his house either his son-in-law, his daughter-in-law, or his father-in-law, or his stepson; one is surrounded by his nephews or even his grand-nephews; one cultivates his vines, another his fields; they speak different tongues, and have already all managed to understand each other. The most varied idioms are now common to all those nations and races utterly unlike each other live together in trust.

But the Crusaders still remained in touch, at least in spiritual touch, with the cities of the West and this sometimes led to a kind of "twinning" between Eastern and Western churches. An example of this is to be found in the ties of prayer and friendship, expressed by exchanges of gifts, which linked the Church of Rheims with that of Bethlehem, as the following letter* witnesses:

Anselm, by the grace of God Bishop of Bethlehem, to Leon, venerable Dean of Rheims. . . .
We have learnt, from the letters you have sent us, of your desire to be spiritually united with the glorious church of the Nativity of the Lord. . . . We rejoice to know we are joining as brothers in the prayers of the holy Church of Rheims and we have decided, as your charity has demanded of us, that henceforth your holy company shall share in the joyful devotion of the Church of

* Published in *Archives de l'Orient Latin.* Paris 1881, Vol. I, p. 385

Bethlehem. The beautiful psalter which we have received as a very welcome offering from you will be a remembrance to us of your pious spirit.

Sometimes relics were sent. Thus in 1108 Anseau, the precentor of the church of the Holy Sepulchre in Jerusalem, sent to the canons of Notre Dame in Paris, by his servitor Anselm, a piece of the wood of the True Cross, with a letter* certifying the authenticity of the relic by giving details of the way in which it had come into his hands:

This cross belonged to David, King of Georgia, who holds the mouths of the Caspian . . . and whose land and kingdom are for us like a rampart against the Medes and Persians. As long as he lived he guarded it with great veneration and pious adoration. When he died and was succeeded by his son, his wife, who was revered more for her saintliness than for her noble birth, had her head shaved and took the veil; then taking this cross and much gold, she retired to Jerusalem with some companions . . . to end her days there in retirement, silence and prayer. She gave a part of the gold she had brought to the monasteries of the Holy City, and alms from it to the poor and the pilgrims. Then, on the advice of the Patriarch, she entered a congregation of Georgian nuns in Jerusalem and a little while afterwards, at the request of the sisters and of the Patriarch, she became the head of the community. She had spent all she had brought in alms and on the divers needs of the community, so when a scarcity began to be felt in our region, she and her nuns began to lack necessities . . . and she was constrained to do for the service of the community, what she would never have done for herself. Thus it was that for mere money was bought this wood without price, that I now send to you.

A later letter, sent at the request of the canons, gave further explanations, telling how, at the entry of the Arabs into Jerusalem, the fragment of the True Cross had been cut up so as to be more easily hidden and the pieces dispersed among several princes or Christian cities. This was the reason why one of these relics had been in the possession of the King of Georgia.

* The manuscript of this letter, and also of that referred to in the next commentary, are in the Musée de l'Histoire de France at the Archives Nationales in Paris. (A.E. II. 125, 6.) See the old catalogue of the Musée.

THE MOSLEMS DISCOVER THEIR
MASTERS

❋❋❋❋❋❋❋❋❋❋❋❋❋❋❋❋❋❋❋❋❋❋❋❋❋❋❋❋❋❋❋❋❋❋❋❋❋

*T*HE RELATIONS *of the Crusaders with the Moslem peoples were inevitably those of victors with vanquished. And the Saracens of Syria were later as glad to shake off the Frankish domination as the Christians of Spain were of that* Reconquista *that freed them from Moslem tutelage at the same time. For all that, it would be totally wrong to suppose that there was a reign of terror, or indeed even exploitation such as that which the Indian populations of the New World experienced, exterminated as they were in North America, or reduced to a condition of near slavery, as they were in South America. The obligations imposed on the Moslems were: one day of forced labour a year for every seventy-five acres of cultivable land, plus the surrender of a proportion of the crops, varying from a quarter to a half according to the district. This was altogether a much better lot than that imposed, for instance, on the tenant farmers of seventeenth-century France, not to mention those of the nineteenth. And what is astonishing is that the humble Frankish people, who had remained in the country, mostly paid heavier dues, for they were subject to the ecclesiastical tithe from which the Moslems were exempt. The narrative of Ibn Jubayr, which we have already quoted, contains the following passages on the situation of the Moslems in the territory controlled by the Franks, as he was able to see it for himself on his return journey from Mecca, between Damascus and Acre:*

We left Tibnin [Toron] by a road flanked throughout its length with farms inhabited by Moslems, who live in great prosperity under the Franks—may Allah preserve us from similar temptation! The conditions imposed on them are the surrender of half their crops at the time of harvest and the payment of a poll-tax of one dinar seven qirats,* as well as a light tax on fruit-trees. The Moslems are masters in their own dwellings and order their affairs as they think best. Such is the constitution of the farms and big villages that they inhabit in the Frankish territory. Many Moslems long in their hearts to settle here, when they see the condition of their brethren in districts under Moslem government, for the state of these latter is the very opposite of comfortable. It is unfortunate for the Moslems that, in countries governed by their co-religionists, they have always to complain of the injustices of their rulers, whereas they have nothing but praise for the conduct of the Franks, on whose justice they can always rely.

Another Moslem writer, Usama ibn Munqidh, writing of the year 1140, pays a similar tribute to Frankish justice—though making quite clear the antipathy he feels for the Franks:

The Franks (may Allah forsake them!) have none of the better qualities of men, except courage. Only the knights among them have any special standing or pre-eminence. The knights are really their only men, and it is therefore they who are the arbiters of their counsels, judgments and decisions. One day I sought redress from them for the flocks of sheep that the lord of Paneas [Banyas]† had carried off in the forest. Now, I was then living in Damascus and there was peace between them and us. I said to King Fulk,‡ son of Fulk, "This lord has committed a hostile act against me and seized our flocks. He did this at the season when the sheep were lambing and their lambs were still-born. After he had caused the loss of their young he gave them back to us."

The King at once said to six or seven knights, "Go and sit in judgment for him!" They left the hall, retired and deliberated until they had reached agreement, and then returned to the hall where the King was giving audience and said: "We have decided that the lord of Paneas must repay the amount he has caused them to lose through the death of their lambs." The King ordered him to discharge this debt; but he pleaded with me, insisting and

* One dinar and seven qirats corresponds to a bezant.

† Rainier of Brus.

‡ Fulk of Anjou, the fourth king of Jerusalem, son of Fulk IV, Count of Anjou, who came to the throne on August 31st, 1131.

imploring so much that in the end I accepted four hundred dinars from him as payment. Now, once the knights have pronounced a decision, neither the King nor any Frankish leader can alter or attenuate it, so great is the importance of the knights in their eyes!

Usama also related two anecdotes which reveal that the people who were frankly hostile to the Moslems as such, were the westerners who had newly landed in the country. The others had learnt to live with them:

Not a single one of those who have recently settled in the territories of the Franks but shows himself more inhuman than his predecessors already established among us and used to the Moslems.

What happened to me when I visited Jerusalem is a proof of the hardness of the Franks (may Allah crush them!). I was going into the Mosque al-Aqsa. Beside it there was a little mosque that the Franks had turned into a church. When I entered the Mosque al-Aqsa, which was occupied by the Templars, who were friends of mine, they told me that I could say my prayers in this little mosque. One day I went in and glorified Allah. I was deep in my prayer when one of the Franks fell upon me, laid hold of me and turned my face to the east, saying: "That is the way to pray!" A troop of Templars rushed at him, seized him and thrust him out. I began to pray again. This same man, escaping from their supervision, fell on me again, turned my face to the east once more, repeating: "That is the way to pray!" The Templars once again rushed at him and thrust him out; then they excused themselves to me, and said: "He is a foreigner, who arrived a few days ago from the lands of the Franks. He has never seen anyone pray without turning to the east." I replied: "I have prayed enough for today." And I left, surprised at seeing what a contorted face that devil had, how he trembled, and what an impression it had made on him to see someone pray facing the *kibla* [Mecca].

And here is his second anecdote.

This is what my compatriot told me: "I went with him and we entered the house of a knight who was one of the knights of the old school, who had arrived with the first expedition of the Franks. His name had been removed from the tax lists, he was exempted from all military service, and in addition he had been endowed with a fief at Antioch, which was his means of liveli-hood. On his orders a magnificent table was brought, set with dishes of the utmost delicacy and absolute perfection. My host nevertheless noticed that I refrained from eating. "Eat," he said to me, "you will like it. For I too do not eat the food of the Franks, but I have Egyptian cooks, and I only eat what they cook. What is more, the flesh of pigs never enters my house." So I ate, but with cirumspection. Afterwards, we took leave of our host. A few days later I was crossing the market-place when a Frankish woman attached herself to me, uttering barbarous cries in their language, and I did not understand a word of what she was saying. A crowd gathered round us. They were Franks and I felt certain that my death was near. But thereupon the same knight came up. He saw me, drew near and said to the woman: "What is this Moslem to do with you?" She answered: "He is the murderer of my brother Hurso." Now, Hurso was a knight from Apamea, who had been killed by a soldier of the army of Hama. The Christian knight reproached the woman, saying to her: "The man before you is a burgher, that is to say a merchant, who does not fight and is not even present at battles." He then reprim-anded the crowd, which dispersed. Then he took me by the hand and went with me. It was therefore thanks to this meal that I escaped from certain death.

Another of Usama's stories reveals that the Franks at least often felt a genuine friendship for the Arabs:

I am going to tell you a few things about the Franks and the surprise their minds often caused me.

There was in the army of King Fulk, the son of Fulk, a worthy Frankish knight who had come from their country to make the pilgrimage and then return. He made my acquaintance and became so attached to me that he called me his brother. We were fond of each other and spent our time together. When he was preparing to cross the sea again to return to his own country, he said to me: "O my brother, I am going home and I would like, if you will let me, to take your son and show him our part of

the world (I had with me my boy of fourteen). He will see our
knights there, he will learn wisdom and the science of chivalry.
When he returns he will have the bearing of an intelligent man."
These words, which were not the words of a sensible man,
wounded my ears. For even if my son had been made prisoner,
captivity could have brought him no other calamity than to be
transported to the land of the Franks. I answered: "As you live,
that was what I meant to do, but I have been prevented by my
son's affection for his grandmother, my mother. She only let him
come with me because I swore to bring him back." "Is your
mother still alive?" he asked me. "Yes," I answered. And he
said to me: "Do not upset her."

*It was religion, not race, that created barriers between Franks and
Saracens, as Usama's story of these marriages proves:*

Some young Frankish girl captives had been brought to the
house of my father (may Allah have pity on him!). These Franks
(may Allah curse them!) belong to an accursed race, which does
not join itself in marriage with those of another race. My father
singled out a beautiful young girl, in the flower of youth, and
said to the housekeeper: "Make her take a bath, tidy her person
and dress her for a journey." The housekeeper obeyed. My father
entrusted the young girl to one of his equerries and had her taken
to the Emir Shihab ed-Din Malik ibn Salim ibn Malik, lord of
Kal'at Dja'bar, one of his friends, to whom he wrote: "We have
taken booty from the Franks and I send you a share of it." The
young girl pleased and charmed the Emir. He kept her for himself
and she bore him a son whom he called Badran. His father made
him his heir presumptive. He grew up and his father died. Badran
governed the town and the people, his mother keeping the right
to command and forbid. With the connivance of a few men she
slid down a rope from the top of Ka'lat Dja'bar. These men
accompanied her as far as Saruj, which then belonged to the
Franks. She married a Frankish shoemaker, while her son was
lord of Kal'at Dja'bar.

Among the Frankish women who had been sent to my father's
house, there was an old woman with one of her daughters, young
and well built, and a sturdy son. The son became a Moslem and his
Islamism was genuine, to judge by his show of prayer and fasting.

He learnt the art of working marble at the school of an artist who was paving my father's house with marble. Then, as his sojourn continued, my father gave him in marriage to a woman from a pious family and provided him with all he needed for his wedding and to set up house. His wife bore him two sons, who grew up amongst us. They were five and six years old when their father, the workman Raoul, whose joy they were, left with them and their mother, taking everything that was in the house to go and join the Franks at Apamea. He became a Christian once more and his children with him, after years of Islamism, prayer and faith. May Allah the All-High cleanse the world of that breed!

Glory to Allah, the author of all things, the creator! Whoever has become acquainted with what concerns the Franks cannot but praise with me and sanctify Allah the All-Powerful; for he has seen in them creatures who are superior in courage and ardour in battle, but in nothing else, just as animals are superior in strength and aggression.

THE KNIGHTS DEFEND THEIR
FRONTIERS

✤✤✤

*T*HE EXISTENCE of the Latin kingdoms was precarious and constantly threatened. It was the existence of a handful of men whose safety was in fact only assured from one outpost to another, each protected by castles or fortified towns that they had hastened to build. Their activity as builders astonishes us nowadays. The splendid witnesses of it that remain under the Syrian sun after centuries and centuries—Krak of the Knights, Margat, Saone, and many more—are still impressive. They met a need: sheltered by those bastions, a few men were enough to bar the route to an army. They did in fact assure the survival of Frankish Syria; and those fortresses tell the story of the Kingdom of Jerusalem.

From time to time reinforcements arrived in the shape of the flood of pilgrims which had never entirely ceased and from then on became larger than it ever had been, since to take the crusading vow had become an act of piety, encouraged by the Church. It is true that each flux was followed by a reflux, since the greater part of the Crusaders only remained for a short time in Syria; but at least some of them settled there, so that the population of Western origin ended by being relatively abundant, even in humble folk, traders and artisans, established in the towns. In Jerusalem, when Saladin retook the city, there were about 20,000 persons who could not pay ransom. There was as well the far from negligible addition of the Italian traders, who little by little established themselves in the coastal cities of the prosperous colonies. But above all from time to time there arrived barons who had taken the cross and brought with them a certain number of men-at-arms.

A very artificial system of classification has sometimes been laid down for the history of the Crusades, and it is traditional to write and repeat that there were eight Crusades in 200 years. This reckoning cannot *be justified; there was in reality a continual influx, followed by returns almost as frequent; a coming and going that thenceforth linked the East and the West. Every noble family whose history we can follow—for example the two families of the chroniclers Villehardouin and Joinville —show us a departure for the Crusades in each generation. The eight Crusades of tradition were only rather more important expeditions than the others, inspired by outstanding events such as the loss of Edessa or Jerusalem. The history of the first reigns of the Latin kingdoms consists chiefly of small skirmishes of limited importance which consolidated the conquest. Thus, between 1101 and 1110 the ports of Caesarea, Acre, Beirut and Sidon were conquered—all coastal places facilitating the arrival of help if occasion arose; consequently the pilgrims thenceforward took the sea-route. Fulcher of Chartres has recalled for us a few episodes of combats, such as the one that took place before Ascalon:*

We must tell how, in this same year, the King of Babylon assembled a great army and sent it, under the leadership of the general of his militia, to Ascalon, to combat the Christian faith, planning and thinking he would be able to exterminate us from the Holy Land down to the last man. He had been told that we were reduced to a very small number and that we no longer received, as we used to, new levies of pilgrims. So at Ascalon there assembled Arab horsemen, Ethiopian foot-soldiers and about a thousand Turks from Damascus, excellent archers. When King Baldwin learnt of it, he summoned all his people to Joppa [Jaffa] and there prepared to withstand the attack. Of necessity, no man able to bear arms remained in our towns; they all left for the war, except the sentinels who were indispensable to guard the walls during the night. At that a sharp fear seized us and we trembled lest the infidels should either surprise some one of our cities thus bereft of any garrison, or in the end manage to overcome our King and his little troop. It was the month of August. At first both parties adopted ruses, putting off the fight; and both sides stayed where they were, we without marching against them and they without attacking us. But finally and, I believe, at the time fixed by Providence, the impious brood of pagans left Ascalon and drew near to the country we occupied. As soon as the King heard this he left Joppa and, mounted on his charger, went as far as the town of Ramleh. As it was needful that all our people should unite in the Lord in every way possible,

placing in him their firm hope, Baldwin, inspired by God
Himself, first sent a messenger with all speed to urge the Patriarch,
the clergy and the humble folk also, to implore with fervour the
mercy of the All-Powerful, that He might deign, from the heights
of heaven, to lend His aid to His Christians, placed in so difficult a
position. This messenger could by no means be brought to
accept any reward, for fear lest he should be surprised and slain
on his way by the enemy; he wisely chose rather to rely on the
Lord to reward him for his pains and, recommending his soul
and body to God, he mounted and rode in all haste to Jerusalem.
He had hardly entered the Holy City before he made known his
mission and what the situation demanded: as soon as he had
explained his request, the Patriarch ordered that the greatest bell
should be rung and all the people assemble before him. "O my
brethren," he then said, "you, my friends and the servitors of
God, this war, that you were told would soon break out, is now to
begin; this messenger has just announced it to us and, beyond any
doubt it is nearly upon us. Without God's help we should
certainly be in no state to resist in any way the horde of enemies
that threaten us. You must all then implore the Lord's clemency
so that, in the fight that is being prepared, He will deign to show
Himself favourable and merciful to our King Baldwin and all his
people. Our prince preferred not to give battle today, as he tells
us by this messenger, so that he might give it more safely tomorrow, Sunday, the day when Christ rose from the dead. And
he has waited for our alms and prayers to ensure him the support
of the Lord, in whom alone he trusts. Therefore, in accordance
with the words of the Apostle, watch throughout this night,
remain firm in the faith, and all that you do, do with love.
Tomorrow go barefoot to the Holy Places, rend your hearts,
abase yourselves, address ardent supplications to the Lord your
God that He may deliver us from the hands of His enemies. As for
me, I am leaving you, to go to this battle that is about to begin;
and if among you there still remains one who wishes to take
arms, let him come with me, for our King lacks men." What
more is there to say? All who could mounted their horses; there
were a hundred and fifty of them, both horsemen and foot-
soldiers. At nightfall they set out, marching rapidly, and reached
the town of Ramleh before daylight. As for those who remained
in Jerusalem, they gave themselves fervently to prayer, alms and

tears; until midday they went on visiting the churches; they wept in singing, and sang as they wept; and all this they did in procession. I myself was with them, barefoot.

The battle begins:

The Saracens, surrounding us on all sides, thought they would be able to penetrate our ranks and throw them into complete disorder. Already indeed the Turks, coming up behind our last squadron, were raining a hail of arrows upon them; and then, ceasing to use their bows, they drew their swords from the scabbard and struck our men with them at close range. Seeing this the King, carried away by his own courage, wrenched his white banner from the hands of one of his knights and, followed only by a few of his men, ran with all speed to that place to bring help to those of our men who were so cruelly overwhelmed. Soon, with the help of the Lord, he scattered the Turks by the force of his attack, killed a great number of them and returned to the places where the greatest crowd of Saracens and Ethiopians was fighting. Then the Arabs, Turks and Ethiopians all fled together; some reached the mountains, and the others remained dead on the field of battle. It was because I was afraid that all these deeds might not be written down and so become forgotten, because of the negligence or incompetence of those able to write—rare people in any case I imagine, and all absorbed in their own affairs—that I, Fulcher, although my learning is rude and my capacity feeble, thought that I ought to run the risk of being taxed with temerity rather than not publish those marvellous works of the Lord. I have therefore collected all that I saw with my own eyes, or learnt by carefully questioning truthful narrators; and then, so that I might not be the only person able to perceive all these things and take them in at a glance, moved by pious affection I put them together in a proper book, although written in an unpolished style, and handed them on to those who will come after me. So I beg the reader to be indulgent and charitable to my ignorance; let him rectify here and there, if he wishes, the style of this writing, that no orator has corrected; but let him not go and change the crux of it with the idea of giving more dignity and beauty to the arrangement of the parts of this story, lest by some error he should tamper with the truth of the facts. After the events that I have related above, and at the end of the year, all those of us who were then in Jerusalem felt, on the eve of the Birth of the Lord, a violent earthquake, which caused them acute fear.

In the stories of the Arab Usama we find episodes which bring vividly before us that clash of two mentalities, and the series of truces and battles that constituted daily life in Frankish Syria:

Tancred, the first lord of Antioch after Bohemond,* had pitched his tents close to us. After the battle there had been a reconciliation. Tancred came up and asked us to surrender to him a horse belonging to an equerry of my paternal uncle, Izz ed-Din (may Allah have pity on him!). It was a magnificent horse. My uncle had it brought to him, mounted by a Kurd called Hasanoun, a companion of ours and a brave horseman, young, of attractive bearing and slender. He was to make this horse outstrip others under the eyes of Tancred. The horseman started his mount off at full gallop and made him pass all the other horses that had been made to gallop along the road. When Hasanoun was admitted to Tancred's presence, the Frankish knights examined the strength of his forearms, admired his slender waist and his youth and admitted that he was a valiant horseman. Tancred honoured him with presents. Then Hasanoun said: "O my master, I would like to beg an assurance from you. It is that, if ever you take me prisoner in war, you will favour me by releasing me." Tancred granted him what he asked, or at least Hasanoun thought he did, for those men spoke no tongue but that of the Franks and we did not understand the meaning of their words.

A year had passed, or a little more. The truce expired and once again Tancred advanced towards us, at the head of the army of Antioch. The battle was joined beneath the walls of our town. Our horsemen had overtaken the advance-guard of the Franks. One of our Kurdish companions, called Kamil al-Mashtub, rained blows upon them. He and Hasanoun were equally courageous. In the meantime Hasanoun was standing with my father, in a little house that he owned, waiting for his horse that his equerry was to bring him from the veterinary surgeon, and waiting also for his armour. He grew impatient, and upset at

* Tancred succeeded Bohemond I when the latter left for Europe in 1104.

seeing the blows given by Kamil al-Mashtub, and said to my father: "O my master, give me an accoutrement, even a light one." So my father answered: "Those mules are carrying armour. Choose whatever you wish." I was at that moment standing behind my father; I was a youth and it was the first time I had been present at a battle. Hasanoun looked over the breastplates in their cases on the backs of the mules; none fitted him. He foamed with rage in his burning desire to distinguish himself in action, like Kamil al-Mashtub. He went out on the threshold of his little house, wearing no breastplate. A Frankish knight barred his way. Hasanoun struck his enemy's mare on the crupper with his spear. The mare took the bit in her teeth and dragged off Hasanoun, casting him into the middle of a squadron of Franks. They took him captive, inflicted every kind of torture on him, and wanted to put out his left eye. But Tancred (may Allah curse him!) said to them: "Put out his right eye instead so that, when he carries his shield, his left eye being hidden, he will no longer be able to see anything." They put out his right eye, as Tancred had ordered. For his ransom they claimed a thousand dinars and a brown horse belonging to my father, a magnificent horse from Khafadja, that my father parted with to ransom Hasanoun.

Here is another battle, related by the same Arab warrior. The Saracens had dug a mine under the ramparts of Kafartab, held by the Franks, and the wall had collapsed.

After we had rested until midday, a foot-soldier left our ranks, holding his sword and buckler, and advanced towards the fallen wall, whose extremities were like the steps of a ladder. He climbed up it until he had reached the topmost point. When our other soldiers saw him, about ten foot-soldiers, equipped with their arms, rushed after him and quickly climbed up the slope one behind the other until they finally arrived at the fortress without having aroused the attention of the Franks. As soon as we had put on our breastplates we also left our tents and advanced, and the fortress was invaded by a large army before the Franks had gathered themselves together. Then they advanced upon the besiegers, riddling them with their wooden arrows and wounding the man who had climbed up first. He descended while his companions vied with each other in continuing to mount. They found themselves face to face with the Franks on a curtain-wall of the fortress.

Before them was a tower, whose door was guarded by a horse-man wearing a breastplate and carrying his shield and his spear, whose task was to prevent access to it. The massed Franks assailed our men from the flat roof of it, showering wooden arrows and stones thickly on them. A Turk climbed up and we watched him do it; he advanced, braving death, until he was close to the tower and had thrown at the man who stood at the entrance a vessel full of naphtha. I saw the knight, like a burning brand, roll down that pile of stones towards his companions. They threw themselves to the ground for fear of being burnt alive. The Turk then returned towards us.

Another Turk climbed on to that same curtain-wall. He had his sword and buckler. Coming out of the tower at whose door the knight had mounted guard, we saw a Frankish foot-soldier who advanced to meet him, protected by a double coat of mail, brandishing a spear but with no shield. The Turk grappled with him, sword in hand. The Frank struck him a blow; but the Turk, thanks to his shield, thrust far from him the point of the spear and marched up to the Frank to disarm him. But he turned away, bowing and bending his back like a Moslem in prayer, so as to protect his head. The Turk dealt him several blows, which did him no harm, and the Frank went back into the tower unharmed.

The situation of our soldiers gradually improved. Their number kept on increasing. The Franks surrendered the citadel. Then the prisoners were led down to where the tents of Bursuk, son of Bursuk, had been pitched.

Among them I recognised the foot-soldier with the spear who had come out to meet the Turk. He had been brought with the others into the pavilion reserved for Bursuk, son of Bursuk, so that the price for setting each one at liberty might be fixed. The foot-soldier was waiting patiently. He was a sergeant. "How much will you take for me?" he asked. "We ask six hundred gold pieces," he was told. He laughed in their faces and said: "I am a sergeant; my monthly pay consists of two pieces of gold. Where do you think I could get six hundred from?" Then he went back and sat with his companions.

There was a crowd of prisoners there. The Emir, the noble leader, one of the principal emirs of his time, said to my father (may Allah have pity on them both!): "O my brother, you see these people, let us pray Allah that he will protect us from them!"

But the Saracens had to give way before the assaults of the Franks.

My father (may Allah have pity on him!) came to find me. I had taken leave of him when he left Kafartab, and now the Sultan's army had been defeated. As for us, we had the captives brought out two by two, so that they might be led in chains to the inhabitants of Shaizar. One had had half his body burnt and his thigh pierced, another had perished by fire. What had happened to them was a useful lesson to us. We had to decide to leave and return to Shaizar with my father (may Allah have pity on him!). Before going everyone took possession of whatever was within his reach: tents, camels, mules, baggage and everything that could be loaded on the pack animals. Then the army dispersed.

These unexpected setbacks were due to a strategem of the eunuch Lulu, who at that time was powerful in Aleppo. He had undertaken with the master of Antioch* to use trickery to divide the Moslems. The Prince would then only have to lead his army out of Antioch and cut them in pieces. Lulu had sent a message to the generalissimo Bursuk conceived in the following terms: "You must send me an emir with enough forces for me to hand Aleppo over to him, for I greatly fear that the inhabitants will not fall in with my intention to surrender the place. I therefore want the emir to be in command of a troop I can rely upon against the people of Aleppo." Bursuk put into the field the Emir of the Uzbek armies at the head of three thousand horsemen. The next morning Roger (may Allah curse him!) attacked them and cut them in pieces. Thus was the divine will accomplished!

The Franks (may Allah curse them!) returned to Kafartab, rebuilt the town and established themselves there. Allah the All-Powerful had resolved that the captive Franks, taken at Kafartab, should regain their liberty; for the emirs had shared them out among themselves, and then had spared their lives so that they might ransom themselves. The only exceptions were those who had fallen into the hands of the emir of the armies; for, before

* Roger, Prince of Antioch since the end of 1112.

setting out for Aleppo, he had cut off the heads of all the prisoners
who had fallen to his share.

Usama describes the fate of the Frankish hostages:

We had at that time with us at Shaizar, as hostages to guarantee
a debt owed by Baldwin, King of the Franks, to Husam ed-Din
Timurtash, son of Ilghazi (may Allah have pity on him!), some
Frankish and Armenian knights. When the debt was settled and
they were on the point of returning to their country, Khirkhan,
lord of Homs, sent out a troop of horsemen who lay in ambush
outside Shaizar. When the hostages came up, their enemies
appeared and seized them. The public crier informed my father
and my paternal uncle (may Allah have pity on them both!), who
immediately mounted their horses, took up a conspicuous position
and sent all those who joined them to deliver the hostages. I
went too and my father said to me: "Follow in their footsteps
with your companions and do not flinch from death to save your
hostages." I left, arrived just in time, after having galloped for the
greater part of the journey, delivered them and their escort and
took prisoner some of the horsemen from Homs. But above all I
admired my father's words: "Do not flinch from death to save
your hostages."

A battle on the banks of the Orontes, and the discovery of a sorceress:

The son of that devil Bohemond made our men undergo a
terrible ordeal. One day he came with his army and pitched his
tents at our gates. We had already mounted our horses to withstand them. Not one of them advanced to meet us. They did
not leave their tents while we rode along some rising ground,
observing them, and separated from them only by the course of
the Orontes.

The son of one of my paternal uncles, Laith ad-Daula Yaha,
son of Malik, son of Humaid (may Allah have pity on him!),
left our ranks in the direction of the Orontes. We thought he was
going to water his mare. He plunged into the water, crossed the
river and made his way towards a small detachment of the Franks,
motionless by their tents. When he was close to them, one of
their horsemen came to meet him. The two adversaries hurled

themselves upon one another, but each of them avoided the blow
of the spear meant for him.

At that very moment I and some other young men like myself
hurried towards the two combatants. The detachment began to
move. The son of Bohemond mounted his horse, as did his
soldiers. They rushed forward, swift as a torrent. My father's
mare had been struck by a blow from a spear. The first lines of our
horsemen clashed with the first lines of their cavalry. Among our
troops there was a Kurd, called Mika'il, who in his flight had
reached their advance-guard. A Frankish knight, coming up
behind him, had pierced him with his spear. The Kurd, stretched
out before him, groaned loudly, uttering great cries. I went to
him. As for the Frank, he had turned away from the Kurdish
horseman and was galloping far from where I was, in pursuit of
our horsemen, numbers of whom were posted along our bank of
the river. I was behind him, spurring my horse to catch him up so
that I might strike him; but I did not succeed. The Frank paid no
attention to me; he was entirely taken up with our groups of
horsemen. Finally he reached them, always pursued by me.
My companions struck his horse a mortal blow with a spear.
But his companions came hot-foot after him, too many in
number for us to do anything against them. The Frankish
knight went off on his dying horse, met his soldiers, turned
them all back and departed under their protection. Now, this
knight was none other than the son of Bohemond, lord of
Antioch. Being still a youth, his soul had fallen a prey to terror.
If he had let his soldiers act, we should have been put to flight and
thrust back within the walls of our town.

During the battle, an old servant woman called Buraika,
in the service of 'Ali ibn Mahbub, one of our Kurdish companions, was standing among the horsemen on the river bank.
She was holding in her hand a drink to quench her own thirst
and that of the men. The greater part of our companions, when
they saw the Franks advancing in such hordes, turned back towards the town while that old hag remained, in no way appalled
by this grave happening. . . .

What follows was told me by Bakiyya: "I entered the town at
nightfall, anxious to get into my house where I had things to do.
When I got near Shaizar I saw among the tombs, by the light of
the moon, a living creature which seemed to be neither man nor

wild animal. Feeling afraid, I remained at a distance. Then I said
to myself: "Am I not Bakiyya? Why should I fear an isolated
creature?" I laid down my sword, shield and spear that I had with
me, and I advanced step by step, hearing the creature sing and
speak. Then, when I was quite close, I threw myself upon it,
with a dagger in my hand, and took hold of it roughly. And
behold it was Buraika, with her head uncovered, her hair on
end, astride a branch, whinnying and wheeling among the tombs.
I said: "Woe betide you! What are you doing here at this hour?"
She answered: "Sorcery." And I went on: "May Allah abhor you,
may He abhor your sorcery and your tricks beyond all things!"

THE ROMANTIC ESCAPE OF
JOSCELIN OF COURTENAY

⚜⚜⚜⚜⚜⚜⚜⚜⚜⚜⚜⚜⚜⚜⚜⚜⚜⚜⚜⚜⚜⚜⚜⚜⚜⚜⚜⚜⚜⚜⚜⚜⚜⚜⚜⚜⚜

*B*ALDWIN THE FIRST, *King of Jerusalem, died in 1118. Fulcher of Chartres has left us an account of his death:*

In the year 1118 since the Virgin birth, and at the end of the month of March, King Baldwin launched a fierce attack against the town called Pharamia, took it and devastated it. One day after this expedition, when he was walking in a cheerful mood with his companions, he went as far as the river that the Greeks call the Nile, and the Hebrews Geon, close to the place just mentioned. There some of the knights skilfully speared a few young fish with their lances, took them to their lodging in the above-mentioned town and began to eat them. Suddenly the King felt ill inside, because the pains of an ancient wound started again with great violence. The news of this was immediately passed on to his followers; as soon as they learnt of his malady, they were greatly troubled and saddened and full of respectful compassion. It was decided to return to Jerusalem; but as the King could not mount his horse, his followers made him a litter with the tent-poles and laid him on it; then, at the first blast of the herald's horn, orders were given to set out to return to the Holy City. When we reached the town called Laris [el-Arish], Baldwin, wasted to nothing by his ever-increasing illness, breathed his last. His followers then washed him and salted his entrails, and placing his body on a bier they carried it with them to Jerusalem. By God's will, and an inconceivable chance, on the very day when, according to the rules of the Church, it is customary to carry branches of palm, this lugubrious troop bearing the sad remains of the King met the procession at the moment when it was descending from the Mount of Olives towards the valley of Jehoshaphat. At the sight of it, and as soon as the event became known, all present uttered groans instead of songs of triumph and joy; the Franks wept, the Syrians shed tears, and so did even the Saracens who beheld this spectacle: who indeed could have helped giving way to reverent grief? People and clergy all returned to the town, acting as sorrow and custom dictate, and buried Baldwin in Golgotha, close to his brother Duke Godfrey.

His cousin, Baldwin of Le Bourg, succeeded him, as he had already succeeded him as Count of Edessa, a title which he now yielded to a vassal called Joscelin of Courtenay, lord of Tiberias. Like his predecessor, Baldwin had married an Armenian and his whole reign had but one aim: to make the Frankish kingdom strike roots on Syrian soil. It was during this period that those monkish knights, the Templars, became a genuine military force in the kingdom; they had originally been a small band of eight knights who, at the prompting of Hugh of Payens, undertook to safeguard the security of the pilgrims on the road from Jaffa to Jerusalem. Following their example the Hospitallers, who before the foundation of the Latin kingdoms of the Holy Land had been monkish nurses running the hospital of Saint John at Jerusalem, also became a semi-military order to whom fortresses were entrusted.

In 1123, five years after it had begun, the reign of Baldwin II very nearly came to an end, which might well have endangered the very existence of Frankish Syria. For in that year, during a hawking expedition in the valley of the Euphrates, the King was taken prisoner by the Turkish emir Balak who had already, a few months previously, captured Joscelin of Courtenay, Count of Edessa. They were both imprisoned in the citadel of Kharpurt. Some time previously, Roger, the Prince of Antioch, had been killed, and with him his army of 700 knights and 3,000 foot-soldiers had been massacred to the last man, with unheard-of refinements of cruelty, by a Turkish emir, Ilghazi, who had attacked him with very superior forces. The Patriarch of Antioch, Bernard of Valence, had organised the resistance of the city as best he could, but the fact remained that, of the four principalities which made up Frankish Syria, only one, that of Tripoli, still kept its prince—at that time Pons of Tripoli—at the head of his government.

Baldwin and Joscelin were rescued in the most romantic way, with the help of the Armenian population of Kharpurt.

Fulcher of Chartres:

Towards the middle of the month of August, thanks to the goodness of divine Providence, Baldwin, King of Jerusalem, got out of prison and was freed from the irons in which Balak had kept him in a certain castle [Kharpurt, in Kurdistan] that was very strong because of its situation, inaccessible because of its height, and difficult to take. Joscelin, Count of Edessa, was also imprisoned there, with a few other captives. The story of the rescue of this prince is rather long, but remarkable because of the divine interventions that assisted it, and starred with miracles. After they had languished for a long time, hidden away in this castle, deprived of all help and a prey to cruel sufferings, those unhappy creatures began to concoct a thousand plans whereby, in some clever way, they might manage to escape. To that end, with the help of faithful messengers, they never ceased to beg for assistance in every place where they had friends. A few Armenians lived in the neighbourhood of their prison; the messengers strove to win over these people and secure their loyalty in furthering the escape, if they themselves succeeded in obtaining the help of their friends outside. By means of a few presents and many promises, a treaty was concluded and sworn to on both sides under oath. Then fifty ordinary soldiers were sent from the town of Edessa to the castle to help in the rescue of the prisoners. These soldiers disguised themselves as poor folk, loaded wares upon their backs and, while they were selling them, seized favourable occasions to slip in as far as the inner gates of the castle. At a moment when the head of the guards was imprudently playing chess with one of the men devoted to our prisoners, the soldiers cunningly drew closer, as if to complain to him of some insult that they said had been given them. Then, suddenly putting aside all fear and all hesitation, they drew their knives from their sheaths, killed this man in less time than it takes to tell, seized spears that they found to hand and quickly struck and killed everyone they came across. Great cries arose; within and without everyone was in turmoil; the first to run to the place where the tumult was were the first to get massacred; and about a hundred Turks perished in this confusion. The gates were immediately closed and the King, with the other captives, brought out of prison. Some of them, still with irons on their feet, climbed up ladders to the top of the walls and planted the standard of the

Christians on the summit of the citadel, to show all beholders the truth of what had happened. The favourite wife of Balak was in this same citadel. It was not long, however, before the Turks surrounded the castle on all sides, preventing anyone from entering or leaving, and piled up carts against the gates to block all passage. Furthermore, I think I must not pass over in silence how Balak in a dream had a revelation of a certain misfortune that threatened him. As he himself related afterwards to his people, he thought he saw Joscelin plucking out his eyes. His priests, whom he immediately told of this dream, asking them the meaning of it, told him "that this misfortune or another like it would certainly happen to him, if chance decided that he should one day fall into the hands of this Joscelin". At this answer he sent without delay to the castle a messenger empowered to cut Joscelin's throat, so as to make sure that he should not be able to kill him, as it had been foretold he would. But thank God, before this executioner could reach Joscelin, he had got out of captivity.

Meanwhile, King Baldwin and his men were prudently considering together how they could obtain some kind of help. As it seemed the right time to take a risk for that purpose, the Lord Joscelin declared himself ready to face the danger of almost certain death. So, commending himself to the Creator of the universe, he left the castle, followed by three of his servants and, with the help of the moonlight, succeeded, though as full of fear as he was of courage, in passing through the midst of the enemy. Once out of danger he immediately sent back to the King one of his servants, telling him to give his ring to Baldwin as it had been previously agreed between them, so that he should know that he had completely escaped from the Turks who were besieging the castle. Thereafter, fleeing or hiding by turns, and marching more by night than by day, he reached the river Euphrates with his footwear worn to shreds and almost barefoot. Finding no boat there, he did not hesitate for an instant to do what the fear of being pursued dictated to him. What then did he decide? By blowing into two water-skins that he had brought with him, he managed to inflate them, sat himself upon them and so launched himself on the river. As he did not know how to swim, his companions aided him skilfully and, with God's guidance, brought him safe and sound to the bank. Worn out by the fatigue of this extraordinary march, spent with hunger and thirst, and a prey

to keen sufferings, he could hardly breathe; yet there was none
to offer him a helping hand. Overcome by sleep, he decided to
rest for a while the limbs that were worn out by such rough
labours; so covering himself with branches and brushwood in
order not to be seen, he lay down under a nut-tree that he found
on the bank of the river. Meanwhile, he had ordered one of his
servants to try to find some inhabitant of the country and by
means of prayers to make him either give or sell him, for no matter
what price, a piece of bread to appease the hunger that devoured
him. This servant soon found in the fields an Armenian peasant,
laden with wild figs and bunches of grapes. He spoke to him,
but with extreme caution, and led him to his master. This was
just what the famished Count needed; but hardly had the peasant
drawn near than, recognising Joscelin, he fell at his feet and said:
"Hail, Lord Joscelin." At these words, which the Count would
much rather not have heard, he answered, greatly afraid yet very
gently: "I am not he whom you have just named, but may the
All-High help him wherever he may be!" The peasant then
replied: "I beseech you, do not seek to hide from me who you
are; I recognise you perfectly, beyond any doubt. Rather tell me
what misfortune has befallen you in these parts and how it
happened; fear nothing, I beg you." The Count replied: "Whoever you be, have pity on me; do not, I beg you for pity's sake,
tell my enemies of my misfortune. Lead me to a place where I
may be safe, and you will deserve to receive this piece of money in
recompense. I have just, by God's grace, escaped from the prison
where Balak held me, in a castle called Kharpurt, in Mesopotamia,
on the other side of the Euphrates. Now I am a fugitive and a
wanderer. If you help me in this extremity you will be doing a
good work and you will save me from falling again into the hands
of Balak and perishing miserably. If you wish to come with me to
my castle of Turbessel, you shall spend all your remaining days
happily there. Tell me which little house is yours hereabouts, and
what is the value of it; and if you wish it, I will take pains to
provide you instead with a bigger one in my domains." "I ask
nothing from you, Lord," said the peasant, "and I will lead you
safe and sound where you will. I remember your kindness at one
time when you went without bread so that I might eat it, and
that is why I am ready to do the same for you. I have," he added,
"a wife, an only daughter still a child, a donkey, two brothers

and two oxen. I entrust myself wholly to you, who are a prudent man of great wisdom. I will go with you and bring all that I have with me. I have a pig too, and by some means or other I will bring it here to you." "Do nothing of the kind, brother," answered the Count. "You are not accustomed to eating a pig at one meal, and you must not rouse the suspicions of your neighbours by anything out of the ordinary."

So this peasant went away and soon returned, as it had been agreed, with his family and his animals. The Count, accustomed in former times to mount only a superb mule, got on the peasant's ass and carried in front of him the child, who was a girl and not a boy; and so he bore in his arms, as if he had been her father, the girl-child whom he had not begotten; and he carried the child who was no daughter born of his blood with as much care as he would have carried the certain hope of his future race. Nevertheless, the child soon began to distress the Count with its tears and cries. He knew not how to calm it. Its nurse's breast lacked milk and Joscelin had not learnt the art of lulling a child with caresses. So he began to think of ridding himself of a travelling companion who might well harm him, and of travelling alone in greater safety; but noticing that this plan did not please the peasant, he feared to upset him and continued to bear the new anxiety that he had taken on himself until at last they all arrived at Turbessel. The reception of such a guest is a joyful matter indeed. His wife was overjoyed to find again the illustrious companion of her life; the servants exulted at the return of so powerful a master; and our hearts can surely not doubt the pleasure in which all were proud to indulge, or the floods of tears, or the respectful sighs that their joy roused in them. As for the peasant, he received without delay the just reward of his humble devotion, and instead of the single yoke of oxen which he had he was given two. Meanwhile the Count, not able to remain long in his castle, went to Antioch and thence to Jerusalem.

FRENCH AND GERMANS QUARREL:
THE CRUSADE FAILS

++

*T*WENTY YEARS *after this episode, the principality of Edessa
fell into the hands of the governor of Aleppo and Mosul, the famous Zengi. In the meantime Baldwin II had been succeeded by
King Fulk of Jerusalem, who was killed in 1143 by falling from his horse,
leaving two children of whom the elder, Baldwin III, was still only
thirteen. This loss of one of the Frankish principalities gave a new
impetus to the Crusades; and then at Vézelay the great name of Saint
Bernard shed lustre upon them. For the first time not only feudal barons
but reigning kings took the cross. Foremost among these were Louis VII,
King of France, and Conrad III, King of Germany, and a large
number of their respective vassals followed their example.*

*The expedition was not a successful one. From the outset quarrels
arose between the French and the Germans. These quarrels were
further embittered at Constantinople by misunderstandings with the
Byzantines. Finally, the Crusade, badly led, ended in an attack upon
the walls of Damascus that was doomed to failure, so that in the end
nothing at all was achieved.*

Odo of Deuil:

While we were in the humble little town of Brunduse
[Branitchevo] about to cross the desert, we loaded ourselves with
provisions. These provisions came chiefly from Hungary and we
had them brought across the Danube. There were a great number
of ships there which the Germans had brought, so many that the
citizens were able to make use of them for a long time to build
houses, and as firewood. Our men took the smallest of these ships
and, crossing the river, went to look for what they needed in a certain Hungarian castle, situated not far off, and brought back what

they found there. It was there that we saw copper and pewter coins for the first time; for one of these coins we sadly gave, or rather lost, five pennies, and a mark for twelve sous. And then, lo and behold, hardly had we entered the lands of the Greeks than they dishonoured themselves by committing perjury. You will doubtless remember I have already related how the delegates had sworn to us, in the name of their emperor, that we should find good markets and every facility for exchanges. So we crossed the deserts and that very beautiful and very fertile territory that stretches without any interruption as far as Constantinople. It was there that we began to meet with insults. In the other countries the inhabitants honestly sold us all that we needed and we remained on the most peaceable terms with them. Now the Greeks stayed in their towns and castles and sent us the things they sold us by lowering them down the walls with ropes. This was too slow a method of supplying us with provisions to satisfy the great hordes of our pilgrims. So they, finding themselves starving in the midst of plenty, took what they needed by theft and pillage. However, some men thought that this state of things was due to the Germans who had preceded us, and who pillaged everything they found and had even set fire to some outlying districts, as we had had occasion to see for ourselves. For instance (and though it is a pity to have to report such things) there was outside the walls of Philippopolis a noble town belonging to the Latins, which, for money, supplied all arrivals with everything they needed, and in great abundance. There, the Germans went and sat in the taverns, and unfortunately there arrived among them a juggler who, although he did not know their language, sat down too, paid his share and began to drink. When he had been tippling for a long time he drew out of his breast a charmed snake he was carrying and, putting a glass on the ground, he placed the snake on the glass and began to do all sorts of conjuring tricks, in the midst of those people of whom he knew neither the customs nor the tongue. The Germans, who thought they were going to see marvels, suddenly got up in a rage and, throwing themselves on the juggler, tore him in a thousand pieces. Blaming everyone because of this one man, they said that the Greeks had wanted to kill them by poison. The agitation in the district spread to the town, and the governor there came out unarmed in great haste, followed by all his men, to try to calm the tumult. Excited by the wine and their own fury, the Germans did not look to see if the others were carrying arms but, seeing them rush forward, they threw themselves in their anger on those who had come to bring them peace, thinking that they wanted to avenge the murder of the man. So the others fled back into the town and then, taking their bows, which are their arms, they came out, put to flight those from whom they had fled, killing and wounding them and only finally stopping when they had chased all the Germans out of the district. A great number of them perished, chiefly those who had taken refuge in houses or hiding places to save their money. Later on, however, having summoned up their courage again and armed themselves anew, the Germans returned to avenge their men and the death of their companions and burnt almost everything outside the walls.

Even our own men could not bear those Germans. On one occasion some of our people, anxious to avoid the discomfort of the crowd pressing round the King, went on ahead and took lodgings near the Germans. All of them went to the market, but the Germans would not allow our people to buy anything until they had amply provided themselves with everything they wanted. As a result a brawl broke out, the noise of which was appalling; for since neither side could hear the other, they all shouted at the tops of their voices and talked without being able to make themselves understood. Then the French, while raining blows and receiving them too, managed all the same to get out of the market, what was more taking provisions with them. But the Germans, who were very numerous, scorning the arrogance of this handful of Frenchmen, seized their arms, and hurled themselves with rage upon the French who, taking arms also, put up a stiff resistance. God put an end to this criminal struggle by making night soon fall. But even night could not deaden or even calm the fury of the Germans and the next morning they rose to begin all over again with still greater violence. Their wise men cast themselves down before those madmen and finally, by means of prayers and remonstrance, succeeded in checking them.

In such ways the Germans, marching ahead, spread trouble everywhere, so much so that the Greeks fled before our army, which followed after them, no matter how peaceful it was. Nevertheless, the church authorities and the clergy as a body always came out of the towns and, carrying their images and performing all the ceremonies of the Greek rite, came to receive the King, respectfully paying him the honours due to him. The Duke of Hesternit, a relative of the Emperor, accompanied the King everywhere he went, kept peace among the inhabitants and saw to it that the markets were at least partly stocked with the things the pilgrims needed. He supplied the King liberally enough with provisions, keeping very little or even none at all for himself, and had the rest distributed sometimes among the rich, sometimes among the poor. Thus with him peace was very strictly observed, because there were fewer needs and because he inspired more fear. But there were many army corps marching in front of him or behind, and these were always looking for abundant supplies either in the markets, when they were able to procure them there, or through pillage, which they found an easier method. . . .

On the place of the money-changers, at Constantinople:

One day a man from Flanders, who deserved to be beaten with rods or burnt by flames, seeing those immense riches and blinded by unbridled greed, began to raise a hue and cry; then, carrying off everything that took his fancy, he excited his fellows partly by his own daring, and partly by the attractions of such precious loot, to commit the same crime. While those foolish men were running all over the place, the others, who were trying to save their money, also rushed in all directions. Shouts and cries of rage grew louder and louder, tables were overturned, gold trampled underfoot and stolen; despoiled, and fearing death, the money-changers fled; ships received the fugitives and, immediately pushing off from the shore, brought them back to the town, with many of our men who were going there to buy supplies. When they arrived they were beaten and stripped; all those who still remained in the town as guests were pillaged as if they were enemies. When the King heard of these things he was inflamed with anger and at once sent for the first evildoer, who was handed over to him by the Count of Flanders and hanged on the spot before the whole town. Then the King zealously ordered that everything that had been lost should be sought, granted pardon to those who came to return anything, and threatened with severest punishment those who kept back merely one stolen object. And so that they might not have to dread his presence, or to blush before him, the King ordered that everything should be taken to the Bishop of Langres. The next day those who had fled were recalled, and every single thing which they stated under oath they had lost was given back to them. The greater number of them claimed more than was their due; but the King preferred to make up himself what was lacking rather than upset the peaceful state of his army.

The "abominable mountain":

. . . We left Laodicea, after having lost a day, and with the Turks and the Greeks always close to us, both before and behind our army.

The mountains we were crossing were still all soaked with the blood of the Germans, and we saw appearing before us the same enemies who had massacred them. The King, more enlightened than those who had preceded him (though as it turned out fruit-lessly), seeing the enemy squadrons on one side and the corpses of the Germans on the other, disposed his army in order of battle. And in this matter we shall for ever bear a grudge against Geoffrey of Rancon, whom the King himself had sent in advance with his uncle the Count of Maurienne. Towards midday of our second day's march, an abominable mountain difficult to cross confronted us. The King had decided to spend a whole day crossing it, and not to stop and pitch camp there. Those who got there first, and rather early in the day, not being encumbered by anything, and for-getting the King, who was then looking after the rear-guard, scaled the mountain and, while the rest were only following them a long way off, put up their tents on the other side, about the ninth hour. The mountain was precipitous and covered with rocks; we had to climb it by a steep slope, its summit seemed to us to reach the skies, and the torrent which flowed at the bottom of the valley looked as if it must be not far from the underworld; for all that, the crowd piled up on the same spot and, pressing close on each other's heels, stopped and settled there, without thought of the knights who had gone on before, remaining as though they belonged there rather than as if they were on the march. The pack animals fell from the steep rocks, dragging those they met in their fall right down to the depths of the abyss. The rocks themselves, constantly dislodged, caused great damage, and those of our people who scattered in all directions to find better paths were in danger both of falling themselves and being dragged down by others.

Meanwhile the Turks and the Greeks, ceaselessly shooting their arrows to prevent those who had fallen from getting up again, joined forces to make for the other corps, greatly rejoicing at a sight from which they hoped to gain much advantage by evening. The day declined and the abyss became fuller and fuller of the wreckage of our army. But soon those successes no longer satisfied our enemies and, taking fresh courage, they returned again to our main army corps, for they had already ceased to fear those who formed the advance-guard and had not yet seen those who formed the rear-guard. So they struck and overthrew, and the poor people, deprived of arms, fell, or fled like a flock of sheep. Then great cries rose to heaven and came at the same time to the ears of the King. He did all that was possible in the circumstances; but Heaven sent him no help, unless it were that nevertheless night fell, putting some stop to our ills.

During this time since I, as a monk, could do nothing but call on the Lord or encourage the others to fight, I was sent to the camp of the advance-guard, where I told them what was happening. Filled with consternation they all seized their arms; they would all have liked to retrace their steps with all speed, but they could barely walk, partly because of the roughness of the ground and partly because the enemy, marching towards them, prevented them from advancing.

During this same time the King was abandoned in the midst of the danger with a few of his nobles, but with neither knights in his pay nor equerries armed with bows near him (for he had not made ready to cross the passes, since it had been agreed that they should not be crossed until the next day). Nevertheless, forgetting his own life to save those who were perishing in crowds, he made his way through the outer ranks and vigorously resisted the enemy, who were furiously attacking the main body. Most recklessly did he then assail the infidels, a hundred times stronger than himself and helped as well by the advantage of the terrain. Because of this indeed the horses were unable, I will not say to gallop, but even to stand still, and the unavoidable slowness of the attack made it more difficult to aim the blows with certainty.

Being on slippery ground, our men brandished their spears with all their might, but were deprived of the force of their horses; the enemy in the meantime shot their arrows in all safety, supporting themselves against trees or rocks. Meanwhile, the crowd, freed by the King, fled, carrying off their baggage or taking with them those who were carrying it; but also leaving in their place the King and the Counts exposed to every peril. It would truly be too deplorable to see lords die to save the lives of their servitors, if we did not know that the Lord of all had also given a like example. Here then the fairest flowers of France faded before they had been able to bear fruit in the city of Damascus. This story alone makes me dissolve in tears and I groan from the depths of my heart. Yet a wise spirit can find some consolation in this thought, that the memory of their past valour will live as long as the world, and that having died in burning faith and purified of their errors, they have deserved by such an end the crown of martyrdom. So they fought, and each one of them, so as at least not to die without vengeance, piled up corpses around him; but the enemy, constantly joined by fresh recruits, always remained greatly superior to them in numbers. They killed the knights' horses which, if they could not gallop, at least served to carry the weight of their arms. The Crusaders, become foot-soldiers, and covered with armour, were submerged by the dense ranks of the enemy as by a sea and, separated from each other, were soon stripped bare.

In this confusion the King lost his escort, few in number but renowned. Whereupon, remaining always a king in heart, and as agile as he was strong, he seized the branches of a tree that God had placed there to save him, and threw himself from the top of a rock. A great number of the enemy flung themselves after him to seize his person, while others, further off, aimed their arrows at him. But by the will of God his breastplate preserved him from the arrows and, defending his rock to defend his liberty, with his bloody sword he cut off the hands and heads of many of the enemy. Finally, these, not knowing who he was and seeing that it would be difficult to take him, fearing too that other fighting men might appear, gave up attacking him and made off so as to remove the spoils from the battlefield before nightfall.

All this bravery had been in vain. When the Crusaders finally reached the Holy Land, their leaders made the initial mistake of attacking

Damascus, whose position was impregnable, and whose sultans, what was more, showed the greatest goodwill towards the Christians. Louis VII had especially persisted in doing so, scorning the advice of the Prince of Antioch, Raymond of Poitiers, perhaps to set at defiance this prince, whose conduct with the King's wife, Eleanor of Aquitaine, was giving him some anxiety. The seige of Damascus failed almost before it had begun, and as a result the Crusade collapsed. It will be remembered that, on his return to France the following year, Louis VII divorced Eleanor, who quickly got married again to the Plantagenet Count of Anjou, who had just recovered the Duchy of Normandy and was soon to become Henry II of England.

THE STRUGGLE FOR ASCALON:
THE DECADENT CALIPHS OF EGYPT

✠✠✠✠✠✠✠✠✠✠✠✠✠✠✠✠✠✠✠✠✠✠✠✠✠✠✠✠✠✠✠✠✠✠✠✠✠

*I*N SPITE *of the failure of the Crusade of 1148, the reign of Baldwin III, fourth king of Jerusalem, did much to better the situation in general. In 1153 he brought off a master-stroke by taking Ascalon, the "Virgin of Syria", considered as impregnable. The possession of this fortified town secured the protection of the kingdom on the Egyptian side. Usama has left us an account of this conquest and painted the decadent state of the Court of Egypt at that time:*

We reached Ascalon one morning at daybreak. We had hardly stowed our arms and our baggage away near the public square where prayer took place, than the Franks greeted us by attacking us as soon as the sun had risen. Nasr ed-Daula Yakut, governor of Ascalon, ran towards us saying: "Quick, quick, take your baggage away!" I answered him: "Are you then afraid? The Franks will certainly not take it from us." "It is true," he answered, "that I am afraid." I comforted him by saying: "Fear nothing. They saw us advancing along the plain and tried to bar our way when we had not yet reached Ascalon. We did not fear them then. Why should we fear them today when we are close to a town that belongs to us?"

For a time the Franks remained without moving a short way off; then they returned to their own regions, gathered together an army and came to attack us with horsemen, foot-soldiers and camping equipment, in order to surround Ascalon. We had gone out to attack them and the foot-soldiers of Ascalon had also carried out a sortie. I made the tour of this troop of foot-soldiers and said to them: "O our companions-in-arms, return behind your walls and leave us to grapple with the Franks. If we conquer them, you will rejoin us. If they are victorious, you will be there in reserve, safe and sound within the walls. In that case, take care not to return to the charge."

I left them and went towards the Franks. They had already traced out the site of their encampment and were preparing to pitch their tents. Surrounded and harried by us, they had not time to fold them up again. They abandoned them, unfolded as they were, and retreated.

When the Franks had left the town, a certain number of the inhabitants, who had returned to their homes, set out in pursuit, renouncing the defence of the place and their own safety. The Franks turned, fell upon them and killed a good number. The foot-soldiers, whom I had kept apart, were routed, could not retreat, and cast their shields on the ground. We in our turn began once more to fight the Franks, who were vanquished and went back to their regions, in the neighbourhood of Ascalon. As for the foot-soldiers who were put to flight, they began, on their way back, to turn on each other, saying: "Ibn Munqidh showed he had more experience than we. He advised us to turn back, and we did nothing of the kind until we were repulsed and had suffered a disgrace."

My brother 'Izz ad-Daula Abu'l-Hasan Ali (on whom Allah have pity!), with his companions in arms, was among those who had come with me from Damascus to Ascalon. He was one of the most brilliant of the Moslem knights. He fought for the cause of religion, not for worldly considerations. One day we had left Ascalon to make a foray and attempt an attack against Beit Djibril. When we were on our way back, after getting there and attacking it, I saw that something serious must be happening before Ascalon. I ordered my companions to halt. Fire had been lit and thrown on the heaps of mown corn. So we changed our positions. I remained in the rear of our troops. The Franks (may Allah curse them!) had left all their fortresses in the neighbourhood, where their numerous cavalry were massed, and were concentrating on the siege of Ascalon without respite, day and night. It was they who, this time, had taken the offensive against our companions.

One of the latter came to me at the gallop and said to me: "The Franks are here." I rejoined our companions and already they were face to face with the advance-guard of the Franks, who are (may Allah curse them!) the most cautious warriors in the world. They had climbed a hill and stationed themselves there; we on our side had climbed another opposite them. In between, a crowd of our disbanded companions, and the men in charge of our mounts on the lead, were passing along below the Franks. Not one of their horsemen went down to them for fear of an ambush or some warlike trickery. If they had gone down they would have captured our companions to the last man.

We were facing the Franks with inferior forces, as our troops had previously been routed. The Franks remained motionless on the hill they were occupying until our companions had ceased to file past. Then they rushed upon us and we were repulsed by them, as they had only us to contend with. They needed no great efforts to assail us, for those whose horses stood their ground were killed, while those whose horses collapsed were led away prisoner. Thereafter, the Franks left the battlefield.

Allah (may he be exalted!) decreed salvation for us, thanks to their habit of temporising. If we had been as numerous as they and had been victorious over them as they had been over us, we should have exterminated them.

I remained four months in Ascalon to fight the Franks. During that campaign we made a surprise attack on Yubna, killed about a hundred men there and took captives. At the end of that period I received a letter from al-Malik al-Adil, recalling me. I returned to Misr. My brother, 'Izz ad-Daula Abu'l-Hasan Ali, remained in Ascalon up to the moment when the army of that town left to conquer Gaza. It was there that my brother met a martyr's death. He ranked among the scholars, the cavaliers and the devout.

As for the mutiny in which al-Adil [the Caliph] was killed (may Allah have pity on him!) he had sent to Bilbeis troops, commanded by Abbas the son of his wife, to protect the region against the Franks. Abbas had brought his son Nasr (may Allah have pity on him!) who stayed a few days with his father at the head of the troops, and then returned to Cairo without having received from al-Adil either authorisation or leave. Al-Adil disapproved of his return and ordered him to rejoin the army, thinking that the young man had gone back to Cairo to amuse and enjoy himself and because he was bored by a prolonged stay in a garrison.

But Nasr, son of Abbas, had plotted with al-Zafir and, by
agreement with him, had enrolled some young equerries of the
Caliph who, he had decided, should attack al-Adil in his palace at
the moment when, after entering his harem in the evening, he
had fallen asleep. Nasr would then be waiting to kill him and had
arranged with one of the chamberlains of the palace that he should
inform him immediately his master was asleep. The control of
the house was in the hands of the wife of al-Adil, who was the
grandmother of Nasr, and to whose presence he was admitted
without having to ask for an audience.

When al-Adil was asleep, the chamberlain brought the news to
Nasr who, with six of his men, fell upon him in the house where
he lay, and killed him. Nasr cut off his head, which he took to al-
Zafir. This event took place on Thursday the 6th of Muharram
in the year 548 [April 3rd, 1153].

Al-Adil had in his palace his mameluks and the troops on
sentry-duty, about a thousand men, but they were in the Palace
of Refuge and he was killed in the women's apartments. They
came out of the palace and a struggle broke out between them and
the partisans of al-Zafir and Nasr. But it died down as soon as the
latter brought the head of al-Adil on the point of his lance. On
seeing it, those who had been faithful to al-Adil, split into two
parties: one left Cairo to offer their services and swear obedience
to Abbas; the other threw away their arms, presented themselves
before Nasr, son of Abbas, kissed the dust and attached themselves
to his person.

A few days later his father Abbas returned one morning
to Cairo and installed himself in the Vizier's palace. Al-Zafir
[the new Caliph] put on him the mantle of honour and entrusted
the direction of affairs to him. As for Nasr, he was continually
with the Caliph and was on intimate terms with him, to the great
displeasure of Abbas, who was indignant with his son because he
knew the system which consists of setting men against each other,
so that each in turn strips the other of all he possesses and reduces
him to nothing until the two adversaries have destroyed each
other. . . .

Then al-Zafir conceived the idea of prompting Nasr to kill his
father, to whom he would succeed as Vizier. The Caliph heaped
the richest possible presents on Nasr. I was in his house one day
when he received from al-Zafir twenty silver salvers holding

twenty thousand dinars. A few days passed without presents, and then a new consignment arrived containing a collection of garments of all kinds, the like of which I had never before seen. Then after an interruption of a few days, the Caliph sent silver salvers holding fifty thousand dinars. After another, very short, delay he sent thirty saddle-mules and forty camels with their gear, their grain sacks and their bridles.

A messenger called Murtafi, son of Fahl, passed continually between al-Zafir and Nasr. I was on such intimate terms with the son of Abbas that he would not let me leave him either night or day. I slept with my head on his pillow.

One evening I was with him in the palace of the Sabura when Murtafi arrived. They talked together during the first third of the night, while I kept apart. Then Nasr turned round, asked me to draw near and said to me: "Where were you?" "Near the window," I answered, "reading the Koran, for today I have not had time to finish my daily reading." Then Nasr began to reveal to me some points of their conversation, to see what I would think of them; he wanted me to strengthen him in the guilty resolution that al-Zafir was trying to make him take. I said to him: "O my master, let not Satan make you stumble! May you not let yourself be deceived by those who wish to lead you astray! For the murder of your father is a different matter from the murder of al-Adil. So do not do something for which you will be accursed until the day of the last judgment." Nasr bowed his head, cutting short our conversation, and then it was time for the two of us to go to sleep.

Abbas was aware of the plots that his son had hatched against him. He coaxed him, tried to win him and planned with him to put al-Zafir to death. The Caliph and Nasr were companions of the same age. They would go out together at night without being recognised by anyone. One day Nasr invited the Caliph to come to his house, which was in the Bazaar of the sword-makers. He had posted a handful of his companions in one of the wings of his house. When the company had seated themselves, these men rushed upon the Caliph and killed him. This event took place on the evening before Thursday, the last day of the month of mouharram in the year 549 [April 15th, 1154].

Nasr threw the corpse of al-Zafir into a vault under his house. The Caliph had come accompanied by a black slave who never left him, and who was called Sa'id ad-Daula. He was put to death too.

Egypt was the country towards which Baldwin III and his brother Amalric, who was to succeed him as head of the Kingdom of Jerusalem, were principally to turn. Frankish Syria lay between the two chief Moslem territories which were, on the one hand, Moslem Syria, where the Saracens remained masters of the two strong cities of Aleppo and Damascus, and on the other, Egypt. If the two became united, Frankish Syria could only be crushed. The Franks were therefore showing very acute political sense in seeking an alliance with Egypt, an alliance which incidentally was desired by the last, and utterly decadent, descendants of the Fatimid dynasty in Cairo.

William of Tyre has related the interview that took place in the palace of the Caliph of Egypt between the Caliph, under the direction his Vizier Shawar, and two Frankish knights, the Templar Geoffrey and Hugh of Caesarea:

There were marble basins there, filled with the most limpid water, and one heard the various warblings of a multitude of birds unknown in our world. . . . There were galleries to walk in, with marble columns, embellished with gold and inlaid with carving; the pavements were of divers substances and the whole extent of those galleries was in truth worthy of the royal power. . . . As they proceeded still further under the guidance of the chief of the eunuchs, they found other buildings still more elegant than the ones before. . . . There was there an astonishing variety of quadrupeds, such as it would tempt a painter to represent, or a poet to describe; a variety such as the imagination of a sleeping man might invent in his nightly dreams; such in short as really exists in the lands of the East or the South, whereas the West has never seen anything to compare with it. . . .

In this noble setting, the Vizier Shawar presented the emissaries of the King of Jerusalem to his lord:

. . . With amazing swiftness they drew curtains of cloth of gold, adorned with an infinite variety of precious stones, which hung in the middle of the room, enclosing the throne. The Caliph then appeared, showing his face to all beholders, sitting on a gilded throne, wearing garments more magnificent than those of kings, and surrounded by a small number of retainers and household eunuchs. Then the Vizier, advancing meekly, with the greatest respect humbly kissed the feet of the sovereign sitting on his throne, set forth the reasons why the delegates had come and reported the tenor of the treaties he had concluded.

When our delegates asked that the Caliph should confirm his words with his own hand, the intimate confidants and officers who surrounded his person seemed unable to hear this proposal without horror, as an unheard-of thing; nevertheless, after a long deliberation, and as a result of repeated representations by the Sultan, the Caliph stretched out his hand with great reluctance and presented it covered with a veil. Then, to the great surprise of the Egyptians, who could not conceal their astonishment that anyone should dare to speak so freely to a sovereign prince, Hugh of Caesarea said to the Caliph: "Lord, where trust is concerned, there can be no deviation; when princes bind themselves to each other by agreements, all must be revealed; . . . that is why either you must present your hand bare, or I shall be obliged to think that you have some ulterior motive and less sincerity than I would wish." At last, forced very much in spite of himself, and as though he were offending his dignity, yet smiling, the Caliph put his bare hand in the hand of Hugh of Caesarea and, while the latter dictated to him the words of his oath, he promised, pronouncing after him the same syllables, to observe the conventions according to their tenor, in good faith, without fraud or evil intention.

This Caliph was in the first flower of his youth, of a blackish-brown complexion, tall, with a beautiful face, and a very generous disposition. He had an infinite number of wives.

For a time the Frankish army and the Egyptian army joined forces against the armies of Shirkuh, lieutenant of the governor of Aleppo, the terrible Nur ed-Din who in 1154 had managed to unite Moslem Syria by taking Damascus. An episode of this fight has been recounted by the Arab historian Ibn abi Tayyi:

Shirkuh set out in the month of January. His march was so secret that Shawar only heard of it through the warning that the Franks gave me about it. He at once begged King Amalric to bring him help on the same conditions as in the preceding expedition, and this was granted. So the King set out and followed the coast. Shirkuh, on the contrary, had taken the desert road; his plan was to head for Bilbeis; but as he was outdistanced by the Franks, whom the Egyptians had joined, he turned in another direction and, taking the mountain road, arrived near Atfih, on the Nile, to the south of Cairo, whence he proceeded as far as Sheroune in Upper Egypt, always pursued by the Franks and Egyptians. In this place he crossed the Nile on boats, and returned down the banks of the river as far as Giza opposite Cairo. Then, fearing the consequences of his enterprise, he wrote in these terms to the Vizier: "I swear to you by the God who has no equal, and by all that binds the Moslems together, that I am ready to leave Egypt; that I will never return here and that I will not allow anyone to bring war here, having decided to join forces with you against anyone who comes to attack you, provided you promise me to take in hand the cause of Islam. Now, the enemy is in the heart of the kingdom, he is cut off from all help, it will be difficult for him to escape. Let us unite our efforts to overwhelm him. The occasion is favourable; perhaps there will never be another; so let us exterminate this nation." But Shawar communicated the letter to the Christians and put to death the man who had brought it. On hearing this, Shirkuh gnawed his fingers in grief. "If Shawar had only believed me," he said, "there would not have been a single Western Christian left."

Meanwhile, Shirkuh pitched his tents at Giza where he returned for more than fifty days. As for the Franks and the Egyptians, they established themselves in the outskirts of Cairo: the Nile separated the two armies. The Vizier had a bridge built between the neighbouring island and Giza, and tried to turn the army of Shirkuh. In this contingency Shirkuh succeeded in winning to his cause the inhabitants of Alexandria, who were indignant at seeing the Vizier acting in concert with the Christians and making such a bad use of the treasures of Islamism. Nevertheless, the situation of Nur ed-Din's army became ever more critical. The Sharif Edrisi, a citizen of Aleppo, who at that moment happened to be in Alexandria and was about to announce to Shirkuh, in the name of the inhabitants, the prompt despatch of help, told me that, two days after his arrival at Giza, Shirkuh thought he was going to be overcome by the Egyptians and the

Franks: he only just had time to leave precipitately, abandoning his tents and his baggage. The army once again set out in the direction of Upper Egypt. One night they found themselves so closely beset that hardly had they stopped to rest than they had to take the road again, which they did in darkness and by torchlight: and in this way they arrived at Dalga. Already the enemy had reached Ashmunein, and it was not long before the two armies found themselves face to face and had to begin to fight.

THE NEW MAN OF ISLAM: SALADIN

✦✦

*T*HERE WAS *thus a sort of Frankish protectorate in Egypt in the time of King Amalric. The Caliph's army and that of the Franks joined forces to resist the claims of the Syrian Moslems. The historian Ibn al-Athir, relating the campaign of 1167, describes the first exploits of the man whose name was to become the most celebrated of all in the annals of the East: Saladin. He was a young man at that time: a nephew of Shirkuh, the lieutenant of the Sultan Nur ed-Din, he distinguished himself during an encounter of which his compatriot Ibn al-Athir tells us:*

Saladin was in command of the centre, and his uncle said to him: "The enemy will probably think that I am in the centre and will make for it. You will put up a feeble resistance and then flee before him; when he stops pursuing you, you will retrace your steps." Shirkuh chose the most valiant of the soldiers, especially those whose audacity and coolness he knew, and took up his position with them on the right wing. When the action began the Franks, as he had foreseen, made for the centre; Saladin put up a slight resistance and began to give way, but without breaking his ranks and always pursued by the enemy. Then Shirkuh flung himself on the troops opposing him and caused great carnage among them. When the Christians came back they found their brethren slain or routed and they too took flight. One thing well worth remarking is that Shirkuh only needed one or two thousand horsemen to triumph over the Franks and the Egyptians. . . .

Edrisi:

Afterwards, Shawar and his army retreated to Elmonia, a neighbouring town. As for Shirkuh, he crossed the province of

Fayyum to Alexandria, where he deposited his wounded and his prisoners. Then, fearing that he might soon be besieged in that town, he left Saladin there with part of the army and, after making the inhabitants swear loyalty, he returned to Upper Egypt. He remained there until he heard that the Franks and the Egyptians, after joining forces in Cairo, had gone to lay siege to Alexandria and were on the verge of capturing it. At that he left Cous, on the banks of the Nile, in Upper Egypt, taking with him a great number of Arabs and ordinary people who had sided with him. While this was happening, the Vizier and the Franks proposed peace. It was made through the intermediary of King Amalric. It was agreed that Shirkuh should keep the money he had raised from the provinces. On his side Shawar promised thirty thousand pieces of gold to the Franks to compensate them for the toils of war; and everyone promised to return to his own place.

This Alexandrian campaign is curious for more than one reason, and chiefly because of the fraternisation that took place after the combat between Franks, Egyptians and Syrians.

Edrisi:

The inhabitants of Alexandria, depressed and emaciated by the hardships of a long siege . . . left the town to ease their anxieties and pass the time in conversing familiarly with those whom such a short while before they had dreaded as harbingers of danger and ministers of death. Our men on their side also made haste to enter the town, which they had so longed to see: they walked about freely, visiting the streets, the ports, the ramparts, examining everything carefully so as to be able, when they returned home, to give long accounts to their compatriots, and delight their friends with interesting tales.

The behaviour of King Amalric on this occasion must be mentioned. Saladin took refuge with him at the time of the triumph of the Egyptians, and it was the King of Jerusalem who obtained a complete amnesty for his partisans of Alexandria. It was he again who offered his ships to take back to Syria the wounded of Nur ed-Din's Kurdo-Arab army.

However, the good understanding between Shawar and Amalric did not last long. Disagreement began to break out in 1168 when Amalric revealed his intention of undertaking new campaigns. The historian

Ibn al-Athir relates a picturesque dialogue between the King of Jeru-
salem and the son of the Vizier. The latter had been asked to indicate a
place where the Frankish armies could camp. He answered: "On
the point of our spears. Do you imagine that Bilbeis [*a town for*
which the Frankish armies were making] is a cheese to be gobbled
up?" "Unquestionably," *answered the Christian king,* "and Cairo
is the cream of it."

By way of reprisals his troops sacked this town of Bilbeis in a manner as
bloody as it was impolitic. "If the Franks had treated Bilbeis well,"
remarked Ibn al-Athir, "they would certainly have taken Fostat and
Cairo." *But Shawar preferred to set fire to the city to prevent them*
from taking it. And then he entered into negotiations with Nur ed-Din.

THE LEPER-KING

❋❋❋

*L*ITTLE BY LITTLE *the Moslem armies of Syria established themselves in Egypt and on January 18th, 1169, Saladin assassinated Shawar, and two months later took his place as Vizier to the Caliph al-Adil. The historian and poet Usama addressed a poem to him on this occasion.*

Through him Egypt, bowed by age, has found again the beauty and brilliance of her youth.

How many suitors unworthy of her has she not repulsed, until she was asked in marriage by a suitor who, as a dowry, offered her his sword.

He has defended her as the lion defends his den.

He has protected her as the rim of the eyelid protects an eye against the attack of a wisp of straw. . . .

Saladin, however, did not take long to depose the Caliph, the last descendant of the Fatimids (1171), and so the corrupt court was succeeded by a military government, bound to Moslem Syria by the closest of ties. From that moment it was easy to see that the weak Latin kingdom would soon be surrounded, hemmed in as it was between two Moslem States. This was what happened when Nur ed-Din himself died at Damascus on March 15th, 1174, leaving as his sole heir a child of fifteen, Malik-as-Salih Ismail. Saladin could not fail to take advantage of this to make an alliance which was a veritable death sentence for the Franks. As a crowning misfortune King Amalric died on July 11th in the same year, carried off by typhus at the age of thirty-nine. From then on the Frankish principalities were in a highly critical position. All the same they held out for thirteen years, in unbelievable conditions, since Saladin's only opponent was a little leper-king of thirteen, Baldwin IV. It was under this king, the victim of an illness that carried him off at the age of twenty-four after eleven years of martyrdom, that the most heroic exploits in the history of Frankish Syria took place: among others, on November 27th, 1177, the victory of Montgisard, the most splendid victory of the Crusades, in which Baldwin IV, with 500 knights, who were joined by 80 Templars—3,000 combatants in all, counting the foot-soldiers—won a complete victory over the 30,000 mameluks grouped round Saladin.

This young leper-king had certainly been trained in a good school, since his tutor was none other than William of Tyre, that admirable prelate as remarkable for his learning—he spoke Greek and Arabic in addition to French and Latin, and read Hebrew—as for the saintliness of his life and his talent as a historian. When he was Canon of Tyre, King Amalric had asked him to undertake the history of his reign. Later he entrusted him with the education of his son Baldwin, and it was while he was engaged on this that William composed his Historia Rerum in Partibus Transmarinis Gestarum which remains one of our best sources for the study of the Latin Kingdoms. A proof of his indefatigable curiosity is that he also wrote a history of the deeds of the Eastern Princes, which related the whole history of the Arabs from the time of Mahomet, and which has unfortunately been lost. In his book he tells the story of Baldwin's youth, and how the teacher discovered the illness which afflicted his royal pupil:

We devoted as much care to forming his character as to making him study literature. He was always playing with his companions the young nobles, and, as children of that age do when they are amusing themselves together, they pinched each other on the arms or hands. Then when they felt the pain they began to cry, but the young Baldwin bore these games with extraordinary patience, as if he felt no hurt. . . . I thought at first that this was due to patience in him, and not a lack of sensibility. I called him. . . and finally discovered that his right arm and hand were insensitive. . . . It was the first symptom of a much more serious and utterly incurable illness. When he had reached the age of puberty—one cannot speak of it without weeping—it was realised that the young man was suffering from leprosy.

Not all the men who surrounded Baldwin were of the stamp of William of Tyre. During his reign the pernicious influences of those who were to bring the kingdom to ruin began to reveal themselves. The worst of them was the Patriarch of Jerusalem, Heraclius, who owed his

*appointment to the queen-mother, Agnes of Courtenay. His private life
was most scandalous (everyone in Jerusalem knew his mistress, who was
known as the patriarchess and used to walk about the town covered with
jewels); and he was later to head the plot which, on the death of
Baldwin IV, set aside the provisions he had made in his will to secure
the survival of the kingdom. There was also the Grand Master of the
Temple, Gerard of Ridfort. The chronicles tell how he became the
inveterate enemy of Raymond III, Count of Tripoli, the only man whom
Baldwin the Leper considered capable of keeping order and peace among
the other barons after his death, in face of the unity of the Arab world:*

"Estoire d'Eracles":

When the Master of the Temple first arrived in Syria he was a
worldly knight-errant, and he was hired by King Amalric and
Count Raymond of Tripoli who made a great friend of him. For a
time he was on familiar terms with the Count, who granted and
promised him the first good marriage that should be available in
his domain. Not long after that William Dorel, who was lord of
Botrun, died. . . . He had had a daughter by his first wife. After
his death, a rich man from Pisa arrived there, called Plivano. This
Plivano had brought great riches with him. He asked the Count
of Tripoli for the hand of this young woman who was the heiress
of Botrun. Although the Count had promised her to Gerard of
Ridfort, he chose rather to give her to Plivano than to Gerard
because Plivano paid the Count well for this marriage. It is said
that he had the girl put on a balance with gold on the other side;
and the gold that she weighed was given to the Count; and for
these great riches the Count granted the girl to Plivano. When
Gerard of Ridfort saw that the Count had refused him the marriage, he was greatly wroth at it because he had given her, he said,
to a villein. For the people of France hold those of Italy in contempt, and however rich and however valiant anyone may be they
still consider him a villein; for the majority of Italians are usurers
or corsairs or merchants, and for that reason those who are knights
hold them in contempt. So he was waxed wroth with the Count of
Tripoli and departed in anger and went to Jerusalem. There a slight
malady took him and so he went to the house of the Temple.
Hardly any time after, Brother Arnold of Torosa, who was
Master of the House of the Temple, died, and the brothers elected
Gerard of Ridfort Master.

GUY OF LUSIGNAN BECOMES KING OF JERUSALEM

****

*S*YBILLA, THE sister of Baldwin IV, had first married a baron called William Long-Sword, by whom she had had a son. He was the heir of his uncle, who, before he died on March 16th, 1185, had made his barons swear to remain faithful to the child who was to succeed him, and to the Count of Tripoli whom he named as regent. Unfortunately, the little Baldwin V died in the September of the following year. Now after the death of her husband Sybilla had married a baron of Poitou called Guy of Lusignan, who during the reign of Baldwin IV had turned all the barons against him, partly by his stupidity (sometimes reinforced by cruelty, for he had one day had some Bedouin tributaries of the King massacred while they were peacefully grazing their flocks in the neighbourhood of Ascalon), and partly by that obstinacy of the weak which he sometimes showed.

On the death of Baldwin IV, while the barons were assembled in Nablus round Raymond of Tripoli, Sybilla, supported by the clan who had been hostile to the Leper-King—Gerard of Ridfort, Reynald of Châtillon and the Patriarch Heraclius—had herself crowned queen in Jerusalem, in the course of an improvised ceremony, and then handed the crown to her husband, Guy of Lusignan.

"Estoire d'Eracles":

The barons who were at Nablus answered that they would not go [to the coronation of Sybilla]; but they sent two priests from Cîteaux to the Patriarch and to the Masters of the Temple and the Hospital at Jerusalem, forbidding them in the name of God and of the Pope of Rome to crown the Countess of Jaffa before they had held a council, according to the oath that they had taken in the time of the Leper-King. The priests went to Jerusalem with two knights and delivered their message. The Patriarch and the Master of the Temple and Prince Reynald said they would keep neither oath nor troth, but that they would crown the lady as queen. The Master of the Hospital did not wish to join with them and said that he would not go, since they were acting against God and against their oath. Then the gates of the city were closed, so that none might go out or enter, for they feared lest the barons who were at Nablus, twelve miles from there, should enter the city while they were crowning the lady, and that a conflict should ensue. When the barons learnt that the city was thus closed and that one could neither enter nor leave it, they dressed a sergeant, who had been born in Jerusalem, as a monk and sent him to Jerusalem to keep watch on the crowning of the lady. He set off but was not able to enter Jerusalem by any gate. He therefore went to the Madeleine of the Jacobites of Jerusalem, which adjoined the walls of the city. There was there a little postern by which one could enter the city. He worked to such good purpose that the abbot of the Madeleine opened this postern for him. He went to the Holy Sepulchre and remained there all the time to see and find out all that he had been sent for. The Master of the Temple and Prince Reynald took the lady and led her to the Patriarch in the Holy Sepulchre to be crowned. Prince Reynald went up to the upper part of the church and said to the people: "Lords, you know well that King Baldwin the Leper is dead, and after him his nephew whom he had had crowned, and the kingdom has been left without an heir and without a governor. We would like with your approval to crown Sybilla, who is here and who is daughter to King Amalric and sister to King Baldwin the Leper, for she is the most apparent and the most direct heiress of the kingdom." The people who were there said with one voice that they liked King Amalric better than any other. They had all forgotten the oath they had sworn to the Count of Tripoli and all the trouble came from that. When the lady was at the Holy Sepulchre, the Patriarch came to the Master of the Temple and asked him for the key of the Treasury where the crown was. The Master of the Temple willingly gave it to him. Then they asked the Master of the Hospital to bring his key. And the Master of the Hospital said that he would not obey and that he would not set foot there unless it were with the agreement of the barons of the land. Then the Patriarch and the Master of the Temple and Prince Reynald went to ask the Master of the Hospital for his key. When he knew that they were coming to him, he hid himself in his house and it was nearly the hour of nones before they found him and were able to speak to him. And when they had found him they begged him to give them the key; but he said that he would not give it to them. They begged him and pestered him so much that he grew angry and ended by throwing into the middle of the room the keys he was holding in his hand, for fear lest someone of the house should take them and give them to the Patriarch. Then the Master of the Temple and Prince Reynald took the key and went to the Treasury; they took out two crowns and carried them to the Patriarch. The Patriarch put one of them on the altar of the Holy Sepulchre and with the other crowned the Countess of Jaffa. When the lady was crowned queen, the Patriarch said to her: "Madame, you are a woman; it is fitting that you should have someone to help you govern your kingdom and who should be a male. Here is a crown. Take it and give it to such a man as can help you govern your kingdom and knows how to govern." She came and took the crown and called her lord Guy of Lusignan who was before her and said to him: "Sire, come, receive this crown, for I could not use it better." He knelt down before her and she put the crown on his head. The Master of the Temple put his hand on it and helped her place it, saying: "This crown compensates for the Botrun marriage." After that the Patriarch anointed them both and she was queen and he was king.

This took place on a Friday, in the year of Our Lord 1186. And never before had a king been crowned in Jerusalem on a Friday, nor when the gates were closed. When the sergeant dressed as a monk had seen the coronation, he left by the postern through which he had entered the city, and departed. Then he went to Nablus, to the Count of Tripoli and the barons who had sent him, and told them what he had seen.

When Baldwin of Ramleh [Baldwin of Ibelin] learnt that Guy of Lusignan was King of Jerusalem, he said: "I will wager that he will be king for less than a year." And it was true; for he was crowned in mid-September and lost the kingdom on the day of Saint-Martin-the-Impetuous, which falls at the beginning of the month of July [July 4th]. And Baldwin said to the Count of Tripoli and the barons of the land: "Fair lords, do the best you can, for the country is lost; for my part I shall leave it, for I do not wish to incur either reproach or blame for having been present at the loss of the Holy Land. For I know the king who is there now well enough as both mad and bad to be sure that he will do nothing on my advice or yours; that is why I shall leave the country." Then said the Count of Tripoli: "Sir Baldwin, for God's sake have pity on Christendom and let us take counsel how we may protect the land. We have here a daughter of King Amalric* and her baron Humphrey. We will crown them, we will go to Jerusalem; we have on our side the strength of the barons of this land and of the Master of the Hospital, except for Prince Reynald who is with the King at Jerusalem. I can make truces with the Saracens and with their king, as I wish; they will not attack us and if need be they will even help us." To this they all agreed and decided that the next day they would crown Humphrey as king.

When Humphrey knew that they wanted to crown him king, he thought that he would not be able to bear the strain of it. At nightfall he mounted his horse with his knights and they rode all night and so came to Jerusalem. In the morning of the next day the barons rose and prepared to crown Humphrey. Then they learnt that he had fled and gone to Jerusalem. And when Humphrey reached Jerusalem, he went into the presence of the Queen, whose sister he had to wife, and greeted her. She did not greet him because he had been against her and because he had not been present at her coronation. He began to scratch his head like a child who is ashamed and said: "Lady, I know not what to do, for they wanted to make me king by force." And the Queen said to him: "Lord Humphrey, you are right and, since you have acted thus, I forgive you; go and do your homage to the King." Humphrey thanked the Queen for pardoning him; he did homage to the King and remained in Jerusalem.

When the Count of Tripoli and the barons who were at Nablus learnt that Humphrey had done homage to the King, they were filled with sorrow and knew not what to do. Then the barons came to the Count of Tripoli and said to him: "Sire, in God's name, advise us concerning the oath that the Leper-King made us take, for we do not wish to do anything for which we may be blamed or reproached." The Count told them to keep their word as they had done and that he did not know what other counsel to give them.

* Isabella, half-sister of Sybilla and Baldwin, married to Humphrey of Toron.

SARACEN HONOUR AND CHRISTIAN TREACHERY

❋❋❋❋❋❋❋❋❋❋❋❋❋❋❋❋❋❋❋❋❋❋❋❋❋❋❋❋❋❋❋❋❋❋❋❋❋

*T*HE BARONS *had been doubly tricked; first by the coronation of Guy of Lusignan, and then by Humphrey's escape. From that moment it was easy to see what was going to happen in Frankish Syria, a disunited country, headed by an incapable and little-respected king, and gripped as in a vice between Egypt and Moslem Syria united under Saladin.*

Who was this Saladin? One anecdote gives us some idea, and at the same time depicts the chivalrous relations that he maintained with his Christian adversary. It refers to an event some years earlier, when Stephanie, the Lady of Kerak, was celebrating the wedding of her son Humphrey to Isabella, sister of Sybilla.

From her son's wedding the princess sent Saladin bread and wine, oxen and sheep and, in greeting him, reminded him that he had often carried her in his arms when he was a slave in the castle as a prisoner and she was a child. When Saladin saw the present, he was greatly delighted. He accepted it, expressing his thanks openly; and he asked all those who had brought the present which tower the wedded pair occupied, and they pointed it out to him. Thereupon, Saladin proclaimed throughout his army that none should be so rash as to shoot at that tower or to attack it.

And here is Saladin seen by one of his companions, Beha ed-Din:

Here is a story in which I was myself involved, and which gives a high idea of the religious zeal of Saladin. Towards the end of the year 584 when, after taking Caucab, Saladin had disbanded his army, he wished to visit Ascalon and the coastal places, to put them in a state of defence. I accompanied him on this voyage; we were then in winter, the sea was angry and, as the Koran says, the waves were tall as mountains. It was the first time that I saw the sea and the sight of it made the greatest possible impression on me. I said to myself that, not for the whole world would I ever consent to go even for a mile on that element; and I was ready to consider as madmen those who, for a miserable sum of gold or silver, embark without fear. In short, I joined the ranks of those who think that, because a man trusts himself to the sea he must be considered out of his mind and his evidence no longer legally valid. Suddenly, while I was plunged in these thoughts, the Sultan, turning towards me, said: "I am going to tell you what is in my heart. When God has given into my hands the rest of the Christian towns, I shall divide my States among my children; I shall leave them my last instructions and then, bidding them farewell, I shall embark on that sea to go and subdue the isles and the countries of the West. I do not want to lay down my arms until there is no longer a single infidel on earth, unless between now and that time death prevents me." These words astonished me so much that, immediately forgetting the thoughts that were occupying me, I said to the Sultan: "In truth there is on earth no courage, no strength of soul and no zeal for divine religion like those of the Sultan. The proof of his courage is that he is in no way hindered by the sight of that furious sea; as for his zeal for religion, the Sultan, not content with driving the enemies of God from one part of the land, such as Palestine, wants to rid the whole world of them." Then, recalling the terror that the sight of the sea had at first caused me, I added: "Nothing could be more splendid than the Sultan's plan; nevertheless, it would be better for him to content himself with sending his armies, and to stay here himself, for fear of putting his life in danger; for he is the rampart of Islam and its unique resource." Whereupon the Sultan continued: "But I make you judge of it: which is the more glorious death?" I answered that it was without question that in which one died for the cause of God. So he replied: "Then I am right in desiring that kind of death."

Unfortunately, one of the Christian barons broke the pledge that had been given to Saladin and thus all was lost, including honour.

There was among the Crusaders a certain Reynald of Châtillon who, it will be remembered, played a prominent part at the coronation of Sybilla. Like Gerard of Ridfort, Reynald was typical of those adventurers of lowly origin who sought and found fortune in the kingdoms of the Crusaders. A capricious widow, Constance, Princess of Antioch, dazzled by the handsome adventurer, had in a moment of folly made him head of one of the most splendid principalities of the kingdom. The only use that he made of his authority was to give free rein to his pillaging instincts; and the stories of William of Tyre recall his exploits as a brigand lord—astonishing exploits, such as transporting to the Red Sea, in separate parts on the backs of camels, a fleet with which he hoped to pillage Mecca—and those acts of insubordination which brought the kingdom to ruin as soon as there were no longer men as firm and heroic as King Baldwin at the head of it.

After the death of Constance of Antioch, Reynald of Châtillon married Stephanie, the Lady of Kerak. One day, according to the Estoire d'Eracles, which relates the whole story:

. . . a spy came to Prince Reynald and told him that a great caravan was coming from Babylon to Damascus and would pass by the land of Kerak. The prince immediately mounted his horse, went to Kerak, collected as many people as he could, and went and seized this caravan and with it the sister of Saladin who was with it. When Saladin heard that Prince Reynald had seized his caravan and his sister, he was sorely vexed and grieved. He at once sent messengers to the new king, demanding the caravan and his sister, and saying that he did not want to break the truce that he had made in the time of the little king. King Guy ordered Prince Reynald to give back to Saladin the caravan he had taken, and his sister. He answered that he would not give them back, that he was lord of his land, as the King was of his, and that he had made no truce with the Saracens. The taking of this caravan led to the loss of the Kingdom of Jerusalem.

The situation in which the Crusaders found themselves was so desperate that in the end Guy of Lusignan felt he must become reconciled with the very man he had ousted, Raymond III of Tripoli, the bravest of the barons of the Holy Land and the most experienced warrior.

So the King summoned the Master of the Temple, Gerard of Ridfort, and the Master of the Hospital, Brother Roger of Les

Moulins, and Josias, Archbishop of Tyre, and Balian of Ibelin and Reynald of Sidon, and ordered them to go to the Count of Tripoli in Tiberias and make peace. And whatever peace they made between them, he would keep. So they departed, and four of them went to spend the night at Nablus; but Reynald of Sidon went by another road. Now, while they were at Nablus the first night, Balian of Ibelin went to find the Master of the Temple and the Master of the Hospital and the Archbishop of Tyre and said to them that their journey next day would be short, so he would stay at Nablus where he had something to do, and would leave at night and ride all night so as to be with them at daybreak. So they separated and Balian remained behind.

In the meantime Saladin's son had asked Raymond of Tripoli to let him pass through his land. He was granted this on condition that he went and returned between sunrise and sunset, and that he took nothing, either in any town or any house. Raymond thought that in this way the Christians would be so well protected that they would lose nothing by his coming.

The son of Saladin promised this. When the next morning came he crossed the river and went towards Tiberias. He entered the land of the Christians, and the Count of Tripoli had the gates of the city closed so that none should go out to attack them. The Count had learnt the day before that messengers from King Guy were coming to him. He had letters prepared and sent messengers to Nazareth to the knights who were garrisoned there, and everywhere else where he knew that the Saracens would pass, to say that, whatever things they might see or hear, they should not that day leave their towns or their houses, for the Saracens were entering the land; that if the people lay low and did not leave their towns, the Saracens would pay no attention to them but that, if they found them in the fields, they might seize and kill them. Thus did the Count of Tripoli guarantee them peace.

The messenger went to the castle of La Fève and handed the letters of the Count of Tripoli to the Master of the Temple and the Master of the Hospital and the Archbishop of Tyre. When the Master of the Temple learnt that the Saracens were going to enter the country the next day, he took a messenger and sent him post-haste to the House of the Temple, which was four miles from there in a town called Kakum. In the letter he sent he ordered them, as soon as they received it, to mount and come to him, for the next day the Saracens would enter their territory. Immediately the Templars received this command from the Master, they mounted and got there before midnight, and lodged in front of the castle; and when the next morning came they went to Nazareth. There were ninety of them there, and ten members of the Hospital who were with the Master, and in Nazareth they took forty knights who were garrisoned there and went two good miles beyond Nazareth towards Tiberias, and found the Saracens at a fountain called the Springs of Cresson. They were on their way back to cross the river without doing any injury to the Christians. For the Christians considered themselves safe, as the Count had told them. The Master of the Temple was a bold knight, very sure of himself and, like those who are overbearing, he despised all other people. He would not believe the advice either of the Master of the Hospital, Brother Roger of Les Moulins, or of Brother James of Mailly, who was Master of the Temple; he scolded him, telling him he spoke like a man who is trying to flee, and saying: "You're too fond of that blond head of yours, that you want to keep at any cost." To which the marshal replied that he would not flee from the battle but would remain on the field like a brave man, and that it was the Master who would flee like a bad renegade. Then the Master of the Temple and the knights who were with him went and attacked the Saracens; and after them the Master of the Hospital did the same. The Saracens received them joyfully and surrounded them so completely that the Christians were unable to resist; for the Saracens had seven thousand armed horsemen and the Christians were only a hundred and forty. There the Master of the Hospital had his head cut off and all the knights of the Temple too, save only the Master, who escaped with three knights. And the forty knights who were garrisoned at Nazareth were all taken prisoner. When the equerries of the Temple and of the Hospital saw that the knights were surrounded by the Saracens, they took flight with all their harness so that none of the Christians' harness was lost.

Now I will tell you what the Master of the Temple did. When he passed Nazareth, fleeing from the Saracens, he sent a mounted sergeant back to have it cried throughout Nazareth that all who could bear arms should follow him to the booty, for they had routed the Saracens. So all those who could go left Nazareth and made such haste that they came where the battle had been. They found the Christians dead and defeated and the Saracens attacked them and took them all prisoner. When the Saracens had defeated and killed the Christians, they took the heads of the Christian knights whom they had slain and set them on the points of their lances; they led the prisoners bound and passed in front of Tiberias. When the Christians who were in Tiberias saw that the Christians had been taken prisoner and defeated, and that the Saracens were carrying their heads on their lances and leading them prisoner and bound, they were filled with sorrow at the sight. . . . They came near to taking their own lives. And so the son of Saladin departed, crossing the river again by day before sunset. He kept his promise to the Count of Tripoli well, for they did no damage either in castle or town or house, except to those whom they found in the fields. This battle took place on a Friday; it was the day of the feast of Saint James and Saint Philip, the first of May. It was because of the caravan which Prince Reynald had taken in the land of Kerak and it was the beginning of the loss of the kingdom.

Balian, who was at Nablus when night fell, set out, as he had promised the Master of the Temple and the Master of the Hospital, to go and rejoin them. When he had gone two miles he came to a city called Sebastea. Remembering it was a feast day he thought that he would not go further without having heard Mass. So he went to the house of the bishop, made him get up and sat talking with him until the watch had proclaimed the day. Then the bishop bade one of his chaplains robe himself and say Mass. When Balian had heard Mass he went off with all haste after the Master of the Temple and did not stop until he came to the castle. He found the awnings of the house up, but there was no one inside. He marvelled greatly at it and found no one whom he could ask what was the matter. Then he made his valet enter the castle to see if he could find anyone who could tell him what had happened. The valet went and called throughout the castle; he saw no one who could give him any news; there were only two sick men, who lay in a room and could tell him nothing. So he returned to his lord and told him he had found no one who could say what had happened. Then Balian ordered him to mount and they rode towards Nazareth. When they were a little way off from the castle, there appeared in the distance a brother of the Temple on horseback who called to them to wait for him. They waited. Balian of Ibelin asked him what was the news and he answered: "Bad." And he told him that the Master of the Hospital had had his head cut off and all the knights of the Temple too; that only the Master of the Temple and three of his knights had escaped; and the knights whom the king had garrisoned at Nazareth were all taken prisoner. When Balian of Ibelin heard this news, he was sorely grieved; he called a sergeant and sent him back to Nablus, to the queen his wife,* to give her the news and tell her to order all his knights at Nablus to join him that night at Nazareth . . . and that for a surety if he had not gone to Sebastea to hear Mass, he would have arrived in time for the battle. When Balian reached Nazareth he heard great mourning being made for those of the city who had been slain or taken in the battle, and few were the houses where there was not someone dead or prisoner; but he did not find there the Master of the Temple, who had escaped. He took lodging there and waited until his knights had arrived and then informed the Count of Tripoli that he was at Nazareth. When the Count knew that Balian was at Nazareth and that he had not been in the battle, he was overjoyed.

King Guy becomes reconciled with the Count of Tripoli and prepares to resist Saladin:

The King ordered the Patriarch to take the True Cross to the army. The Patriarch took the Cross, brought it out of Jerusalem and handed it to the Prior of the Holy Sepulchre. He told him to take it to the King, as he was busy and could not go; for he had no wish to go to the army. So the prophecy was true, that the Archbishop of Tyre had made when the Patriarch was elected: that Heraclius had won the Cross from the Persians and brought it to Jerusalem, and that Heraclius would take it out of Jerusalem and that in his time it would be lost. In that hour Heraclius sent the Cross out of Jerusalem and never again was it taken back.

---

* Balian's wife was Marie Comnena, a Greek princess, whose first husband had been King Amalric I of Jerusalem.

THE DISASTER OF HATTIN

✢✢

*S*ALADIN HAD *raised "an army without number, like to the Ocean" (80,000 men) and invaded Galilee in the direction of Tiberias, where he captured the lower town within an hour. The inhabitants took refuge in the citadel. Tiberias was one of the fiefs of Raymond of Tripoli, whose wife, Countess Eschiva, was there with her children. Nevertheless, when Raymond was invited by Guy of Lusignan to give his advice on the measures to be taken, he did not hesitate to advise against marching on Tiberias, in a desert region in the height of the hot season.*

"*Estoire D'Eracles*":

The Count answered like a wise man and said: "Sire, know that any damage done to Tiberias is my affair and falls on me and no other; for my wife, the lady of Tiberias, and my children are there before the castle, and I would not for anything in the world that harm should come to them. So I have advised them, if they see that the forces of Saladin are too great for them to withstand, to go on board their ships and seek refuge on the sea until such time as we can come to their aid. Having said that, Sire, if you wish to enter into combat with Saladin, let us go and lodge before Acre so as to be near our fortresses. I know that Saladin is so proud that he will not leave the kingdom until he has joined battle with you, and if he comes to fight you before Acre and things go ill (from which God preserve us), we can call on Acre and the other cities near by to help us. And if God gives us the victory, so that we may defeat him before he has regained his own territory, we shall have so vanquished and broken him that he will never be able to recover." When the Count had finished speaking the Master of the Temple said to him: "I spy treason." When the Count heard that, he immediately said to the King: "Sire, I urge

and beg you to go to the help of Tiberias." He replied that he
would willingly go. Thereupon the Countess of Tiberias sent
messengers to the King to come and help her, for she and her
people were sorely pressed. When they heard this news, a cry
rose among the knights in the army, saying: "Let us go and
succour the ladies and maidens of Tiberias." . . .

*On the advice of the Count of Tripoli and the barons, the army
decided to camp where they were, in a fortified place, since the forces
of Saladin were far superior to those of the King.*

. . . When night came, the Master of the Temple went to the
King and said to him: "Sire, do not believe the advice of the
Count, for he is a traitor and you know well that he does not
like you and would like you to suffer shame and lose the kingdom.
I therefore counsel you to go from hence, and we with you, and
that we should go and defeat Saladin. For that is the first task you
have undertaken, according to your own will. If you do not leave
this lodging, Saladin will come and attack you here, and if you
leave here because of his attack, the shame and reproach of it will
be the greater." When the King heard that, he ordered his army
to get under way. When the barons of the army heard that the
King was commanding them to move off, they were astonished
and went to him, saying: "Sire, your counsel was to the effect
that you and we had decided not to stir from here. By what
counsel are you making the army move?" He said to them:
"It is not for you to ask me by what counsel I am doing it. I
want you to mount your horses and prepare yourselves immediately to go to Tiberias." They, like serious and loyal men,
obeyed the King and did his bidding. It may be that, if they had
gainsaid the command he gave them, it would have been better
for Christendom. I must not fail to tell you of a miracle that
happened in this army. The pack animals of the Christian army,
the day before and the night when they left the fountain of
Saphori in the great heat that prevailed, would never drink nor
touch water, but behaved like men who are sad and grieving.
And so the next day, when they were setting to work, to the
general dismay they began to grow weak and failed their masters
and died for lack of water.

I must not omit to tell you of an adventure that befell the

people of this army, although it seems like a fable and the Holy Church forbids us to believe it. When the army set out from the fountain of Saphori and had left Nazareth two miles behind, the sergeants of the army came across an old Saracen woman on a donkey. The sergeants thought she was a slave who had fled from her master, and they took her prisoner. Some of them could tell that she was from Nazareth; they asked her where she was going at such an hour, but she was unable to give a clear answer to their question. They threatened her and frightened her and she then owned that she was the slave of a Syrian of Nazareth. They asked her where she was going. She told them she was going to Saladin to get her reward for a service she had done him. Then they maltreated her even more to find out what the service she rendered Saladin had been. She said that she was a sorceress and that she had put a spell on the men of the army: for three nights she had gone all round about them and she had cast her spell in the name of the devil . . . and she told them they were in a bad way and heading for their own ruin, for few among them would escape. . . .

It was indeed true that few of that cavalcade escaped from death or being taken prisoner. . . . They collected thorns and couch grass and made a great fire and threw her into it; she jumped out of the fire two or three times. There was a sergeant who had a Danish axe; he gave her such a great blow on the head with it that he clave her in two, and she was then thrown into the fire and burnt. Saladin heard tell of it and it weighed sorely on him, and if she had not been burnt he would have ransomed her at a great price. . . .

The disaster of Hattin, on July 4th, 1187, marks the end of the Kingdom of Jerusalem.

. . . So King Guy asked the Count what he counselled for him and for Christendom, and the Count of Tripoli said that if the King had followed his advice the first time as he wanted to now, it would have greatly profited him and he would have saved Christendom; but now it was too late. "Because of that," he said, "I cannot now think of any other counsel than to pretend that we are staying here and that the King should have his tent pitched on the summit of this mountain." Then King Guy had faith in his advice and did what the Count said. On the summit of that mountain, where King Guy was taken, Saladin had a mosque built, which still stands there in praise of him and in memory of his victory.

When the Saracens saw that the Christians were staying there they were overjoyed at it and established their camp round the Christian army, so close that they could speak to each other; if a cat had escaped from the army of the Christians, it could not have got away without the Saracens taking it. . . .

All that night the Christians remained armed and suffered greatly from thirst. The next day they held themselves ready to fight and so did the Saracens. But the Saracens retreated and did not wish to fight until the heat had begun. And I will tell you what they did. In the middle of the plain of Baruf there was a great stretch of heathland covered with herbage, and the wind had risen very strongly from that direction; so the Saracens came and set fire to it all round them to increase their discomfort further still, from the fire as well as the sun. And they kept them in this state until after the hour of tierce. Then five knights left the ranks of the Count of Tripoli and went to Saladin and said to him: "Sire, what are you waiting for, fall upon them; they can no longer help themselves; they are all dead." And the foot-sergeants surrendered to the Saracens, their mouths open because of the pangs of thirst. When the King saw the distress and anguish of our people, and that the sergeants were going to give themselves up to the Saracens, he ordered the Count of Tripoli to fall on the Saracens, for the battle was taking place on his territory and it was for him to deliver the first attack. The Count of Tripoli fell upon the Saracens and harried them on a hillside adjoining a valley. And as soon as the Saracens saw the Christians bearing down on them, they moved aside and made way for them, as their custom is; and the Count rode beyond them, whereupon they reformed their ranks and hurried after the King who had remained where he was; and they took him and all who were with him, save only those in the rear-guard who escaped. . . .

The same battle of Hattin, as seen by an Arab, Ibn al-Athir:

On the Saturday morning, the Moslems left their camp in order of battle; the Franks advanced too, but already weakened by the thirst which tormented them. On both sides the action began furiously. The first Moslem line let fly a cloud of arrows, like a cloud of grasshoppers. The arrows worked havoc among the Christian cavalry. The Christian infantry had moved off in the direction of the lake to get water. Saladin immediately hurried to block their passage, urging on the Moslems by his voice and gestures. All at once one of the young mameluks of the Sultan, carried away by his ardour, hurled himself upon the Christians and, after prodigies of courage, was killed. The Moslems advanced to avenge his death, and wrought great carnage among the infidels. Soon there was no longer any hope of salvation for the Christians. The Count of Tripoli tried to break his way through: Taki ed-Din, nephew of the Sultan, was opposite him; when he saw the Count advancing like one out of his mind, he had the ranks opened and the Count got away with his suite. The Christian army was then in a horrible situation. As the ground where it was fighting was covered with heather and dry weeds, the Moslems set fire to it and kindled a vast conflagration. And so the smoke and the heat of the fire, that of the day and that of the fight, all combined against the Christians. They were so dismayed that they were within an ace of asking for quarter. Finally, seeing that there was no salvation left, they flung themselves on the Moslems with such impetuosity that, without the help of God, one could not have resisted them. However, with every attack they lost men and grew weaker; at last they were surrounded on every side and pushed back as far as a neighbouring hill, near the hamlet of Hattin. There they tried to pitch some tents and defend themselves. . . . Soon the King had round him on the hill no more than a hundred and fifty of the bravest knights. Afdal was at that moment with the Sultan his father. He himself said afterwards: "I was beside my father when the King of the Franks retreated to the hill; the brave men who were round him fell on us and pushed the Moslems back to the bottom of the hill. Then I looked at my father and saw the sadness on his face. 'Give the devil the lie!' he shouted to the soldiers, tugging at his beard. At those words our army hurled itself on the enemy and forced him back to the summit of the hill, while I shouted: "They flee! they flee!" But the Franks returned to the charge and advanced once again to the bottom of the hill, where they were once again repulsed; and again I cried: 'They flee, they flee!' Then my father looked at me and said: 'Be silent; they will not be truly defeated until the King's tent falls.' Now he had barely finished speaking when the tent collapsed. My father immediately got down from his horse, prostrated himself before God and gave thanks to Him, weeping tears of joy."

This is how the King's tent fell. When the Franks, on the hill, attacked the Moslems with such fury, it was because they were suffering horribly from thirst and wanted to break their way through. Finding themselves repulsed, they got down from their horses and sat on the ground. Then the Moslems climbed the hill and overthrew the King's tent. All the Christians who were there were made prisoner. Among the number, besides the King, there was his brother Prince Geoffrey, Reynald, Lord of Kerak, the Lord of Jebail, the son of Humphrey, the Grand Master of the Templars and many Hospitallers and Templars. When one saw how many were dead, one could not believe there were any prisoners; and when one saw the prisoners, one could not believe there were any dead. Never since their invasion of Palestine had the Franks suffered such a defeat. I myself crossed the battlefield a year later and saw there the piles of bones. There were also some scattered here and there, not to mention what torrents and carnivorous animals had carried away to the mountains and valleys.

The account of another Arab chronicler, Imad ed-Din:

This battle took place on a Saturday. The Christians were lions at the beginning of the fight, and at the end were no more than scattered sheep. Of so many thousands of men, only a small number were saved. The battlefield was covered with dead and dying; I myself crossed Mount Hattin; it presented a horrible sight. I saw all that a happy nation had done to an unfortunate people. I saw the condition of its leaders; who could describe it? I saw severed heads, eyes dulled or gouged out, bodies covered with dust, dismembered limbs, severed arms, split bones, cloven necks, loins smashed, feet hanging by a thread from legs, bodies cut in two, torn lips, smashed foreheads. Seeing those faces glued to the earth and covered with blood and wounds, I recalled those words of the Koran: "The infidel shall say: Why am I not dust! What a sweet odour rose from that terrible victory!"

The vengeance of Saladin, seen by a Crusader:

"Estoire d'Eracles":

When the Saracens had overcome the Christians, Saladin gave thanks to God for the honour He had done him, and had it cried throughout the army that the knights taken prisoner were to be brought to his tent. . . . When he saw the King and the other barons who were at his mercy, he rejoiced greatly; he saw that the King was hot and knew well that he was thirsty and would gladly drink; he had a cupful of syrup to drink brought to refresh him. When the King had drunk, he handed the cup to Prince Reynald [Reynald of Châtillon], who was sitting beside him, that he might drink. When Saladin saw that the King had given the drink to Prince Reynald, who was the man he hated most on earth, he was greatly incensed and grieved thereby, and said to the King: "It displeases me that you gave him to drink." But since it had been given to him, he let him drink. But it was on condition that he should never again drink anything; for for no riches that anyone might be able to give him, would he let him live any longer without cutting off his head with his own hand: for never had he [Reynald] kept his word or faith in the truces that he had concluded with him. When Prince Reynald had drunk, Saladin had him seized and led out of his tent. He asked for a sword and they brought it him and he took it and cut off his head. And then he ordered that the head should be dragged through every city and every castle of his land. And so it was.

THE HOLY LAND IS ALL BUT LOST:
SALADIN REMAINS A NOBLE FOE

✳✳✳

*A*FTER WREAKING *vengeance on Reynald of Châtillon, Sala-din marched on Acre. On July 13th a small fleet belonging to the Piedmontese Marquis, Conrad of Montferrat, appeared off the town. The Marquis was astonished not to hear the bells ringing, as they usually did to greet Christian ships. When the crew looked more carefully at the people they could see on the shore, they soon realised that they were not Christians but Saracens. Acre had sur-rendered to Saladin, without resistance, on July 9th, less than a week after his victory at Hattin. After taking Acre, Saladin undertook the conquest of the towns of the Holy Land one after the other, and Nazareth, Caesarea, Sidon and Ascalon soon fell into his hands. Next he marched on Jerusalem. There a baron whose name we have already come across, Balian of Ibelin who had escaped the slaughter near Nazareth and joined Raymond of Tripoli, had constituted himself defender of the Holy City. Balian had armed sixty burghers as knights so that they could take part in the defence of the city. But it was obvious that Jerusalem would not resist for long.*

A Saracen witness, Ibn al-Athir, records:

Jerusalem was then a very strong city. The attack took place on the northern side, towards the Gate of Amud or the Gate of the Column, not far from the Church of Sion. That was where the Sultan's quarters were. The machines were set up during the night, and the attack took place the next day.

The Franks at first showed great bravery. On both sides this war was regarded as a religious matter. The soldiers needed no orders from their leaders to rouse their ardour; all defended their positions fearlessly; all attacked without looking behind them. The besieged made sorties each day and descended to the plain.

In one of these attacks, after a distinguished emir had been killed, the Moslems all advanced together as one man to avenge his death, and they put the Christians to flight; they then approached the moat of the place and made a breach. Archers posted nearby repulsed the Christians on top of the ramparts with shots from their arrows, and so protected the workers. At the same time they dug a subterranean passage and when it was hollowed out they filled it with wood, which they then only had to set alight. In this plight the leaders of the Christians thought it best to capitulate. The chief inhabitants were sent in a deputation to Saladin, who answered: "I shall treat you as the Christians treated the Moslems when they took the Holy City, which means that I shall put the men to the sword, and reduce the rest to slavery: in a word, I shall return evil for evil." On getting this answer Balian, a son of Basran, who commanded in Jerusalem, demanded a safe conduct to go and treat with the Sultan himself. His request was granted. He presented himself to Saladin and made representations to him. As Saladin showed himself inflexible, Balian stooped to supplications and prayers. As Saladin remained inexorable he cast caution to the winds and said: "Know, O Sultan, that we are infinite in number and that God alone can guess what our number is. The inhabitants are reluctant to fight, because they hope for a capitulation, such as you have granted to so many others. They fear death and cling to life; but once death becomes inevitable, I swear by the God who hears us, we shall kill our women and our children, we shall burn our riches and we shall not leave you an écu. You will find no more women to reduce to slavery, or men to put in irons. We shall destroy the Chapel of the Sakkra [the Dome of the Rock] and the Mosque al-Aqsa, with all the holy places. We shall slaughter all the Moslems, to the number of five thousand, who are imprisoned in our walls. We shall not leave a single beast of burden alive. We shall come out against you, and we shall fight like people fighting for their lives. For one of us who perishes, many of yours will fall. We shall die free or we shall triumph with glory." At these words Saladin consulted his emirs, who considered that they should agree to capitulation. "The Christians," they said, "must come out on foot and bring nothing without showing it to us. We shall treat them like captives who are at our mercy, and they will ransom themselves at a price to be decided." These words entirely satisfied Saladin. It was agreed with the Christians that every man in the town, rich or poor, should pay for his ransom ten pieces of gold, the women, five, and the children of both sexes, two. A delay of forty days was granted for the payment of this tribute. At the end of this time, all those who had not paid would be considered as slaves. On the other hand, as soon as anyone paid the tribute he was free and could go where he would. With regard to the poor of the town, whose number was fixed at approximately eighteen thousand, Balian bound himself to pay thirty thousand pieces of gold for them. All being thus agreed, the Holy City opened its doors and the Moslem standard was hoisted on the walls. It was then Friday, the 24th of Rajab [early October, 1187].

Ibn al-Athir complains of the cupidity of the emirs and their underlings who, instead of handing this money to the Sultan, kept back a part of it for themselves:

If they had behaved loyally, the Treasury would have been filled. The number of Christians in the town able to bear arms had been estimated at sixty thousand, without counting the women and children. For the town was in fact a big one and the population had been swollen by the inhabitants of Ascalon, Ramleh and other towns in the neighbourhood. The people overcrowded the streets and the churches and it was difficult to find room. This multitude proved that a very great number had paid the tribute and were sent back free. Eighteen thousand poor folk had also come out, for whom Balian had given thirty thousand pieces of gold; for all that there remained sixteen thousand Christians who, for want of a ransom, were made slaves. There can be no uncertainty about this fact, which is taken from the public registers. Add to that that a large number of inhabitants got out under false pretences, without paying the tribute. Some slid stealthily down from the top of the walls with the help of ropes; others borrowed Moslem clothes for money, but left without paying anything. Lastly, some emirs claimed a certain number of Christians as belonging to them, and themselves took the price of their ransom. In short, it was only the smallest part of that money which found its way into the Treasury. . . .

Jerusalem is lost indeed.

... There was on the cupola of the Sakkra a great cross of gold. The day the town surrendered, many Moslems climbed up to pull it down. Christians and Moslems alike gazed up at that sight. When the cross fell, cries arose from everyone in the town and the surrounding districts; they were cries of joy from the Moslems, and cries of grief and rage from the Christians; the noise was such that one might have thought that the end of the world had come. ...

The Christians mourn.

... In Aleppo I had as a slave a Christian woman, taken at Jaffa, who had a child one year old. One day that child fell and bruised its face and the mother began to weep great tears; and as I was trying to calm her, telling her that her child's hurt was slight, she answered: "I am not weeping for the child, but for the evils we have suffered; I had six brothers who have all perished; I had a husband and two sisters, and I do not know what has become of them." This was what had happened to one person only, but many others had suffered the same misfortunes as this woman. Another day I saw in Aleppo a Christian slave-girl who was accompanying her master to a neighbouring house; all at once another woman appeared at the door: the first gave a great cry; they embraced each other tenderly and then sat down and began to talk together. They were two sisters who had been reduced to slavery and taken without knowing it to the same town.

But the old Crusaders did not wish to leave. Ambroise, a Christian chronicler, tells us:

When Saladin took Jerusalem it happened that he found in the city two ancient men. One was called Robert of Coudre, who had been with Godfrey of Bouillon at the conquest; the other was called Fulk Fiole; he had been born in Jerusalem after the first conquest, as soon as it was conquered. Saladin found those two men in the city of Jerusalem; because they were very old people he took pity on them. They asked him to let them stay and end their lives in the city of Jerusalem. He gladly granted this and ordered that they should be given what they needed, as much as they wanted; and they ended their lives there.

*But even so, all was not lost. When, on the previous July 13th,
Conrad of Montferrat realised that Acre had fallen to Saladin, he set
sail again and moored alongside the fortified town of Tyre which, because
it was well defended both by its natural position and by its ramparts,
was still in the hands of the Christians. But he was only just in time,
for its defenders had just entered into negotiations with the envoys of
Saladin, whose banner was already floating on one of the towers.
Conrad's arrival was to change the destiny of the city and make the
fortress of Tyre the starting point of the resistance. In vain did Saladin
tell Conrad that in exchange for Tyre he would free his father, who had
been made prisoner at Hattin. Conrad answered that he was not
disposed to give even a stone of the walls of Tyre in exchange for the
liberty of his father. Moreover, Saladin found that he was up against
several pockets of resistance which, either by force or by guile, put
obstacles in the way of his conquest. An example of this is the story of the
fortress of Beaufort, as told by the Arab chronicler, Beha ed-Din:*

The first time that Reynald [Lord of Beaufort] appeared before
the Sultan [Saladin], he pretended to have come without followers
and without warning, in short, on a sudden impulse. Saladin
was at that moment at table and he made him eat with him.
Reynald knew Arabic very well, and even had some knowledge
of our chroniclers. He is said to have taken into his service a
Moslem so that he might learn our language from him. He
offered to hand over Beaufort to Saladin, declaring that he would
be content with a house at Damascus, with enough land to let
him live comfortably, with his family. In the meantime he
often came to see us and we argued about religion; he wanted to
prove to us that the Christian religion was the better; we on the
contrary maintained that it was worthless. In any case it was
pleasant to converse with him, and his language showed that he
was educated. ...

This lord had a subtle and wily mind. As he feared that he
would not be able to resist openly, he ... made great protestations
of friendship [to the Sultan]. "I like you," he said to him, "and
I recognise my obligations to you; but my children and my
parents are at this moment in Tyre, and I fear that the marquis
in command there, when he learns of my relations with you, may
revenge himself on them. So grant me a delay and give me time
to bring them here. As soon as they arrive I will hand over

Beaufort to you, and we will all enter your service; we will accept whatever you are good enough to give us." These words flattered Saladin greatly and he granted Reynald a delay of three months...

Saladin then learnt that the Christians of Tyre were marching on his army.

. . . This news greatly distressed Saladin: he no longer knew which way to turn. He would have liked to go straightway to Tyre and halt the Christians in their march. On the other hand he dared not leave in his rear a place as important as Beaufort; for if he departed it was to be feared that Reynald might provision it and prepare to defend it. Neither could he break his word and ask for Beaufort to be handed over to him before the three months had expired. In this conjuncture he received a letter from the army corps which was on the look-out before Tyre, telling him that the Franks were about to set out, and that they were going to attack Sidon. Saladin left some troops before Beaufort and took the road with his fighting men; but he was unable to arrive in time. The Franks had already left Tyre and, surprising the Moslems in a defile, they delivered such a terrible attack on them that it would have made children's hair turn white with fear. This combat was equally deadly for both armies. Finally the Christians, meeting with stubborn resistance, retraced their steps and returned to the walls of Tyre.

The outcome of this fight strongly affected Saladin; he was impatient to come to blows again in order to avenge the carnage of his troops. One day he mounted his horse and went with a handful of followers to the top of a hill to observe the enemy. When they saw this, the shepherds of the neighbourhood, the Arabs, and the volunteers in the army thought that battle was going to be joined again, whereupon they took fright and fled with all speed. In vain did the Sultan send people hurrying after them; the foolhardy creatures, listening to no remonstrances, let themselves be surprised by the Franks and sent to their last sleep; Allah have pity on their souls! Among those Moslems were some persons of distinction. Saladin was greatly grieved by this accident: he himself saw this massacre from the top of the hill and hastened there with all speed. He pursued the Franks right up to the walls of Tyre, but the Franks entered the town again and the Sultan went to see the great works which were being done in Acre.

A short time after, Saladin was told that the Christians were making ready to come out again to seek for wood and fodder. He immediately had some troops placed in ambush in valleys and narrow places, and charged some of his braves to go and provoke the Christians and lure them into a fight. Unfortunately, when those braves were face to face with the Franks, instead of pretending to flee, as they had been ordered, they made it a point of honour to fight where they were. The troops in ambush, growing tired of waiting, went to take part in the action and the design miscarried. During this engagement a mameluk of the Sultan's, who was seen to have been wounded by many arrows, was left for dead: the next day the Moslems, passing by that place, heard him groan and realised that he was still alive: they wrapped him in a cloak; and as his state was such as to leave no hope, they urged him to make his profession of faith and to die like a good Moslem, congratulating him on his glorious end.

While these things were happening the delay granted to Reynald lord of Beaufort expired. Unfortunately, Reynald had profited by the interval to buy provisions in our camp and had prepared himself to make a stout defence. From time to time Saladin had been warned of this trick but he refused to believe in such bad faith, and would think nothing but good of Reynald. When anyone spoke to him on this subject and told him that Reynald was only trying to gain time, and that before long he would show his hand openly, he refused to believe it. At last, when the truce was about to expire, and Saladin had sent to ask Reynald to hand over the place, Reynald came to find him and said that he had not yet received his children from Tyre; in short, he asked for another delay. The Sultan then had him arrested and called on him to keep his word forthwith. Reynald promised to do so and asked to speak to a priest whom he said he wished to send to the garrison to urge it to surrender. The priest was called; he had a secret interview with Reynald. He was allowed to enter the fortress and from that moment the garrison defended itself with more energy than ever. Indignant, Saladin sent Reynald loaded with chains to Damascus and began a regular siege against the fortress of Beaufort.

The Siege of Tyre thereafter continued for several months, but without result, for on January 2nd, 1188, Saladin was obliged to raise it.

THE RESISTANCE IS ORGANISED:
THE SIEGE OF ACRE

✢✢✢✢✢✢✢✢✢✢✢✢✢✢✢✢✢✢✢✢✢✢✢✢✢✢✢✢✢✢✢✢✢✢✢✢✢✢

*T*HE *WEST* had been greatly moved by the news of the fall *of Jerusalem. It was then that what is traditionally known as the Third Crusade was decided upon. As had happened a half-century previously, the chief sovereigns took the cross. The King of France, Philip Augustus, the King of England, Henry Plantagenet, then his son and successor Richard Cœur-de-Lion, and the German Emperor Frederick Barbarossa, all decided to answer the call of the Pope. Frederick Barbarossa was the first to set out, on May 11th, 1189, at the head of an army which, according to contemporary accounts, numbered 100,000 men. It was moreover remarkably well organised, revictualling posts having been established in advance along the route to be covered, But on June 10th, 1190, the Emperor was drowned near Seleucia. From then on his splendid army, which had in advance struck terror into the Moslem world and had already seized Konya, a capital of the Seljuk Turks, literally fell to pieces; the greater number of the soldiers returned to Europe, others went to join the Christians before Tyre or before Acre.*

After Saladin had raised the siege of Tyre on January 2nd, 1188, all the efforts of the Christian army were concentrated before Acre, which was reconquered after a siege of two years (August 20th, 1189–July 12th, 1191) with all the frustration of alternating setbacks and successes and also, from time to time, curious episodes of fraternisation between the opposing camps. This siege of Acre has been recounted by the Arab chroniclers in particular:

Imad ed-Din:

When Saladin took Acre, two years earlier, several emirs had counselled him to raze this town to the ground and remove all traces of it, claiming that, as long as it remained standing, the

Christians would be tempted to come and recapture it. For a time Saladin was disposed to take this advice; but others thought it would be a pity to destroy so great and beautiful a city, and that it would be enough to surround it with good fortifications. Saladin sent to Egypt for the Emir Beha ed-Din Caracusch, who had built the walls of Cairo, and was considered a great expert on building. Caracusch had at his disposal a large number of Christian prisoners; he had the machines he needed brought from Egypt. The walls were repaired, the towers raised, and the town surrounded with redoubtable fortifications. When the siege began Caracusch was still in the town and he remained there until the end. . . .

Beha ed-Din:

The attack was fixed for the Friday, at the hour of public prayer. The emirs wanted it to be on a Friday, while the katibs or preachers were in their pulpits, sure that so holy an hour would bring them good fortune; but all the efforts of the Moslems were vain. Night separated the combatants; the two armies spent that night under arms and the battle began again next day. They fought until midday with no decisive victory. Finally, the Moslem right wing, commanded by Taki ed-Din, made a last effort and hurled itself on the Christians towards the north of the town, near the sea-shore: this was the last place that the Franks had occupied and they had not yet had time to entrench themselves there. Taki ed-Din broke in on them and made a way through right into the town. From that moment communications were re-established. The Sultan quickly sent reinforcements into the town and entered it himself, hastening along the ramparts to observe the Christian army. I went up too and was happy to let fly a few arrows at the Christians. The garrison also made a sortie and chased the Christians before it. This day would have been decisive if our warriors had continued the fight; unfortunately, when they saw that communications were re-established, they thought they had done enough and went to rest. The attack was put off till the next day; but in the interval the Christians took heart again and it became impossible to drive them off. As for the Sultan, nothing affected his ardour: he was in a perpetual agitation like a lioness who has lost her young. I know from his doctor that he went from the Friday to the Sunday with hardly any food. . . .

The siege lasted a long time, and the armies fraternised:

. . . As each side was continually attacking the other, the
Christians and the Moslems ended by drawing closer, getting
to know each other, and talking together. When they were tired,
they laid down their arms and mingled together; they sang,
danced and gave themselves up to enjoyment; in a word, the two
sides became friendly until, a moment later, the war started
again. One day when, after fighting for a long time, both sides
were trying to relax after their hardships, a Christian said to the
soldiers of the garrison: "How long are we men going to go on
fighting? Why don't we make the children fight too? Come now,
let your children come to blows with ours." Thereupon, several
Moslem children went outside the town, the Christians brought
theirs and the fight began. Those children fought with the utmost
courage. One Moslem child in particular seized hold of his
antagonist with all his might, lifted him off the ground and
threw him. One unusual thing was that the vanquished was considered a prisoner, and his parents gave two pieces of gold to
ransom him. It was no use for the victor to make difficulties
about accepting them; he was told that the vanquished was his
prisoner and he took the money.

Imad ed-Din describes an assault:

On Wednesday the 21st of Shaban [end of September, 1189]
the Franks advanced with their crosses as eagerly as horses running
to the pasture, and came to our hill. In one moment they were all
over it like a deluge or a raging sea. Their impact was such that
the earth trembled and the air was darkened. At that time I was
on the hill with some pious Moslems, looking at the two armies.
We never thought the enemy would come as far as us. When
we saw the Christians approaching and about to close in on us,
we had to think of our safety, for we were on our mules, with
no defence. Dreading a disaster, we retreated and galloped without
stopping as far as Tiberias, where we crossed the Jordan; and as
every country we passed through was in a state of terror, we
continued galloping, always heading east, heart-broken at the
defeat of the Moslem army. None of us thought of eating; none
was tempted to stop. Hardly breathing, and with heavy hearts,

we gripped the bridle of our horses. Several even fled as far as Damascus. But for our part, we finally tried to get some rest, our hearts full of fear and offering vows to God. Meanwhile, certain rumours began to spread. People were saying: The Moslems have regained courage; Islamism is avenged; the infidel has been broken; the left flank has stood fast; the Sultan's mameluks have repulsed the enemy. These statements were repeated; messengers confirmed them; finally, on the morning of the next day, I suddenly heard the voice of a mameluk crying: "Where is Imad ed-Din? The victory he longed for has been won." At these words, we ran to the mameluk and plied him with question after question: "How had this victory happened? How had the Sultan won it? How had God's will prevailed?" Then our spirits calmed and we regretted that we had fled so quickly.

In spite of his victory, Saladin was a prey to the keenest anxieties: he had just learnt that in the West a new army was getting ready to leave for the Crusade. The Sultan was afraid he might not be able to resist so many united forces, and hastened to write to the Caliph of Baghdad and all the Moslem princes. An Arab chronicler, Abu Shama, has preserved his letters to the Caliph:

"We hope that God in His goodness will let the danger in which we stand rouse the zeal of the Moslems, and that they will strive to quell the ardour of our enemies and overthrow the edifice that the Franks have raised. As long as our enemies are hastening hither by sea and land, our country is threatened by the greatest disasters; and we see with amazement the pugnacity of the infidels and the indifference of the true believers. Does a single Moslem respond to our entreaty and come when he is called? Yet look at the Christians; see how they come in throngs, how they hurry to vie with each other, how they support each other, how they sacrifice their riches, how they subscribe together, how they submit to the greatest possible privations! With them there is not a king, not a lord, not an island or a city, not a man of the least importance, who does not send to this war his peasants and his subjects, and make them act in this theatre of bravery; not a powerful man who does not take part in this expedition; all of them desire to work for the aim to which they are devoted. They think that by so doing they serve their religion; that is why they consecrate their lives and their riches to this war. In all that their one aim is the cause of Him whom they adore, the glory of Him in whom they believe; it never even occurs to them that perhaps the whole of Palestine may be subjugated, that the veil of the Christians' honour may be rent, and that they may lose their domains and see them pass into other hands. The Moslems, on the contrary, are feeble, discouraged, apathetic, indifferent, stupefied, without zeal for religion, so much so that if, which God forbid! those who guide Islamism were to lead it astray, neither in the East nor the West, nor far from here nor near, would one find a single man willing to devote himself to the cause of the religion of God, and undertake to defend the truth against error. Nevertheless, we have now reached a point where procrastination is no longer opportune, where we need the help of all the friends of religion, in distant as in near-by lands. Let us hope that God will be good enough to grant us His support; that the infidels, by God's grace, will be exterminated; and that the true believers will be saved, and removed from danger."

Not content with this urgent letter, Saladin sent a man he trusted to speed up the despatch of the help he was asking.

It was I, Beha ed-Din, whom he chose for that mission. I went immediately to the princes of Sinjar, Gezira, Mosul and other towns of Mesopotamia, and I exhorted all the Moslems to come and take part in the holy war. I went to Baghdad too, on the same mission. God favoured my journey; I saw all those princes and all promised to do what I asked.

Another Arab chronicler, Imad ed-Din, tells how the Moslems besieged in Acre corresponded with their brethren by carrier pigeon:

Summer had returned; the sea became calm again, and the Christian vessels took up their positions anew in front of Acre. Our fleet was obliged to put out to sea and withdraw to Egypt; all direct communication with the town ceased. All we could do was to employ clever swimmers who, excited by the lure of rewards, carried money and provisions to the garrison in their belts; they were also responsible for the letters and the pigeons, and the garrison sent replies under the wing of those pigeons.

There was at that time in the army a man who amused himself by training those pigeons; he made them fly round his tent and taught them to come back when they were called. This man was very useful to us in our predicament: we used to ask him for pigeons day and night, so much so that they finally became scarce.

Saladin's camp, seen by another Arab, Abd el-Latif:

In the middle of the camp there was a vast place containing as many as a hundred and forty smithies of farriers; one can judge of the rest in proportion. In a single kitchen there were twenty-eight cooking-pots, each of which could hold a whole sheep. I myself made a list of the shops registered with the inspector of the market: I counted as many as seven thousand of them. And note that they were not shops like the shops in our towns: one of those in the camp would have made a hundred of ours: and they were all well stocked. I have heard tell that, when Saladin changed camps to withdraw to Karuba, although the distance was quite short, it cost a single butter-seller seventy pieces of gold to transport his shop. As for the market of old and new clothes, that is something which passes imagination. There were also in the camp more than a thousand baths: most of them were kept by Africans, generally in groups of two or three. Water was to be found at a depth of two cubits. The baths were of clay, surrounded by a palisade and matting so that the bathers could not be seen by the public; the wood was brought from gardens in the neighbourhood. It cost a piece of silver or a little more to have a bath.

The Christians as usual displayed their skill as engineers:

Beha ed-Din:

Fortunately, God sent us something to console us. The Christian army had constructed a machine four storeys high, of which the first was of wood, the second of lead, the third of iron and the fourth of bronze; this machine over-topped the ramparts of Acre, and was already about five cubits away from the walls, as least as far as the eye could judge. The garrison was in a state of despondency and all were thinking of surrendering, when God allowed this machine to take fire. At this sight we abandoned ourselves to joy and gave fervent thanks to God.

This was because the Saracens had at their disposal the resource of "Greek fire":

Ibn al-Athir:

There was in the army a man from Damascus whose favourite pastime was manipulating naphtha and studying substances that could kindle fire. For a long time he was blamed for this and he used to answer: "I am not doing it as a profession. I spend my time on this study because I enjoy it." Now it was God's will that that man should be in the town at that moment. He kept on studying inflammable substances, among others those that could overcome the resistance of vinegar and clay. When he had finished his experiments he went to find the Emir Caracusch, governor of the town, and said to him: "Order the man in charge of the machines to do what I shall tell him; if he throws what I give him against the towers, they will catch fire." Caracusch was at that moment a prey to fear and anger. His fear that he might not be able to hold out much longer made him receive this man very badly and he said to him: "Many others besides you, and very clever people, have already failed." However, when one of those present remarked that there would be no harm in trying, and that perhaps God had put into the hands of that man the fate of the Christian army, Caracusch resisted no longer. In order to deceive the Christians the man from Damascus first threw at one of the towers pots of naphtha and other substances not alight, which produced no effect. The Christians, full of confidence, immediately climbed to the top of the tower with an air of triumph, and overwhelmed the Moslems with raillery. In the meantime, the man from Damascus waited until the substance contained in the pots had spread over everything. When that moment arrived, he hurled a new pot all in flames; the fire at once spread everywhere, the tower was consumed and the outbreak was so prompt that the Christians had not even time to descend; men, arms, everything was burnt. God willed it thus, so that the Christians might burn in the fire of this world before burning in the next. The two other towers were consumed in the same manner; but this time the Christians had time to take flight. That day surpassed everything that had ever been seen; the joy of the Moslems was past telling. At the moment when the fire broke out, they were all looking in that direction; their faces, that had been sad and drawn, beamed with pleasure; and they all rejoiced at the help that God had sent them and at the deliverance of the town. For in truth there was no one in the army who had not some relation or friend in Acre. Meanwhile, the man from Damascus was brought before the Sultan, who offered him money and wide lands; he refused them, saying: "I did it for the love of God; I look to Him alone for my reward." This glad news was sent to all the Moslem provinces.

Meanwhile, the reinforcements the Christians had so long hoped for finally arrived from the West. First the King of France, Philip Augustus, came in sight of Acre on April 20th, 1191, and then the King of England, Richard Cœur-de-Lion, disembarked two months later, having taken the island of Cyprus on the way.

Ambroise:

The King of France, with the Christian army, was there from Easter until the noble feast of Pentecost, and then the King of England, who had taken Cyprus, arrived too. . . . When King Richard of England arrived in the Holy Land . . . he performed an act of generosity such as deserves to be recounted. The King of France had promised and granted to his people that every month each one of them should have from his treasury three bezants of gold. This was much talked of. When King Richard arrived and heard this great news, he had it cried throughout the army that every knight, from whatever country he came, who joined his army should have four gold bezants, and that thus he promised them.

These rivalries did not prevent them from pursuing the siege actively. Not only siege machines but every method of mining and sapping then known was put into operation. Ambroise relates that:

The miners belonging to the French King, who had sworn to help him, dug so far under the ground that they found the foundations of the wall. They supported it with props to which they subsequently set fire, so that a great section of the wall fell; but this was not without danger for them, for before falling it tilted forward so that everyone was greatly afraid. When they saw the wall collapse, the enemy crowded there. There you could see the great throng of those accursed pagans with their banners and their standards; you could see them advancing and casting fire at us; you could see the struggle round the ladders that we placed against the wall. A mighty deed of valour was done there and it was Aubry Clément who did it:

> "There was done a mighty deed
> And Aubery Clément did it.
> He said that day that he would die
> Or he would enter Acre.
> He ever scorned to tell a lie,
> And there became a martyr."*

The whole army was grieved because of Aubry Clément and they abandoned the attack that day to mourn and pity him. It was not long after the death of Aubry Clément when the miners arrived at the Accursed Tower of which I have told you, and propped it up from underneath; it was already much shaken. The besieged on their side made a countermine, trying to reach the miners. Finally, they met and mutually agreed on a truce. Now among the counterminers there were some Christians in irons [prisoners]: they spoke with our men, to such purpose that they escaped. When the Turks of the town learnt this, they were greatly grieved at it.

It was no easy feat to overcome the resistance of the walls of Acre which, according to a fourteenth-century traveller, were so wide that two chariots could easily pass each other on them. The siege therefore saw a great display of machines of every kind, which the chroniclers describe for us.

Ambroise:

Our perriers were brought down from the ships. They were disembarked piece by piece and the valiant King of England in person, together with his companions, carried on their shoulders—we saw it—the wooden parts of them, on foot, their faces covered

---

* Nothing is known of this Aubry, or Aubery Clément, who was perhaps a friend of the chronicler.

with sweat, for nearly a league on the sand, laden like horses or mares.

. . . The perriers battered the walls incessantly night and day; the King of France had one called Male Voisine; but in Acre was Male Cousine [another machine built by the Moslems and so named by the Franks] which was always damaging it, and he [the King] had it constantly repaired; and it was so well repaired that it shattered the principal wall and also caused much damage in the Accursed Tower. The Duke of Burgundy's perrier did its work equally well. The one belonging to the good Knights of the Temple struck many Turks on the head; that of the Hospitallers delivered blows that satisfied everyone. A perrier called the Perrier of God had been set up. To get it made, a good priest collected so much money, by sermons that heartened the whole army, that it was big enough to demolish more than two perches [11 yards] of the wall near the Accursed Tower. When the Count of Flanders was alive, his was the best that could be found. The King of England had it after him, and he had as well a small one that was considered very good. The two together attacked a tower over a gate where the Turks were thronging; they pounded it and battered it to such an extent that they demolished half of it. The King had had two new ones made, so well built that wherever they went they were able to do their slinging entirely under cover; and he had had a belfry set up which greatly disquieted the Turks. It was so well covered and protected with leather, wood and ropes that it could defy everything that was cast at it, stone or Greek fire. He had two mangonels* made also, one of which was so stable, that any stone it hurled flew into the town as far as the Butchery. This stone-slinger hurled stones night and day without stopping and it is as true as we stand here that one stone killed twelve men, and was taken and shown to Saladin. Those stones had been brought to the country by the King of England: they were pebbles that he had got at Messina to kill the Saracens.

Thus each tried to outdo the other in ingenuity. To obviate victualling difficulties, the Crusaders had a windmill constructed on the spot, the first to be made in Syria; that was why the name Turkish Mill *was*

---

* Another kind of engine for slinging stones, hurling them from a spoon-ended bar by the force of twisted ropes.

afterwards given to these entirely new wind-driven mills. Ambroise tells how much this new kind of engine alarmed the Arabs:

> First they built with a will
> The very first wind-mill
>   That was in Syria made,
> At sight of it the race that curses God
> Gazed at it agog,
>   And were greatly afraid.

Saladin's magnanimity.

Beha ed-Din:

One day when I was present, forty-five Christian prisoners taken in the neighbourhood of Berytus [Beirut] were brought to the Sultan. Among them was a decrepit old man who had lost all his teeth and could hardly move; the Sultan was astonished and had him asked through his interpreter where he came from and what he wanted. The old man replied: "It is several months' march from here to my country; as for the motive that brought me, it was the desire to make pilgrimage to the Holy Sepulchre." At these words Saladin took pity on this man and had him taken back to the camp of the Christians on horseback.

The same day, when the Sultan's youngest children, still of tender years, happened to see one of these prisoners, they wanted to cut off his head; they bade me go and ask their father's permission to do so, which I did; but the Sultan was against it; and when I asked him why, he answered: "I do not want them to get used to shedding blood so young; at their age they do not know what it means to be a Moslem or an infidel, and they will grow accustomed to trifling with the lives of others."

King Richard, for his part, had made a deep impression on the Moslems, to judge by the following description:

Beha ed-Din:

This king was of terrible strength, proven valour and indomitable character; he had already gained a great reputation by his past wars: in dignity and power he was inferior to the King of France, but he was richer than he and braver, and of greater experience in war. His fleet was composed of twenty-five large ships full of warriors and munitions of war. He had taken the island of Cyprus on his way. He arrived before Acre on Saturday 13th of Jumada I [June 8th].

At the beginning, courteous relations were established between the adversaries, as this story of Richard's illness illustrates:

Beha ed-Din:

The messenger [of the King of England] who had really come to ask for different things his master needed in his illness, spoke thus: "It is the custom between our kings to give each other presents, even in time of war: my master is in a position to give some which are worthy of the Sultan; will you allow me to bring them to you? Will they be welcome to you, if they come through a delegate?" To which al-Adil [Saladin's brother] replied: "The present will be well received, provided we are allowed to offer others in return." The delegate went on: "We brought with us falcons and other birds of prey which suffered greatly on the voyage, and are dying of want; would it please you to give us hens and chickens to feed them? As soon as they are restored to health we will offer them in homage to the Sultan." "Say rather," went on al-Adil, "that your master is ill and that he needs chickens to regain his health. In any case there is no obstacle; he shall have as many of them as he wants: let us speak of other things." But the conversation went no further. A few days later the King of England returned to the Sultan a Moslem prisoner, and Saladin handed to the messenger a robe of honour. Subsequently the King sent to ask for fruit and snow, which were given him.

Surprising negotiations also took place between Richard and Saladin's brother and eventual successor, al-Adil. The King offered him his own sister in marriage: she would bring him as her dowry the town of Acre and all the coastal possessions of the Christians, while al-Adil would receive from his brother Jerusalem and the territories which the Moslems had regained. He and she would receive the titles of King and Queen of Jerusalem; prisoners on both sides would be returned, while the Templars and Hospitallers would be re-established in their domains. Al-Adil, greatly flattered by the proposal, charged Beha ed-Din to inform Saladin of it. But Richard's sister [widow of the former king of Sicily] absolutely

refused to marry a Moslem; so the King suggested to al-Adil that he
should turn Christian if he wished to pursue the project.

In the meantime sorties and skirmishes never stopped:

Beha ed-Din:

The Christian army was divided into three corps, each ready to defend itself. The first was commanded by the former King of Jerusalem, and formed the advance-guard; the second, placed in the centre, was composed of the English and the French; the rest formed the rear-guard. In the midst of the army there rose a sort of rolling tower, like one of our great minarets, placed on a wagon; it was the standard of the Christians. In addition to this main division, the three corps were each subdivided into two parts: one, marching at a certain distance from the sea, opposed the Moslem soldiers and repelled their attacks; the other, marching along the sea-shore, was covered by the former and protected from our attacks. When the first were exhausted, the second took their place. As for the cavalry, it remained always in the middle surrounded by the infantry as by a wall, and never leaving its ranks save in exceptional circumstances. The soldiers were clothed in a kind of thick felt, and coats of mail as ample as they were strong, which protected them against arrows. I have seen soldiers with up to twenty-one arrows stuck on their bodies marching no less easily for that. They on the contrary pierced us with their spears, killing horse and rider at the same time. I am speaking here of what I have seen, or of what deserters and prisoners have told me. The Franks kept the same order whether they were marching or fighting; they never left the main body of the army, no matter what attempt was made to draw them out of the ranks. The three army corps mutually supported each other; when one was threatened, the others went to its help. They marched slowly, for they were keeping pace with the fleet which was following the coast, laden with supplies and provisions. The day's march was short because of the infantry; for among those foot-soldiers, some were confronting the Moslem army while the others, who were hugging the shore, carried on their backs, for want of pack animals, the baggage and the tents. Observe the steadfastness of this people, exposing themselves in this way to the most painful fatigues, without being paid or gaining any real advantage.

As a general rule the Moslems attacked the Christian army on three different sides, on the east, the north and the south; only the side towards the sea remained free. During these attacks I have seen the Sultan galloping between the two armies, in the middle of a shower of arrows, with only one or two equerries beside him as he went from one rank to another. I have seen him inspiring his warriors and inflaming them with ardour. The air resounded with the noise of drums and trumpets and the cries of our soldiers exciting each other with the words: Allah is great! Allah is great! Nevertheless, the Christian army kept its ranks; it never faltered; it never disturbed its order; it never broke up; it overwhelmed our horses and their riders with arrows and wounds. The attack nearly always continued while they were marching; but once the Christian army stopped to camp, we had to retire; our men could have gained nothing by attacking it and the safest plan was to move off.

Saladin makes a last attempt to save the besieged:

Ibn al-Athir:

The Sultan wrote to the soldiers of the garrison to come out all together the next day, and carve themselves a passage through the Christian army. He charged them to follow the sea-shore and to load themselves with everything that they could carry, promising that for his part he would go to meet them with his troops and help their retreat. The besieged made ready to evacuate the town; each one set aside what he wanted to save; unfortunately, these preparations lasted till daylight and the Christians, forewarned of the plan, occupied all the exits. A few soldiers climbed on the ramparts and waved a flag; it was the signal for the attack. Saladin immediately dashed to the Christian camp to create a diversion; but all was in vain; the Christians resisted both the garrison and the army of the Sultan. All the Moslems were in tears; Saladin came and went, encouraging his warriors; he was within an ace of breaking through the enemy camp but, in the end, he was repulsed by their number.

Here is how the same chronicler describes the taking of Acre:

When Mashtub saw the desperate state of the town and the

impossibility of defending it, he went to treat with the Franks. It was agreed that the inhabitants and the garrison should depart in freedom with their goods in exchange for the sum of two hundred thousand pieces of gold, the freeing of two thousand five hundred Christian prisoners, five hundred of them of high rank, and the restitution of the Cross of the crucifixion. In addition Mashtub promised ten thousand pieces of gold for the Marquis of Tyre and four thousand for his people. A certain delay was granted for the payment of the money and the handing over of the prisoners. When all was thus agreed, the two parties swore to carry out the treaty and the Franks entered the town.

RICHARD CŒUR–DE–LION AND SALADIN

✠✠

*I*MMEDIATELY AFTER *the taking of Acre, Philip Augustus made ready to leave the Holy Land and return to the West. This caused great anger and disappointment in the army of the Crusaders. Acre was a solid bastion, but was not the aim of the Crusade the reconquest of Jerusalem?*

Ambroise:

The barons of France were full of fury and anger when they saw that the leader, whose followers they were, was so decided that neither tears nor laments could make him agree to remain. And when, in spite of all their efforts, they saw that they were powerless in the matter, they blamed him, I warrant you. And so displeased were they that they came very near to disowning their king and their lord.

Their previous efforts would indeed have been wasted if Richard Cœur-de-Lion, displaying a generosity that seems to have been totally lacking in the King of France, had not remained in the Holy Land to consolidate the reconquest. Moreover, he had some difficulty in persuading his troops to go on with the campaign, so absorbed were they in the delights of Acre which have been described by the poet-chronicler, Ambroise.

> So delightful was the town,
> So good the wine, so fair the maids,
> That the soldiers laid them down
> And forgot their warlike raids.
> Wine and women cast their spell
> Sunk in pleasures did they dwell.
> Lechery and vice and sin

All were found that town within,
So that wise men looked with shame
On what the soldiers thought a game.

Nevertheless, Richard went on with the campaign, performing such extraordinary feats of arms that all Saladin could do was to avoid direct action and lay waste the land before the armies of King Richard. However on July 26th, 1192, he was able by a stroke of luck to make a surprise attack on Jaffa, where the King had left only a weak garrison:

Beha ed-Din:

The miners had already sapped the ramparts, propping up with wood the part that seemed likely to fall; at a given signal they set fire to it and the wall collapsed; but at the same moment we discovered behind it a terrible fire protecting the breach; the Christians had made a kind of rampart of it. In vain did the Sultan give the order to charge; the Franks opposed a stubborn resistance. O my God, what men! What courage! What bravery! What strength of soul! In spite of the danger they gave no thought to their lives: they did not trouble to close the gates of the place; they stood outside the walls, disputing every foot of ground with us; only with night did the combat cease. Then the Sultan regretted that he had not accepted the capitulation; but the moment had passed. The next day, Friday, the assault began afresh; the whole army attacked at once, uttering great shouts; the drums and trumpets made a terrifying noise; the machines went into action, the miners sapped the ramparts; finally, the walls collapsed and the din was such that you would have thought the world was coming to an end. Immediately, a great shout arose and the Moslems rushed to the attack; but the Christians stood firm at their posts: the dust and the smoke had at first concealed them from us; when the cloud cleared we saw them standing behind the breach, forming a forest of impenetrable pikes and spears. The Moslems were at first appalled by this spectacle, for in truth the enemy showed astonishing steadfastness. I myself saw two Christians on top of the breach, repulsing the assailants; when one of them was killed the other took his place and fought with the same coolness. Meanwhile, as the town was open on every side, the Christians sent one of their number to the Sultan to offer to surrender. As the fighting was continuing, they asked that it should be stopped. "I cannot do that," answered the Sultan. "Let the besieged shut themselves up in the citadel. As for the town, the soldiers are in such a state that it is impossible to save it from pillage." When the messenger returned with this reply the Christians abandoned the town and withdrew into the citadel; but our troops were so roused that, while the Christians were retreating, they killed many of them. The town was immediately occupied and put to the sack.

While this was happening the Sultan received from one of his lieutenants a letter telling him that the King [Richard], on hearing of the danger that threatened Jaffa, had abandoned his plan of attacking Berytus and straightway put to sea with his fleet at Acre to go to the help of his people. Saladin was anxious to occupy the citadel; but the army was so weary that it was thought better to put off the enterprise until the next day. It was then a Friday. Early in the morning of the next day, the Sultan charged me to have the citadel evacuated. We could already begin to see in the distance the King's fleet advancing at full sail; but they were too far off for us to make out how many vessels there were. When I presented myself at the gate of the citadel the Christians, who had at first sounded the trumpet, made no resistance and promised to come out. As our soldiers were still scattered throughout the town, indulging in the worst excesses of looting, and it was therefore to be feared that the Christians might be insulted as they passed, the emir who accompanied me thought that the first thing to do was to evacuate the town. Unfortunately, the soldiers were without leaders and without discipline, and it was impossible to make them hear reason. The emir was obliged to use force and even blows; and it was therefore broad day when the Christians began to evacuate the citadel. They came out at first without offering any resistance, leading their horses, their wives and their children; about forty-nine of them came out. But in the end those who remained perceived, as the Crusaders' fleet drew near, that the number of vessels was more considerable than they had at first thought. In fact the fleet was composed of more than fifty ships, among which was the King's galley, painted red with sails of the same colour. When they saw this they did not doubt that the King would at once set foot on land to deliver them, and they took up their arms again. I descended to warn our people to stand on their guard. Barely an hour had passed when, all at once and as one man, the besieged galloped down from the top of the citadel on horseback, and spread throughout the town. Our men took flight; they were in such panic that many were nearly crushed at the gates; a group who had taken refuge in a church were cut to pieces. Meanwhile, the Moslem flags were still floating on the ramparts. When the King arrived at the entrance to the port he thought at first that all was lost and hesitated to disembark. The noise of the waves and the shouts of the soldiers prevented anything from being heard. The Sultan had had the drum beaten and hastened up with his army; the town had been retaken. Then the Christians passed from complete confidence to the depths of despair; they were so terrified at seeing the fleet keeping out at sea that they sent the patriarch and the chaplain to Saladin to ask him to pardon them and give them the same conditions as before. In the meantime, the fighting continued; a moment more and it would have been all up with the besieged. All at once a Christian, out of devotion to the glory of the Messiah, decided to jump from the top of the citadel on to a heap of sand below; then, taking ship, he went to tell the King of the state of the besieged. Immediately the fleet drew near to the shore; the King was the first to set foot on land and our men took flight. As for me, I ran to the Sultan to tell him what was happening; he was then with the Christian delegates, pen in hand, ready to sign a new capitulation. The rout soon became general; the whole town was evacuated; the Sultan did not even feel himself safe in the place where he was; he sent his baggage away and himself withdrew a certain distance. His own camp was soon occupied by the Christians and the King remained peacefully master of Jaffa.

While this was happening the King, who more than ever longed to return to his kingdom, had occasion to see some mameluks of the Sultan with whom he was familiar and he said to them: "The Sultan is a great prince; without question he is the greatest and most powerful in Islam to-day. Why did he withdraw at my approach? Before God, I was not coming with a warlike train, but only with my ordinary crew of sailors: I am not in a position to undertake anything. Why did he depart?" Later he added: "By the great God, the generous God, I should never have believed the Sultan could take Jaffa in two months, still less in a few days." Then, addressing one of the mameluks in particular, he charged him to go and greet the Sultan in his name and say to him: "In the name of God, grant me peace; it is time that this war ended. My realms are a prey to civil discord. This war cannot be of use either to you or to me."

That took place on Saturday evening the 19th of Rajab, the same day that the King disembarked. On the advice of his council, the Sultan made answer that he did not at all refuse to enter into negotiations; that, since Jaffa was now in ruins, they would leave it in that state and that, in addition, they would raze Ascalon to the ground. Thereupon, the King immediately wrote these words to Saladin: "The custom among the Franks is that a prince who gives a country to another makes him his man and his vassal: by virtue of this I ask you for Ascalon and Jaffa; and I will agree to serve you, with my troops; I will be at your orders when you call me, and I will serve you as you know I know how to. Do not refuse my request." The Sultan answered: "Since you take it in this way, I will surrender Jaffa to you and you shall give me back Ascalon." And since the King still insisted, pointing out that, if his request was refused, he would have to remain that summer and the following winter in Palestine, the Sultan replied that he would never yield. "Concerning the King's departure," he added, "he will hardly be able to leave so soon; for he must know that he only holds the towns he is occupying by force and that I shall seize them as soon as he has gone, or even perhaps before, if Allah pleases. Moreover, since he can resolve to spend the winter here, far from his family and his home, and that in the flower of his manhood and the age of pleasures, why should I hesitate to spend the winter and summer under arms also, I who am in my own realms here, with my children and my family, able, if I wish, to obtain all the sweets of life; especially as I am in my declining years, at the age when one is indifferent to pleasures, nay more, weary of everything and detesting the world? Besides it should be remembered that I am able to renew my troops and to divide them up so that those who serve in the winter do not serve in the summer, a thing which the King is not in a position to do; and that in pursuing this war I believe I am doing a deed pleasing to Allah. For these reasons I am disposed to stand firm until Allah decides between him and me."

Thenceforward, all had to resign themselves to war. The Sultan, learning that the Christian troops left by the King in Acre had set out to join him, resolved to go and intercept them; but he had hardly reached Caesarea before he learnt that the Christian troops had received reinforcements by sea and that the King, hearing of the danger threatening his men, was weakening his own position to support them. He straightway altered his plan, deciding to march against the King and seize this occasion to crush him. The King had remained almost alone; and Jaffa, in her existing state of ruin, could be of no protection to him. So Saladin suddenly appeared in sight of Jaffa, on Thursday the 24th of Rajab, five days after the sack of the town. The King had kept with him only about ten knights and a few hundred foot-soldiers, comprising in all ten tents; however, he was not abashed and he deployed his little troop along the sea shore. The Moslems, having surrounded the Christians on three sides, fell upon them all at the same time and as one man; but the Christians stood fast, grinding their teeth in warlike rage. This courage so amazed our soldiers that they dared not attack them, and were content to caracole round them. The truth is that our soldiers still resented keenly what had happened at Jaffa. Not only, under the pretext of capitulation, had they first been prevented from pillaging; but those who had managed to seize some booty found themselves despoiled of it at the gates of the town; force was even used to make them leave. They now avenged themselves. In vain did the Sultan, roused to indignation, go up and down the ranks to inspire the warriors; in vain did his son Zahir set an example by hurling himself on the enemy; none would obey. There was even an emir called Gehah, brother of Mashtub, who said to the Sultan: "Why do you not talk to your mameluks, who struck the soldiers at the sack of Jaffa and took their booty from them?" When he heard these words, Saladin felt that he would be endangering himself in vain; so he had the retreat sounded and withdrew, in a transport of anger. I have heard tell that, on that same day, the King galloped along the whole front line of the Moslem army with his lance at rest, and that none of our people dared to try conclusions with him.

Twice did Richard approach so close to Jerusalem—within twelve miles—that his knights felt the Holy City was already theirs. But, being a prudent strategist, he knew that his few troops could not resist for long so far from their base. If the King of France had been there, things would have gone differently. Discouraged, Richard Cœur-de-Lion too set sail for his kingdom, on October 9th, 1192; but he had at least made peace with Saladin and obtained from him freedom of pilgrimage in the Holy City for the Christians.

A new chapter was opening in the history of the Crusades. Like the first, it was to cover a hundred years; years when the Kingdom of Jerusalem did not include Jerusalem itself.

A few months after the departure of Richard, on March 4th, 1193, Saladin, the most honourable hero of Islam, died. His brother, al-Adil, succeeded him as Sultan of Damascus and Cairo, but he had not the prestige that Saladin had acquired by his courage as well as his generosity.

As for the Frankish kingdom, it was reduced to a coastal strip; but its position was after all rather favourable, since it had what the first Crusaders had not: free access to the sea, with an excellent base for operations and revictualling in the island of Cyprus, which the King of England had handed over to Guy of Lusignan to compensate him for the loss of his kingdom. In the event the barons had not wanted to keep at their head the man responsible for the disaster of Hattin. The kingship had fallen to Conrad of Montferrat, the famous Piedmontese Marquis responsible for the resistance of Tyre, which had been the point of departure for the reconquest of Frankish Syria. To justify their choice, he had been made to marry Isabella of Jerusalem, who inherited the crown. In order to marry him Isabella had had, against her will, to divorce her husband, the handsome but incapable Humphrey of Toron. But Conrad did not enjoy the crown for long: he was stabbed in the streets of Tyre by the followers of the "Old Man of the Mountain", the head of the terrible sect of the Hashishiyun, or Assassins. A third husband was imposed on Isabella: Count Henry II of Champagne, who had just disembarked in the East—without any intention of remaining there—and who ended by yielding to the barons' pressure; unfortunately, he was killed five years later falling into the street from a window of his palace in Acre. Then a fourth husband had to be found for Isabella, widowed for the third time at twenty-six. This one, curiously enough, was Guy of Lusignan's brother Amalric, who moreover possessed all the qualities that his brother lacked. As Guy had died, Amalric had just succeeded him as King of Cyprus, and so by chance he united the two crowns of Cyprus and Jerusalem.

Amalric distinguished himself both by his courage—he retook the town of Beirut from the Moslems, thus re-establishing communications between Acre and Tripoli—and his wisdom, for in 1204 he renewed the truces concluded with the Sultan al-Adil.

Meanwhile, the Christian territories of Syria, Palestine and the

Near East in general had acquired considerable economic importance. From the time of the First Crusade the Italian cities of Genoa, Pisa, Amalfi and Venice had come to the help of the Crusaders. They were now to reap the benefit.

Other Mediterranean cities: Marseilles, Montpellier, and then Barcelona, had established warehouses in the East. The presence of the Franks in the Holy Land gave them access to those Levantine markets which supplied the most precious of all commodities: spices, perfumes, precious stuffs, silken fabrics and other things, which constituted the wealth of the traders of that time. The political role of the merchant cities only began with the second stage of the Crusades: that of the prosperity that follows conquest. Thus Conrad of Montferrat, to make sure of supporters in Tyre, negotiated with the Western traders, promising them whole quarters of the town where freedom of trade would be guaranteed them; allocating to them in short what in our day would be called concessions, territorial and otherwise. The same thing happened in Acre and from that moment the commercial establishments played a most active part in the relations between the West and the Near East.

PART THREE

CONSTANTINOPLE: THE CRUSADERS
FORGET THE CRUSADE

❧❧

*I*N THE *midst of the preoccupations that blunted the crusading spirit, Pope Innocent III did not forget that his chief aim was the reconquest of Jerusalem. To that end, and to complete the work that the Kings of France and England had merely roughed out, he preached a Crusade during the first years of the thirteenth century. Villehardouin saw the birth of it:*

You must know that one thousand and ninety-eight years after the Incarnation of Our Lord Jesus Christ, in the time of Innocent III, Pope of Rome, of Philip, King of France and of Richard King of England, there was a holy man in France called Fulk of Neuilly. This Neuilly lies between Lagny-sur-Marne and Paris, and he was the parish priest of the town. And this Fulk began that day to speak of God, in France and in other lands, and through him Our Lord performed many miracles.

You must know that the renown of this holy man spread so far that it reached Innocent the Pope of Rome; and the Pope sent him to France and told him to preach the Crusade on his authority, and afterwards he sent him a cardinal, Master Peter of Capua, a Crusader, and by him he sent an indulgence, couched as follows: "All those who shall take the cross and serve God for one year in the army shall be acquitted of all the sins they have sinned and have confessed." At this the hearts of many people were moved, and many took the cross to obtain so great an indulgence.

The year after this wise man Fulk thus spoke of God, there was a tourney in Champagne at a castle called Ecri, and by the grace of God it chanced that Tibald, Count of Champagne and Ecri, took the cross there, as did also the Count Louis of Blois and

Chartres. This was at the beginning of Advent; and you must know that this Count Tibald was a young man of not more than twenty-two and Count Louis was not more than twenty-seven. With those two Counts two important barons of France took the cross also: Simon of Montfort and Reynald of Montmirail. When those two men of rank took the cross, the renown of it was great throughout the land.

This was the tourney of Ecri-sur-Aisne where several high barons did in fact take the cross in answer to the call of Fulk of Neuilly. It is noteworthy of the Crusade then about to begin that it gave rise to the first great prose work written in a "romance" language, in other words in French: the chronicle of Geoffrey of Villehardouin just quoted. Its author was himself one of the most important barons of Champagne, destined to play a preponderant part in the expedition, which also included, as well as other lords, Geoffrey of Joinville, uncle of the Seneschal who left us the story of another Crusade, that of Saint Louis.

The Crusade preached by Innocent III was to be deflected from its goal in a curious way. Even from its outset the expedition had been hindered by unforeseen obstacles. The most serious was the death of Count Tibald of Champagne, who would have been the soul of it, and in spite of his youth would no doubt have had the necessary authority to prevent the deviations that took place. Villehardouin tells us how, on returning from Venice, where he had gone to negotiate the passage of the troops on vessels belonging to Venetian ship-owners, who had become the transporters of the Crusaders, he found "his lord Count Tibald weak and ill; he was overjoyed at his coming, and when Geoffrey told him the news of what they had decided, he was so joyful that he said he would go for a ride, which he had not done for a long time; and he arose and mounted, and alas! it was a great pity that he did, for after that one time he never rode again".

With Tibald dead, the expedition was deprived of its chief. The barons finally approached the Marquis Boniface of Montferrat, brother of Conrad the defender of Tyre; but they did not all support this choice and "many avoided going through Venice and went to Marseilles, which brought much shame upon them and for which they were greatly blamed; and later great misfortune befell them thereby", *says Villehardouin, who explained the events to come by the defection of those Crusaders.*

As soon as they were assembled in Venice, the Crusaders found themselves unable to keep the agreements they had concluded with the city.

Villehardouin:

There was a great falling off in those of the army that went to Venice, and this led to a great misadventure, as you will hear. . . . The army was composed of fine and good people. Never had a finer army been seen, nor a bigger; the Venetians sold them freely all that was needful for the horses and the men; and the ships that they had fitted up were so rich and beautiful that never had any Christian seen any that were richer or more beautiful, either in the way of ships or galleys and transports. . . . Alas! what great pity it was that the others who had embarked in other ports did not come here. . . . The Venetians had kept all their promises faithfully and more besides, and they called on the counts and barons to keep theirs and to give them the sum agreed, for they were ready to set sail.

Thereupon passage-money was collected from the army; there were a good number who said that they could not pay their passage, and the barons took charge of those who could not; in this way they paid what they could of the passage-money; and when they had finished soliciting and collecting, they had not half the sum needed.

The Venetians had settled for 94,000 silver marks, which was to cover the price of transport for 4,500 knights, 9,000 equerries, 20,000 foot-sergeants, and the horses they needed, with provisions for nine months. Now, according to Villehardouin's estimate, they were short of 34,000 silver marks to make up the sum due.

It was then that the Venetians suggested another deal to the Crusaders: that they should go and reconquer on their behalf the little town of Zara, situated on an island in the Adriatic, which had been taken from them by the King of Hungary. This suggestion by no means won the approval of everyone; however the chief barons agreed to it.

Villehardouin:

An assembly then took place on a Sunday, in the church of Saint Mark. It was a very great occasion, all the people of that country and the majority of the barons were there. Before High Mass began the Duke [Doge] of Venice, who was called Enrico

Dandolo, went up to the lectern and spoke to the people, saying:
"Lords, you have here with you the finest people in the world,
and you come for the greatest affair that people have ever undertaken. As for me, I am an old man and weak, and I have need of
rest and am enfeebled in my body; but I see that none would be
able to govern and guide you save I myself, who am your lord.
If you agreed that I should take the sign of the cross to guard and
teach you, and that my son should remain in my place to protect
the land, I would go to live or die with you and the pilgrims."
And when they heard him, they cried all with one voice: "We
pray you in God's name to let us grant you this, and that you
should do as you say and come with us." The people of that
country and the pilgrims then felt great pity and shed many tears,
because this wise old man had such good reasons for remaining
where he was: he was old, and he had very beautiful eyes, but he
could see nothing, for he had lost his sight through a wound in
his head.

During this display of popular emotion Enrico Dandolo, Doge of
Venice, took the cross. He was ninety years old, and blind. According to
some his eyes had been put out by order of the Byzantine Emperor
Manuel Comnenus. Many Venetians took the cross with him that day;
but the events that followed provide strong reasons for suspecting the
purity of their intentions.

So the Crusaders set off to take Zara. The Pope excommunicated
them for this lapse from their crusading vows: "And," says Villehardouin, "you must know that the hearts of the people were not
in harmony; some were working to disunite the army and some to
keep it together. Many humble folk departed in the merchant
ships."

Next, another temptation was put in the way of the Crusaders, this
time one of far greater import. A few years previously the Byzantine
Emperor Isaac Angelus had been dethroned by his brother Alexius,
who had put out his eyes and imprisoned him, and then had himself
crowned Emperor at Constantinople under the name of Alexius III.
Isaac's son, who was also called Alexius, had fled to Europe and
taken refuge with Philip of Swabia, husband of his sister Irene. During
the winter of 1201–1202 the young Alexius came to implore the help
of the Venetians and the Crusaders. He promised the latter considerable sums and led them to hope that the Greek church would return to

the bosom of the Roman Church. It seems that his pleas for help were favourably received by the Venetians, who must have been delighted by the idea of having an emperor devoted to them. In such conditions, then, the fleet of the Crusaders reached Constantinople on June 26th, 1203.

Villehardouin:

You might have beheld the Sound of Saint-George [the Bosphorus] bedecked with ships and galleys and horse-transports, and the beauty of them was a very great marvel. They passed up the Sound of Saint-George until they came to Saint-Stephen, close to an abbey which is three leagues from Constantinople, and there they saw the full extent of Constantinople. Those in charge of the ships and galleys and transports headed for the port and the vessels entered one by one. You may know that many then gazed at Constantinople who had never seen it before, and they were not able to believe that there could be so rich a town in the whole world, when they saw those high walls and mighty towers that enclosed it all around; and those rich palaces and lofty churches, of which there were so many that none could believe it if he had not seen them with his own eyes, and the length and breadth of the town which was the queen of all towns. Know you that there was none so brazen that his heart did not quiver and this was no wonder; for never had people undertaken so great a matter since the world was created.

Yet as early as July 17th the town was taken, the Emperor Alexius III in flight and Isaac Angelus re-established on the throne that he was to share with his son Alexius IV. Villehardouin records the speeches that the Doge of Venice and the Marquis of Montferrat made to the Byzantine people:

They walked all along the walls of Constantinople and showed the young squire [Alexius] to the Greeks and said: "Behold your natural lord and know that we have not come to do you harm, but we come to protect and defend you if you do what you ought; for he whom you obey as lord holds you wrongfully and sinfully, against God and against reason, and you know well how disloyally he had worked against his lord and brother; he has plucked out his eyes and seized his empire; and here is the rightful heir; if you cleave to him you will be doing what you ought, and if you do not, we will do you all the harm in our power.'

A place must be found here for an episode on the fringe of events, related by Robert of Clary, who reveals a true reporter's curiosity, fascinated by all he sees and able to make others see it:

It happened one day that the barons went to the palace for the pleasure of seeing Isaac and the Emperor his son. While they were there there arrived a king whose skin was all black and in the middle of his forehead he had a cross that had been branded on it with a hot iron. This king was staying in a very rich abbey in the city, where Alexius had asked that he should be put, and he was the lord and squire and guest of it as long as he wished to stay. When the Emperor saw him coming, he rose and went towards him and did him great honour; and the Emperor asked the barons: "Do you know who this man is?" "No, sire," said the barons. "In faith," said the Emperor, "he is the King of Nubia, who has come on pilgrimage to this town." They made him talk through interpreters and asked him where his country was. And he answered in his own language through the interpreters that his country lay a hundred days' journey beyond Jerusalem; and that he had come thence to Jerusalem on pilgrimage, and he said that, when he left his country, he had with him sixty of his subjects, and when he reached Jerusalem only ten of them were left alive, and when he reached Constantinople from Jerusalem, there were only two left. And he said that he wanted to go on pilgrimage to Rome, and from Rome to Saint-James [Compostella] and then to return to Jerusalem in the hope of living and dying there. And he said that all the people of his country were Christians and when a child was born and baptised, a cross like his was branded on its forehead. The barons looked on this king as a great marvel.

It then remained for Alexius to keep his promises. This he seems to have shown little eagerness to do, all the more because keeping them would have meant alienating his own people, who were alarmed at having to pay the heavy sums promised to the Crusaders, and uneasy at the presence of their army, billeted in the suburb of Galata.

*Robert of Clary has related the parleys and quarrels that ensued.
He, unlike Villehardouin, was one of the foot-soldiers: he was a
humble knight of Picardy, whose sole possession was six hectares of land
at Clary-les-Pernois. His narrative, less brilliant than that of Villehardouin, has the merit of frankness. He shows us the entourage of the
Emperor Alexius trying to wean him from his alliance with the
Crusaders:*

"Ah, sire, you have paid them too much; do not pay them any
more, you have paid them so much you are quite ruined; make
them depart and send them away from your lands." And Alexius
believed this advice and would not pay them any more. When the
time allowed was up and the French saw that the Emperor was
paying them nothing, the counts and high barons of the army met
together and went to the palace of the Emperor and asked for
payment. And the Emperor answered them that he could in no
wise pay them and the barons answered him that, if he did not
pay them, they would seize so much of his wealth that they
would be well paid. With these words the barons left the palace
and returned to their lodgings, and when they had got back they
took counsel together as to what they should do, until the Doge
of Venice said that he wished to go and speak to him [the Emperor].
He sent him word by messenger to come and see him on the
port. The Emperor went there on horseback and the Doge caused
four galleys to be manned and he went on to the island and made
three of them accompany him to protect him. And when he was
drawing near to the waterfront of the port, he saw the Emperor
who had come on horseback and said to him: "Alexius, why
are you acting thus? Consider that we have saved you from great
captivity; we have made you a lord and had you crowned
emperor. Are you not going to keep your agreements with us,
and will you not do more?" "No," said the Emperor, "I will not
do more than I have done!" "No?" said the Doge. "You wicked
youth! We pulled you out of the mire and we will cast you back
into the mire. I defy you, and be assured that I shall harry you
cruelly to the limit of my powers, from this day onwards!"

*Thereupon the situation rapidly became tragic for the unfortunate
Alexius IV because in January 1204 another Alexius, Alexius Doukas,
surnamed Murzuphlus, took advantage of these disagreements, combined*

with the nervous irritation that the presence of the Latins caused the Greek population, to dethrone him and have himself appointed emperor in his stead, under the name of Alexius V. In the meantime, relations between the Crusaders and the inhabitants became embittered:

Villehardouin:

While the Emperor Alexius [IV] was with his army, a great misfortune befell in Constantinople, for a conflict broke out between the Greeks and the Latins who were quartered there; and some people out of malice set fire to the town, and it was so great and terrible a fire that no man could put it out or diminish it; and when the barons of the army, who were quartered on the other side of the port, saw that, they were greatly grieved and full of pity because of it, for they saw those lofty churches and rich palaces melt and collapse, and those great streets of shops all on fire and they could do nothing about it. The fire began above the port in the densest part of the town and spread as far as the sea on the other side, next to the monastery of Saint-Sophia [the great basilica of Justinian], and it lasted eight days without any man's being able to put it out, and the burning wall of flame stretched for half a league. None could reckon the damage, nor the loss of goods and riches, nor the numbers of men, women and children who were burnt. None of the Latins who were living in Constantinople, from whatever land they came, dared remain there any longer, and they took their wives and children and whatever they could rescue from the fire, and they escaped and went aboard the barques and vessels and left the port to go to where the pilgrims were, and there were certainly fifteen thousand of them, great and small, and they had great need of the pilgrims. And so the Franks and Greeks became estranged, and were no longer such friends as they had been before, and this saddened both sides.

On April 8th, 1204, after the Franks and Venetians had agreed in advance to share between them the booty and the ownership of the city, the second siege of Constantinople began.

Villehardouin:

The Emperor Murzuphlus had come with his forces to camp on an open place before the front line, and had pitched his vermilion tents. Nothing happened until the Monday morning, when the men on board the ships, galleys and transports armed themselves. The people of the town feared them less than they had the first time; and they were so confident that you could see nothing but people on the walls and towers. Then began a violent and marvellous attack; each vessel attacked what lay before it; the cries uttered in the battle were so great that it seemed as if the world were falling into ruin.

The assault continued like this for a long time, until Our Lord caused a wind called Boreas [the North Wind] to arise for them; and this drove the ships and vessels closer to the shore than they had been before, especially two ships which were bound together, one of which was called the *Pèlerine* and the other the *Paradise*; and these came close to the tower, one on one side and the other on the other, according as God and the wind led them, in such a way that the ladder of the *Pèlerine* reached to the tower. Forthwith, a Venetian and a knight of France called Andrew Durboise went into the tower and others began to enter after them. And those who were in the tower were routed and fled.

When the knights who were in the transports saw that, they disembarked and set up ladders against the flat of the wall and forced their way to the top of the wall; and they conquered about four of the towers. And those on the ships and transports and galleys began to jump down, vying with each other who should be first. And they smashed about three of the gates and entered into the town; and they began to drag the horses out of the transports, and the knights began to mount them and rode straight to the camp of the Emperor Murzuphlus. And he had his army-corps drawn up in front of his tents; and when his people saw the knights on horseback coming, they took flight and the Emperor fled through the streets to the Castle of the Lion's Mouth.

Robert of Clary gives more details than Villehardouin about the episodes of the siege, especially that in which he took part with a handful of knights (ten knights and sixty sergeants) who had undertaken to reopen an ancient postern that had been walled up in one of the walls, so as to penetrate through it into the interior of the ramparts:

The Lord Peter of Bracheux [or Bracieux] outdid all others, whether high or low, for not one of them performed so many feats of arms and bodily prowess as did he. When he had returned to this postern, they began to batter it in as hard as they could. Stones flew so thickly and so many were hurled down on them from the top of the walls that it seemed as if they would get buried beneath them; but those below had shields and bucklers with which they protected those who were staving in the postern. And they threw down on them from above pots full of boiling pitch and Greek fire, and enormous stones so that it was a miracle of God that they were not all overwhelmed. Master Peter and his men suffered so greatly from their labour and wounds that it was almost too much; and they so battered that postern with axes and good swords, rods and pikes, that they made a great hole in it; and when this postern was pierced they looked through it and saw so many people high and low that it seemed as if half the world was there and they did not dare make bold to enter. When Aleaume the clerk saw that none dared go in, he leapt in front and said that he would enter there. But a knight there who was his brother, Robert of Clary [the narrator], forbade him and said that he should not enter. And the clerk said that he would and he got inside, crawling on hands and feet; and when his brethren saw that, they took hold of his feet and began to help him so much that, in spite of his brother, right or wrong, the clerk entered; when he was inside, all the Greeks ran upon him and those on top of the walls began to throw enormous stones at him. When the clerk saw that he drew his knife, ran upon them and made them flee before him like animals; and he said to those without, to Lord Peter and his men: "Sire, enter boldly, I can see that they are discomfited and are making off in flight." When Master Peter and his people who were without heard that, Master Peter went in with them, and there was hardly any knight but he, but he had quite sixty sergeants with him and all were there on foot; and when they had got in and those who were in that place saw them, they were so afraid that they did not dare stay there, but they made for the wall and outstripped each other in flight. And the traitor Emperor Murzuphlus was close by there, less than a stone's throw away, and he caused his silver trumpets and gongs to be sounded, and made a great din.

A terrible pillage followed. The story of it was told in the Novgorod Chronicle, *written by a Russian who was passing through Constantinople:*

The Franks entered the town on Monday, April 12th, the anniversary of Saint Basil, and set up their camp in a place where the Emperor of the Greeks had already been, in the sanctuary of the Holy Redeemer, where they spent the night. In the morning, when the sun had risen, they invaded Saint-Sophia and, having torn down the doors, they demolished the choir adorned with silver and with twelve columns of silver, where the priest stood; they smashed four reredoses against the wall decorated with icons, and the Holy Altar and twelve crosses which were upon it, chief among which were the crosses carved like trees, taller than a man; the sides of the altar placed in the middle of the columns were made of embossed silver. They also stole a wonderful table set with precious stones and a great gem, not knowing the evil they were doing. Then they seized forty chalices which were on the altar, and silver candelabra of which there were such a number that I could not count them; and vases of silver which the Greeks used during the greatest festivals. They took the Gospel used to celebrate the mysteries, and the sacred crosses with all the images, and the covering which was on the altar and forty censers of pure gold. And everything they could find in the way of gold and silver, and also of vases of inestimable value, in the cupboards, on the walls and in every place where they were shut up, in such quantities that it would be impossible to count them. All that in the Church of Saint-Sophia alone; but they also pillaged the Church of Saint-Marie des Blachernes . . . and other buildings both within and without the walls, and monasteries whose number and beauty we cannot tell.

The leaders of the army tried to restrain this frenzy of looting.

Villehardouin:

It was then announced throughout the army by the Marquis of Montferrat, who was the army commander, and by the barons and the Duke of Venice, that all these goods should be brought and put together, as it had been agreed and sworn, under pain of excommunication. And three churches were appointed as the places, and guards were stationed there, Frankish and Venetian, the most loyal that could be found. And then each one began to bring his booty and pile it all together.

Some brought the booty well, others badly: for covetousness, which is the root of all evil, continued at work; and the covetous thenceforth began to keep things back, and Our Lord began to like them less.

If we are to believe Robert of Clary, the example was given in high places:

Even those whose duty was to guard took the jewels of gold and whatever they wanted . . . and every rich man took either jewels of gold or silken stuffs, and whatever he liked best he took away . . . and nothing was ever given to the ordinary soldiers, nor to the poor knights, nor to the sergeants who had helped to win it. . . .

The Marquis [of Montferrat] took the palace of Boucoleon and the monastery of Saint-Sophia and the houses of the patriarch; and the other great men took the richest palaces and the richest abbeys that one could have found—for, since the town had been taken, no harm had been done either to the poor or the rich: but whoever wished to go, went, and whoever wished to, remained; and the richest men left the town.

It was ordered that all the booty should be brought to an abbey which was in the city. The goods were brought there and they took ten knights from among the pilgrims, and ten Venetians who were thought to be loyal, and set them to guard the goods. . . .

There was such a quantity of rich vessels of gold and silver, and of cloth of gold, and so many rich jewels, that it was a magnificent marvel of great possessions that was brought to that place; and never since this age has begun has such great wealth, so noble and so rich, been either seen or conquered, either in the time of Alexander or in the time of Charlemagne, or before, or after.

As for the Palace of Boucoleon which the Marquis of Montferrat took for himself:

Robert of Clary:

Within this palace there were at least five hundred rooms connecting with each other, and they were all made of gold mosaic. And there were at least thirty chapels both great and small.

There was one that was called the Holy Chapel, which was so
rich and noble that even the hinges and latchets were not of iron
but all of silver, and there was no column that was not of jasper
or prophyry or rich precious stones. And the pavement of the
chapel was of white marble, so smooth and bright that it seemed
like crystal; and that chapel was so rich and noble that it is
impossible to describe it to you. . . . Within it were to be found
very rich sanctuaries; in them were two pieces of the True Cross, as
thick as a man's leg and a yard long; and there was the head of the
spear that pierced the side of Our Lord and the two nails that
were driven into His hands and feet. . . .

*This chronicler cannot say enough about the marvels of the city; he
intersperses his descriptions with an account of various legends which
were current:*

There was in the city a gate called the Mantle of God. Over
this gate there was a golden globe fashioned by such magic that
the Greeks said that, as long as the globe remained there, no
thunderbolt would fall upon the city On this globe was an image
cast in copper with a gold mantle which it stretched forth over its
arm; there were letters written on it which said that, "All those
who remain in Constantinople for a year should have a gold
mantle like mine."

Elsewhere in the city there was another gate called the Golden
Gate. On that gate there were two elephants cast in copper, so
huge that it was a wondrous marvel. This gate was never opened
except when the Emperor returned from battle and had conquered
lands. When he returned from the battle and had conquered
lands, the clergy of the city came in procession to meet him and
opened this gate for him, and they brought him a golden chariot
made like a four-wheeled chariot and in the middle there was a
lofty bench and on the bench a throne and round the throne there
were four columns supporting a canopy which shaded the throne,
and it seemed that it was all of gold. The Emperor sat on the
throne all crowned and he was led with great rejoicing and
great festivity to his palace. . . . Then again there were elsewhere in
this city still greater marvels, for there were two columns, and it
took at least three men to encircle each column and each was at
least 300 feet tall; and on each of those columns there dwelt a

hermit, in little dwellings that were there, and there was a door in each column, through which one entered and climbed. On the outside these columns were carved, and prophecies were written on them of all the adventures and all the conquests that had happened and would happen in Constantinople. . . . The adventure could not be known before it had taken place, and when it had happened, the people went to talk there and they saw and perceived the adventure: the conquest by the Franks was written and carved there, and the ships by which the city was attacked and taken. . . . And it was seen that the letters inscribed on the carved ships said that there would come out of the West a race with close-cropped heads and coats of mail, who would conquer Constantinople.

The next thing was to elect another emperor. The barons collected the army together.

Villehardouin:
   Then they assembled a parliament and told the rank and file of the army what they wanted to do and how they had reached their decision—and they talked so much that it lasted a second day and on that day were to be chosen the twelve who were to make the election. . . . And when the parliament-day came the parliament assembled, six on one side [the Crusaders] and six on the other [the Venetians], and they swore by the saints that they would well and truly elect him who was most needful and who would best govern the empire. Thus the twelve were chosen and on the day fixed they met in a rich palace, where the Doge of Venice had set up house, one of the most beautiful in the world. There was there so great an assembly of people that such a marvel had never been seen; everyone wanted to see who would be chosen. The twelve who were to make the choice were called and put in a very rich chapel which was in the palace, and the doors were shut outside so that no one should stay with them, and the barons and knights remained in a great palace which was outside. And the council lasted until they reached agreement and among all the others they appointed Nevelon, Bishop of Soissons, who was one of the twelve, to speak. They went outside, where all the barons were, and also the Doge of Venice. And you can understand that many men looked at them to know the result of the election; and the bishop said to

them: "Lords, we have agreed, thank God, to make an emperor and you have all sworn that he whom we would choose for emperor, you would consider him such and that, if someone wished to oppose it, you would not help him. We will name him at the hour when God was born [this proclamation took place at midnight]: the Count Baldwin of Flanders and Hainault." And cries of joy arose in the palace and they carried him from the monastery. . . . And the day for his coronation was fixed at three weeks from Easter.

This coronation was described in all its details by the humble knight, Robert of Clary, obviously awed by its magnificence, and remembering it so vividly that at one point he seems almost unconsciously to adopt the present tense:

So they led the Emperor to the monastery of Saint-Sophia and when they had arrived at the monastery, they led him through a winding part thereof to a bedroom. There they disrobed him and took off his shoes: then he put on hose of vermilion samite and they shod him in slippers all covered with rich stones; then they clothed him in a very rich tunic which was entirely sewn with gold buttons, front and back, from shoulders to chest. Then they put on him the pallium: this is a kind of vestment which fell in front down to the ankles and behind was so long that he wrapped it round him and then passed it behind again over his left arm; and this pallium was very rich and noble and all covered with rich precious stones.

After that, they put on top of it a very rich mantle all covered with precious stones; eagles were embroidered on it, made of precious stones which glittered so much that it seemed as if the mantle was on fire.

When he was thus robed, they led him before the altar and Count Louis [of Blois] carried his imperial standard, the Count of Saint-Pol his sword, and the Marquis Boniface [of Montferrat] his crown; and two bishops supported the two arms of the Marquis carrying the crown, and two other bishops escorted the Emperor; all the barons were very richly clothed and there was neither Frenchman nor Venetian who had not a robe of samite or silken stuff.

The Emperor goes up to the altar. He kneels down, they take off the mantle, then the pallium; he remains in the simple tunic; they undo the gold buttons of the tunic in front and behind and, when he is bare to the chest, they proceed to the anointing. Once he is anointed, they do up the gold buttons, they put the pallium back on him, then the mantle which they fasten on the shoulder. When he is thus robed, two bishops take the crown to the altar, the other bishops join them, all together take the crown, bless it, consecrate it and put it on his head; then they put round his neck a very rich stone mounted as a clasp, for which the Emperor Manuel has paid sixty-two thousand marks.

As soon as he is crowned, they make him sit on a high throne. He stays there while Mass is sung: he holds his sceptre in one hand, a gold orb in the other, with a little cross on top: what he wears on him in the way of ornaments is worth more than the treasures of a powerful king. When the Mass has been said they bring him a white horse, on which he mounts; the barons lead him to his palace of Boucoleon and they make him sit on the throne of Constantine. It is there, sitting on the throne of Constantine, that, as Emperor, he receives the homage of all; and the Greeks who are there honour him as their holy emperor.

This unusual ceremony inaugurated the Latin Empire of Constantinople, destined to last until 1261, a little more than half a century. The Pope had to resign himself before the fait accompli, but this turning of the Crusade against the Christians was a serious matter. It was the beginning of an era during which personal ambition together with commercial covetousness were to be the chief motives of expeditions oversea. Only the Crusades of Saint Louis revived in their purity the spirit of the first years in Frankish Syria, the spirit that had inspired the appeal of Urban II.

Yet that spirit still survived here and there in Europe and occasionally flickered into unexpected flame. An instance of this was in the Children's Crusade of 1212. In May of that year a shepherd boy of twelve called Stephen announced that Christ had told him to go on a Crusade to conquer the Holy Land. As he travelled round France preaching this, his enthusiasm fired the children until, by the time they reached Marseilles, it was said that thirty thousand of them, both rich and poor, had joined him. He had promised them that the seas would open and let them through dryshod and they were bitterly disappointed when this did not happen. Instead they went on board two merchant ships and for eighteen years nothing more was heard of them. Then it was learnt that some had been drowned and the rest sold as slaves in *Algeria* and *Egypt*.

In *Germany* a slightly older boy called Nicolas followed Stephen's example, with equal success. He led his band to *Rome* in the first place and there Pope Innocent received them kindly, but sent them home. Few appear to have returned and in their grief the parents hanged the father of Nicolas, for having encouraged his son.

THE JOURNEY OF THE BISHOP OF
ACRE: THE SIEGE OF DAMIETTA:
FRANCIS OF ASSISI AT DAMIETTA

✦✦✦

*A*LTHOUGH *Pope Innocent did not encourage the children,
he was greatly touched by their zeal and devotion. "The very
children put us to shame" he wrote in one of those persistent
appeals for a Crusade that he never ceased to launch throughout
the thirteenth century. It appears that few contemporaries were aware
of the change that had taken place, whereby the war against Islam,
which had originally been only the means to that reconquest of the holy
places which had first justified the appeal of Urban II, had now become
an end in itself. Little by little, the defence of the Latin Kingdoms—including that Latin Empire of Constantinople won from other Christians
in defiance of the whole crusading idea—began to be considered a
sufficient justification for taking up arms. It may indeed have been
thought that these Latin Kingdoms would one day serve as a base for
the reconquest of Jerusalem. But it is highly significant that this conquest never took place, save through diplomatic channels exploited
by the guile of the Emperor Frederick II of Hohenstaufen.*

*When he took the cross in 1215, the papacy was filled with great
hope. The Crusade had been fixed for June 1st, 1217. Preachers went
everywhere to urge the taking of the cross, following the example of
one of the most illustrious among them, James of Vitry, Bishop of Acre,
who was later to write a History of Jerusalem. A celebrated letter which
he wrote from Genoa in October 1216 tells of his return journey to
Acre and his preaching.*

Just as I arrived in Lombardy, it happened that the devil
flung headlong into a rapid river, terribly deep and swift, the
arms with which I had decided to fight him—in other words my
books—and all the other things I needed. This river, because of the

melting of the snows, had swollen beyond measure and carried away bridges and rocks. One of my coffers, full of books, was borne along on its waters; another coffer, in which was a finger of my mother, Marie d'Oignies, buoyed up my mule, and saved it from drowning. So although there was only one chance in a thousand of escaping that, my mule arrived safe and sound at the bank with the coffer. The other coffer, caught by the trees, was later recovered by a miracle and, what is more miraculous still, although my books were a little damaged, one can nevertheless still read everything.

He then recounts the arrangements he made for the voyage:

I have reserved on a new ship, which has just been built at a cost of four thousand pounds, and has never been to sea, five places for myself and my companions, being a quarter of the upper deck. I shall eat, study my books and stay there all day, unless there is a storm at sea. I have reserved a bedroom to sleep in at night with my companions, another to keep my clothes in and the victuals we shall need for a week; I have reserved another room where my servants will sleep and prepare my food; and another place for the horses that I have brought with me. Finally, in the ship's hold I have stored my bread, with biscuits, meat and other things sufficient to feed us for three months.

As I came from France, and it was winter, and I should soon have to set out again on a journey where I should probably have little respite and much work, and as I felt very tired, I decided to rest a while so as to be better able to undertake my work overseas; all the more because several thousand Crusaders, whom I should have to receive and comfort, had already gone overseas. I planned to preach the word of God to the men of my diocese, and to the others overseas, before the arrival of the great crowd and to warn and exhort them so that they would receive those pilgrims well, and abstain from sin so as not to lead the strangers into wrongdoing by their example. When the great crowd had arrived I should in fact be so taken up with their affairs that I should hardly have any time for the people of Acre who had been particularly entrusted to me, unless I did so previously. . . .

I therefore set out for Genoa. . . . When I got there the citizens of the town, although they gave me a good welcome, took my horses, whether I liked it or not, to go and attack a fortress. It is the custom in that town, whenever they go on an expedition, to take with them horses wherever they find them, no matter to whom they belong. The women had remained in the city. During that time I did what I could and preached the word of God to many women and a few men. A great number of rich and noble women took the cross. The men had taken my horses and I made their wives take the cross. They were so fervent and devout that, from early morning until night, they hardly left me a moment's peace, either because they came to glean edifying words in my company, or because they wished to confess. When the citizens returned from their expedition, and saw that their wives and sons had taken the cross, they too, after hearing my preaching, received the sign of the cross with much fervour and love. I remained in that city of Genoa all September and I often preached on Sundays and feast days to the people of the city. Although I do not know their tongue, thousands of men turned towards God and took the cross.

It must be remembered that no one was authorised to preach a Crusade unless he had himself taken the cross, and that it was obligatory for all the preachers to have read the Koran and to know the Mahomedan religion, before going to the Holy Land.

Counting on expected reinforcements, John of Brienne, King of Jerusalem, was about to set on foot operations against Egypt. It was during this campaign that the siege of Damietta was undertaken.

"*History of the Patriarchs of Alexandria*":

The Franks made haste to pitch their camp and surround themselves with ditches and entrenchments; after which they directed their attacks against the tower of the foul-cable. They were very anxious to get possession of it, for this was the only passage through which their big ships could obtain entry into the interior of Egypt. Eight of their perriers never ceased working day or night; the stones they hurled went as far as Damietta; missiles and arrows were seen flying continually and a great number of Moslems lost their lives. Terror became general. In a trice the villages surrounding Damietta were abandoned and the desolation spread as far as Cairo.

During this time help reached the place from all sides: al-Adil, who had remained in Syria to protect the country, hastened to send all his available troops. Egypt was at that time under the authority of his elder son, al-Kamil. This prince stationed himself in the neighbourhood of Damietta, on the eastern bank of the Nile. In this contingency a great number of Moslems from Cairo and old Cairo took arms, some out of religious sentiment and others because they were forced to do so. The chief citizens subscribed together and some troops were equipped. Such was the fear that reigned in those two towns that already people began stocking wheat, flour, biscuits, rice and other foodstuffs; one would have thought the enemy was at the gates.

On Friday [June 23rd] the Christians launched an attack on the tower of the foul-cable. Seventy of their barques, protected with leather and proof against naphtha and Greek fire, advanced in terrifying array. The assault was keen, but had no success. A new attack took place on Sunday [July 3rd]. That day the Franks employed four ships each surmounted by a tower: three were directed against the foul-cable; the fourth was to proceed against the town. The enemy made the greatest efforts and was on the point of triumphing: already they had set up their ladders when the mast supporting one of the towers broke and all the warriors on it fell into the water; most of them were drowned, weighed down by their arms. This success filled the Moslems with unbounded joy; in Cairo and old Cairo they lit illuminations and the inhabitants gave themselves up to transports of the keenest pleasure. . . .

In the meantime, the attacks against the town and the tower of the foul-cable continued. No day passed without some new assault. The stones flung by the Christians' machines were of a prodigious size; a single one weighed more than three hundred Egyptian pounds. The Franks were working at that time at a kind of pontoon-bridge that they called a maremme: it consisted of two or three ships placed together and joined with beams and planks so as to look like a single ship. The one in question here was made of two ships; on top there rose four masts supporting a wooden tower with look-out slits and battlements, which could be raised or lowered at will by means of straps and pulleys. All these preparations were intended for the tower of the foul-cable. On the day fixed, the Franks advanced with their pontoon, and lowered the drawbridge. In a moment the upper storey [of the tower] was in their hands, and forthwith the bridge which joined the tower to the town was cut. The Moslems who were shut up in the tower, to the number of about three hundred, seeing themselves cut off from help, laid down their arms and were made prisoner; only a few tried to throw themselves into the sea and swam to safety. That was a horrible day. The Christians planted their flags and their crosses on top of the tower; next day they closed the door facing Damietta and on the opposite side built a bridge of boats to join the tower to their camp. From that moment the bed of the Nile was open to them. Four months had passed between the arrival of the Christians and the taking of the tower of the foul-cable.

But no attempt at all was made to exploit this first success. The Sultan of Egypt proposed the cessation of hostilities, and offered to give the Christians Jerusalem and Palestine as the price of their departure. This was an unhoped-for offer that ought to have been seized without delay; it was rejected under the influence of a newcomer, the Cardinal-legate Pelagius, who was to reveal himself as the evil genius of the expedition. Some modern historians have attempted to rehabilitate him; but in fact this obstinate and narrow-minded prelate could only contemplate one form of victory: the unconditional surrender of Islam.

"*Estoire D'Eracles*":

The Pope sent to the army at Damietta two cardinals: Cardinal Robert [of Courson], who was English, and Cardinal Pelagius, who was from Portugal. Cardinal Robert died and Pelagius lived, which was a great pity for he did much harm there.

Pelagius was one of those men who confuse tradition with outworn ideas, apply to the present the formulas of the past, and see in the faith above all a question of authority. It should be added, to explain the state of listlessness which seemed to paralyse the army of the Crusaders, that the offensive against Damietta had only been undertaken in the hope that the Emperor Frederick II, who had taken the cross three years before, would bring the help he had promised. As the unlooked-for proposal of the Sultan was refused by Pelagius, against the advice of John of Brienne, there was nothing for it but to continue hostilities.

In the camp of the besiegers before Damietta there was an unusual Crusader. James of Vitry, who knew him, speaks of him thus:

We saw the first founder and Master of that Order, whom all the others obey as their Grand Prior; he is a simple, unlettered man, beloved of God and men; they call him Brother Francis. . . .

This Brother Francis, the Poor Man of Assisi—and still more his Order—inspired certain apprehensions in James of Vitry:

That Order seemed to me very dangerous, because not only those who are perfect, but also those who are young and imperfect, and who ought to be subject for a time to monastic discipline so as to be tested and made submissive to it, are sent in twos into the world.

All the same the presence of Francis of Assisi before Damietta was significant. It foreshadowed the advent of a new chivalry and confronted a Cardinal Pelagius, clinging to the solution of yesterday, with the solution of tomorrow, the solution that the Blessed Ramon Lull, who was to consecrate his life to it and die for it, so splendidly set forth in his writings.

An episode which then took place was therefore something entirely new, that left both Moslems and Christians nonplussed.

James of Vitry:

When the army of the Christians arrived before Damietta in the land of Egypt, fearless Brother Francis, armed with the buckler of the faith . . . advanced towards the Sultan of Egypt. When the Saracens seized him on his way, he said: "I am a Christian, lead me to your master." When they had brought him there, the fierce beast, on seeing him, was turned to gentleness by the aspect of the man of God and listened very attentively to the sermon on Christ which he preached for several days to him and the people.

The chronicle of John Eleemosyna implies that Francis told the Sultan he was willing to abide the judgment of God by fire:

It is related that he went into the presence of the Sultan, who offered him many gifts and treasures, and when the servant of God would have none of them the Sultan said: "Take them and distribute them to the churches and the Christian poor." But the servant of Christ, despising the things of earth, refused, affirming that divine Providence provided for the needs of the poor. When the blessed Francis began to preach, he offered to enter into the fire with a Saracen priest and in this way to prove to him absolutely that the law of Christ was true. But the Sultan said: "Brother, I do not think that any Saracen priest would enter into the fire for his faith."

Then, fearing lest some of his army, converted to the Lord by the power of his word, should join the army of the Christians, he had him led away with every kind of consideration and in all security to our camp, finally saying to him: "Pray for me, that God may deign to reveal to me the law and the faith which most please him."

As for the siege itself, it ended, in November 1219, in the taking of Damietta, and this had tremendous repercussions in the world of Islam. But this time once again no immediate benefit was drawn from it, since the Legate Pelagius claimed to direct the expedition entirely alone, so much so that John of Brienne, wearied, and made uneasy too by the news reaching him from Syria, where retaliatory expeditions were on the increase, finally went back to Palestine. The army remained idle for a year and a half; then Pelagius, without even warning John of Brienne, ordered it to set out for Cairo in the most unfavourable conditions, and there engaged hostilities. As was to be expected, the result was a disaster. The Crusaders were only too pleased to surrender Damietta in return for the freedom to withdraw, which was granted them.

THE UNHAPPY CRUSADE OF THE
EXCOMMUNICATED EMPEROR

✚✚✚✚✚✚✚✚✚✚✚✚✚✚✚✚✚✚✚✚✚✚✚✚✚✚✚✚✚✚✚✚✚✚✚✚✚✚

*T*HE HELP *expected from the Germanic Roman Empire still
did not arrive. Frederick II was in less and less of a hurry to
set out on the Crusade. On the other hand, he made the greatest
possible haste to take the title of King of Jerusalem, by marrying, in
1228, John of Brienne's daughter Isabella, who had inherited the Kingdom. Philip of Novara has described the marriage of the Emperor to the
little fourteen-year-old princess:*

The marriage was agreed upon and settled on both sides. The
Emperor had twenty galleys fitted up and armed to go to Syria to
bring the damsel who was Queen of Jerusalem . . . and he ordered
knights and squires to embark on the galleys to accompany the
said lady, and the Emperor sent beautiful presents and beautiful
jewels to the lady and to her uncles [John and Philip of Ibelin]
and to her other relations. . . . All the barons and knights and the
commoners and burghers and others apparelled themselves and
had robes and all things suitable made to celebrate so high a
marriage and so solemn a coronation, and brought the damsel to
Tyre. And there she was married [by proxy] and crowned by
Simon, Archbishop of Tyre, and the feast lasted fifteen days
with tourneys and dances and other fêtes of all kinds. . . . And
when the 8th day of July of the year 1224 had come, the said
Queen went on board the galleys that the Emperor had sent her.
On her departure Queen Alice, her sister, Queen of Cyprus, and
the other ladies accompanied her to the sea-shore, weeping as
though they were sure they would never see her again, as indeed
they never did. And when the said Isabella departed, she gazed at
the land and said: "I commend you to God, sweet Syria, that I
shall never more see"; and she was prophesying, for so it was.

Isabella did in fact die three years later in giving birth to a son, Conrad. In the meantime, and contrary to the pact that he had made with John of Brienne, whereby John was to be regent for his lifetime, Frederick II himself took the crown of Jerusalem.

Nevertheless, he did not fulfil his crusading vow until 1228, after he had been excommunicated for failing in it. It was an ill-furnished Crusade; he only took with him six hundred knights and a few thousand foot-soldiers. On the other hand, in the course of the journey he took possession of the island of Cyprus and wrested the suzerainty of it from John of Ibelin, Lord of Beirut and regent during the minority of the young king Henry of Lusignan. Philip of Novara, in the Geste des Chiprois, *tells us of the brutality with which he did it. After he had disembarked at Limasol:*

He sent courteous letters to the Lord of Beirut who was at Nicosia, praying and requesting him, as his dear uncle, to come and speak with him and bring with him the young King and his three children and all his friends; and he sent him another word, and this by the grace of Our Lord was a prophecy, for he told him that he and his friends and his children would be rich and honoured because of his coming. And so they were, thank God, but it was not as he had wished.

The Emperor's messenger was much honoured at Nicosia and his arrival was greatly fêted. The Lord of Beirut gathered his friends together and asked their counsel concerning the young King Henry and himself. All with one voice cried that neither he nor his children should put themselves in the power of the Emperor, nor should they make the King their lord; for the ill deeds of the Emperor were too well known and many times he had said and sent sweet words, while his deeds were horrible and heavy. So they counselled him to excuse himself in some manner, and to say that he and his friends and all the barons of Cyprus would make ready in haste and follow him [the Emperor] to Syria in the service of God. . . . For in Syria were the Temple and the Hospital and other good people who wanted peace and good will and the Emperor would not be able to act there as he liked. The Lord of Beirut answered this advice and said that they had counselled him loyally and in friendship, but that it would be better to die and suffer what God had ordained, than to agree that either he or his lineage or the people of the oversea territories should turn aside from the service of God and the conquest of the Kingdom of Jerusalem and Cyprus; for he had no wish to wrong Our Lord; and that the world should say: "The Emperor of Rome spared no pains to go oversea and would have conquered all, but the Lord of Beirut and other disloyal men oversea love the Saracens better than the Christians, and for that reason they abandoned the Emperor and did not want the Holy Land to be delivered."

So John of Ibelin betook himself with his suite to the Emperor:

He welcomed them warmly, with every appearance of joy, and it seemed that his enemies had misjudged him. He gave scarlet robes to those who were clothed in black,* and jewels, and begged them all to come and eat with him next day. They prepared their robes in haste and the next morning all came dressed in scarlet before the Emperor.

That same night he had a door secretly opened in the wall of a room that gave on to a garden, in the beautiful manor built by Philip [of Ibelin] at Limasol, where he was lodged; through that false postern the Emperor made three thousand armed men and more, both sergeants and crossbowmen and sailors, enter by night secretly, so that almost the whole garrison of his ships was within; they were put in the stables and the bedrooms and the doors closed on them, until it was time to eat, and the tables were laid and the water set out.

The Emperor made the Lord of Beirut and the Constable of Cyprus sit next him, while the two sons of John of Ibelin served "one with the cup and the other with the bowl", *that is, one as cupbearer, the other as carver, according to the custom of the time, when young lords in the suite of princes served at table.*

During the last course, the hidden men-at-arms came out and took up their positions before the doors. The Cypriots "spoke no word and strove to appear at ease". *Then the Emperor dropped the mask and addressed the Lord of Beirut:*

"I require two things of you: one . . . that you should hand over to me the city of Beirut, for you have no right either to have

---

* The Ibelins were wearing mourning for one of their relations, Philip, who died a short while before.

or hold it. The other thing is that you should repay me all that the bailiffship of Cyprus has been worth since the death of King Hugh, that is ten years' rent, for it is my right according to German custom."

The Lord of Beirut replied: "Sire, I believe you are making merry with me and mocking me; and it may well be that some wicked people, who hate me, have advised you to require this of me, and that is why you have thought of it. But please God, you are so good and wise a lord, that you know that we can serve you and will do so willingly, and you will not believe them over this." The Emperor laid his hand on his head and said: "By this head, which many times has worn the crown, I will have my way concerning the two things I have asked, or else you are prisoners." Then the Lord of Beirut arose and said very proudly and with noble mien: "I have and I hold Beirut as my rightful fief, and Madame the Queen Isabella who was my sister and who was the rightful heiress of the Kingdom of Jerusalem gave me Beirut when Christendom had recovered it; and it was in such ruins that the Temple and the Hospital and all the barons of Syria refused it. I strengthened it and maintained it by means of the alms of Christendom and my labour, and every day I have put into it and devoted to it all the rents I have in Cyprus and elsewhere. If you think that I hold it wrongfully, I will furnish you with my reason for it and my right to it before the Court of the Kingdom of Jerusalem. As for what you ask me concerning the rents of the bailiffship of Cyprus, I have never had any; my brother had a lease only of the cross and the work and the government of the kingdom; but Queen Alice, my niece, had the rent and did as she pleased with it, as one who had a right to the bailiffship, according to our custom. . . . And be sure," he added, "that neither for fear of death nor prison will I do more, unless the judgment of a good and fair court should constrain me to do so."

The Emperor was greatly angered, and swore and threatened and finally said: "I always heard and understood, when I was beyond the seas a long time ago, that your words were very fine and polite, and that you are very wise and subtle in speech, but I shall show you well that all your sense and your subtlety and your words will avail nothing against my strength."

The Lord of Beirut answered in such a way that all present marvelled and all his friends were full of fear because of it.

Thus he replied: "Sire, you have already heard of my polite words and, as for me, I have certainly often heard of your doings; and when I was preparing to come here, my whole council told me of the very thing you are now doing. And I would not believe any of them; it was not that I did not suspect it; I come fully aware and I would much rather receive at your hands prison or death than consent that it should be said or thought that Our Lord's worth and the conquest of the Holy Land were neglected be me or my lineage, or by the people of the land where I was. . . . I said this to my council when I left Nicosia to come to you, and I left ready to suffer all that might happen, purely for the love of Our Lord who suffered death for us and will deliver us from it, if it please Him. And if He desires or deigns to allow that we should receive death or prison, I thank Him for it; and I submit to Him in all things." Then he fell silent and sat down.

The Emperor was greatly angered and often changed colour, and the people looked often at the Lord of Beirut, and there were many words and threats. Then the people of religion and other good folk undertook to reconcile them, but they could never bring the Lord of Beirut to renounce what he had said he would do. As for the Emperor, he put forward most strange and dangerous demands.

In the end they agreed to appeal to the court of Jerusalem. The Emperor asked for John's two sons, Balian and Baldwin, as hostages and had them chained "with an iron cross to which they were so firmly attached that they could bend neither arms nor legs, and at night he put other people in irons with them".

A little later, two lords, Anselm of Brie and John's nephew, said to him:

"Sire, go to the Emperor and take us with you, and each of us will have a knife hidden in our hose; as soon as we are with him, we will kill him, and our people, fully armed, will be on horseback before the door. When the Emperor is dead, no one will stir and we will help our cousins." The Lord of Beirut was greatly angered and threatened to strike and kill them if they ever spoke of this, and he said that by such a deed they would be disgraced for ever and all Christendom would cry: "The traitors oversea have slain their Lord Emperor." And afterwards, when he was dead and we alive and well, our right would be wrong and the truth of it would not be believed. He is my lord; whatever he may do we will keep our faith and honour.'

So the Lord of Beirut took his departure. Great was the cry in the camp when he left. The Emperor heard the cry and was much afraid, and left the manor of the Hospital which was close to his ships. . . .

The Emperor and his whole fleet left Cyprus one evening at nightfall and that night even the old Prince of Antioch decamped and fled to a castle called Nephin. There he gave thanks to God that he had escaped from the Emperor; for he had arrived in Cyprus after the Lord of Beirut had made peace, and the Emperor had told him to order all his liegemen of Antioch and Tripoli to pay the homage of allegiance to him, as those of Cyprus had done. The Prince thought himself as good as dead and disinherited, so he pretended to be ill and dumb and cried very loudly: "Ah, ah, ah,"—and remained thus until he [the Emperor] left. But as soon as he got to Nephin, he recovered.

Thus the moving scenes at Cyprus had a comic epilogue: the old Prince of Antioch, passing himself off as a dotard, had hoaxed the Emperor.

In the meantime, the Crusade of Frederick II was beginning badly. He had from the outset estranged the lords oversea; he was excommunicated by the Pope, which lost him the help of the knights of the Temple and the Hospital; finally he had been counting almost solely on the good relations he had maintained with the Sultan of Egypt, al-Kamil. At odds with his brother al-Mu'azzam the Sultan of Damascus, al-Kamil had himself called upon the help of the imperial armies. But while Frederick had kept postponing his Crusade, al-Mu'azzam had died, and the new Sultan of Damascus, the young al-Nasir, was no longer a redoubtable adversary for the Sultan of Egypt; thus the Emperor found himself not wanted by the latter and so completely isolated. He therefore wrote to al-Kamil this supplicating letter; recorded by the historian Maqrisi:

"I am your friend. You are not unaware how much above all the princes of the West I am. It is you who urged me to come here; the kings and the popes have been informed of my journey: if I were to return from it without having obtained anything, I should lose all consideration in their eyes. After all, was not

Jerusalem the city that gave birth to the Christian religion? Is it not you who destroyed her? She is now reduced to the lowest degradation. For pity's sake give her to me in the state in which she is, so that on my return I may hold up my head among the kings. I renounce in advance any advantages that I might obtain from this."

Fortunately for Frederick, the Sultan of Damascus chose this moment to threaten al-Kamil. So after a display of the Crusaders' military force, during which Templars and Hospitallers followed at a distance the little troop of the excommunicated Emperor, whose numerical inferiority put him in great danger, negotiations began which ended in the Treaty of Jaffa, 1229. Al-Kamil gave back to the Christians the three holy towns: Jerusalem, Bethlehem and Nazareth, with a "corridor" giving access to them through Lydda, Ramleh and Emmaus.

It seemed that the goal of Christendom had been attained. In reality the treaty satisfied no one, and with good reason. The Sultan al-Kamil "was unanimously blamed for having acted thus and his conduct was severely judged throughout the country", according to the Arab historian Maqrisi. As for the Christians, they blamed the treaty of Jaffa for having left undecided the essential point, that of the restoration of the walls of the Holy City. And in fact, in the following year, the soundness of this reproach was proved by a raid which caused many casualties among the population of Jerusalem, who had been left without defence against the incursions of pillagers. As early as 1244, an attack by the Khwarismians wrested Jerusalem from the Christians for good.

As for the Emperor Frederick, he had been bent on going to Jerusalem to be crowned but, as he was excommunicated, the Patriarch refused to attend the ceremony; so the Emperor himself took the crown from the Holy Sepulchre and placed it on his head in the presence of the Grand Master of the Order of the Teutonic Knights, Hermann of Salza, the only representative of a religious authority who was with him. After this the Emperor launched an attack against the house of the Templars at Acre, and at the same time against Chastel-Pèlerin, one of the castles that belonged to them. He made every effort to put Frankish Syria in the hands of the German lords and of the Teutonic Order. Then on May 1st, 1229, he re-embarked at Acre.

Philip of Novara:

He departed in a scurvy manner. The Emperor arranged his journey secretly and on the first day of May, before dawn, without letting anyone know, he went to a galley close to the Butchery. Now it happened that the butchers in those streets pursued and pelted him with entrails and offal in a very sordid way. The Lord of Beirut and Master Odo of Montbeliard heard the tumult, ran thither, chased and arrested the men and women who had assaulted him, and called to him from the shore to the galley on which he was that they commended him to God. The Emperor answered them in a very low voice, whether well or ill, I know not. . . . Thus departed from Acre the hated Emperor, accursed and vilified.

SAINT LOUIS

⚜⚜⚜⚜⚜⚜⚜⚜⚜⚜⚜⚜⚜⚜⚜⚜⚜⚜⚜⚜⚜⚜⚜⚜⚜⚜⚜⚜⚜⚜⚜⚜⚜⚜⚜⚜⚜⚜

*T*HE CRUSADE *of Frederick II and his attempt to subject the overseas kingdoms to the Germanic Empire had set up innumerable divisions in Frankish Syria. The loss of Jerusalem completed the disruption of Christendom overseas, and it seemed that it was near its end when, in December 1244, Saint Louis decided to take the cross.*

In him the spirit of the First Crusade lived again in all its purity; and it is strange to think that, before it disappeared for ever, this desire to win back the Holy Land by force of arms should have blossomed once more in the right way, in the person of a spiritually-minded Crusader whose absolute uprightness filled even his enemies with admiration, and for whom the crusading vow meant above all the sacrifice of himself.

It gives some idea of the care with which Saint Louis prepared his expedition that, as he possessed no port of embarkation on the Mediterranean, he began by building one. Such was the origin of Aigues Mortes, which has remained down to our day as a magnificent witness of the King's activity; and a most faithful witness too, since its walls, never having undergone a siege, provide today one of the most perfect examples to be found of a thirteenth-century city. Saint Louis stimulated the building of this city by granting the inhabitants those freedoms and privileges which the citizens of new towns in general enjoyed. He took as much care to provide in advance supplies for his army.

Joinville:

We found in Cyprus a great profusion of the King's stores, namely his cellarage, his money and his granaries. By way of cellarage his people had made in the middle of the fields by the sea-shore great piles of wine casks that they had bought as long ago as two years before the King's arrival; and they had placed them one on top of the other in such a way that, when one saw them from the front it looked as though they were barns. The wheat and barley they had stacked in heaps in the middle of the fields and when one saw them it looked as though they were mountains; for the rain, which had flattened the corn long since, had made it sprout on top, so that all you saw was green grass. What happened when they wanted to take this to Egypt, was that they pulled off the covering layer with the green grass and found the wheat and barley as fresh as if it had been newly threshed.

There were other technical matters to be thought of and the King took with him sappers, carpenters and masters of the ballistas, under the leadership of one of them called Master Joscelin of Cournault. They were to have opportunity to display their skill when it was necessary to construct bridges or build causeways on the branches of the Nile. For this reason Saint Louis' Crusade has been called a "crusade of engineers".

Many French barons took the cross with the King, among others the Seneschal of Champagne, John of Joinville, who many years later related that expedition, in the course of which a solid personal friendship sprang up between the King and himself. Both of them were equally animated by the spirit of chivalry that they brought to its highest pitch. Because of this, Joinville's testimony has the additional interest of being in perfect sympathy with the person of the saint that he evokes.

Joinville embarked at Marseilles. The account he has left of that embarkation has been often quoted, but it is too beautiul to be omitted:

In the month of August we boarded our vessels at the Roche-de-Marseilles.

On the day when we boarded our vessels they opened the ship's hold and put inside all our horses that we were going to take oversea, and then the hold was closed and well stopped up, as when one sinks a barrel because, when the vessel is at sea, the entire hold is under water.

When the horses were inside, our master mariner called to his sailors who were at the prow of the vessel and said to them: "Is all ready?" And they answered: "Yes, sire, let the clerks and priests advance." As soon as they had arrived he called to them: "In the name of God, sing!" And they all cried with one voice: "Veni, Creator Spiritus." And the master called to his mariners: "In the name of God, set sail!" And thus they did.

And before long the wind caught the sails and took us out of sight of land; so that we saw nothing but sky and water, and each day the wind took us further from the lands where we were born.

And I tell you this to show you that he is a rash fool who dares put himself in such peril with other people's money or in mortal sin; for one falls asleep at night not knowing whether by the morning one will not find oneself at the bottom of the sea.

In a letter* to one of his friends, a Crusader related the events that occurred after the embarkation of the King at Aigues-Mortes.

This is to let you know that the King and Queen, the Count of Artois, the Count of Anjou and his wife and I are now full of joy before the city of Damietta that God, by a miracle, and through His mercy and pity, gave back to Christendom on the Sunday of the fortnight of Pentecost.

First I want to tell you the way in which this happened. It chanced that when the King and the army of Christendom had boarded the ships at Aigues Mortes, we set sail on the day of the feast of Saint Augustine at the end of August [1248] and arrived in the island of Cyprus fifteen days before the feast of Saint Rémy, that is to say on the day of the feast of Saint Lambert. The Count of Anjou disembarked at the city of Limasol, and the King and we who were with him, in his ship that was called the *Montjoie*, disembarked next day early in the morning, and the Count of Artois in the third [ship] in this same port. We had very few people in that town with us and we remained there until Ascension to wait for the troops that had not arrived.

After these things the King and the whole army, which consisted of fully 2,500 knights and 5,000 crossbowmen, and many other people on foot and mounted, boarded the ships and stood out to sea at Limasol and in the other ports of Cyprus on the day of the Ascension, which was the thirteenth day of May, to go to the city of Damietta, which was not more than three days' journey from Cyprus. We were at sea for twenty-two days and experienced many vexations and difficulties on the sea.

On the Friday after Trinity, towards the hour of tierce, we arrived before Damietta and a great part of our army with us, although it was not all there. We were still at least three leagues

* Published in Michaud, *Histoire des Croisades*, Paris 1817-22.

from the land. The King had the fleet anchored and sent for all
the barons who were there. They all assembled in *Montjoie*, the
King's ship, and agreed that they would land the next day early in
the morning in spite of their enemies, if they should dare to
oppose them. Orders were given that all the galleys and all the
little ships of the fleet should be made ready and that, very early
next day, all those who could get into them should do so. We
were told that everyone should confess his sins and prepare himself and make his will and put his affairs in order, ready to die if it
pleased Our Lord Jesus Christ.

*It was no doubt at that moment that Saint Louis made the admirable
speech to his companions that another letter* has recorded for us.*

"My faithful friends, if we remain inseparable in our love, we
shall be invincible. We have not been led here, to disembark in
a land so powerfully protected, without the divine permission.
It is not I who am King of France, it is not I who am the Hóly
Church, it is you who are the one and the other. I am only a
man whose life will end like that of other men, when it shall
please God. All is for the best for us, whatever befall us. If we are
vanquished, we are martyrs; if we triumph, the glory of God will
be exalted, as will the glory of France also, and the glory of
Christendom itself."

John Sarrasin:

Very early next day the King heard the service of Our Lord,
and Mass as it is said at sea, and armed himself and ordered that all
should arm and go on board the little ships. The King boarded a
Normandy coche†, as did we and our company with us, and also
the Legate, who held the True Cross and blessed the armed men
who had boarded the little ships to land. The King made Lord
John of Beaumont, Matthew of Marly and Geoffrey of Sargines
go on board the longboat, and he had the banner of My Lord
Saint-Denis set there with them. This longboat went in front and
all the other vessels came after, following the banner and the boat

---

* Written by a Crusader called Guy of Melun, quoted by Matthew Paris
in Vol. VI of *Chronica Majora*, ed. Luard, Rolls Society, 7 vols., London, 1866–9.

† A light boat rounded at prow and stern.

where the King was and the Legate with him carrying the holy True Cross, and we were always just behind.

When we came within crossbowshot of the shore, many well-armed Turks, on foot and on horseback, facing us on the shore, let fly a dense cloud of arrows at us, and we at them. And when we were close to land, at least two thousand Turks who were there, on foot or horseback, waded into the sea against our people, and some others on foot too. When the well-armed men in the ships, and the knights too saw that, they no longer tried to follow the banner of My Lord Saint-Denis, but jumped into the sea on foot fully armed, so that some had water up to their armpits and others breast-high, some being more in the water and some less, according as the sea was deeper in one place than in another. A good number of our men, with great danger, great labour and great bravery, dragged their horses out of the vessels where they were; then our crossbowmen strove their utmost and shot their arrows so fiercely and densely that it was marvellous to see. And so our people reached the shore and landed. When their people saw that, they drew together, speaking in their tongue, and came at us so hard and so proudly that it seemed they must kill us all and cut us to pieces. But our people on the shore did not budge and fought so ardently that it seemed as though they had never endured either toil or distress at sea, by the power of Jesus Christ and of the holy Cross that the Legate held high above his head against the unbelievers.

When the King saw the others jumping down into the sea, he wanted to go with them, but they did not want to let him; all the same he descended against their will and entered the water up to his waist, and all of us with him. And after the King had gone down into the sea the battle lasted a long time. When it had lasted on land and sea from early morning until midday, the Turks withdrew and departed to enter the city of Damietta. The King remained on the shore with the army of Christendom. He had lost few or no Christians in that battle; but of the Turks there were slain quite five hundred and many of their horses. Four emirs were killed. That king who was in command in the battle near Gaza, where the Counts of Bar and Montfort had been routed, was killed in this battle. He was said to have been the greatest lord in the whole land of Egypt after the Sultan, and a splendid knight, bold and wise in war. The next day, namely the Sunday after Pentecost, some Saracens came in the morning to the King and said that all the Saracens had left the city of Damietta, and that they were ready to be hanged if it were not true. The King ordered them to be detained and sent people to learn the truth. Before nones news reached the King that many of our people were already in the city of Damietta and that the King's banner was floating on a high tower. When our people heard this, they gave great praises to Our Lord, and thanked Him for the great goodness He had shown to the Christians: for the city of Damietta was so strong in walls and moats, great strong towers and palisades, barbicans and many machines and arms and provisions, and all that was needful to defend a town, that one could hardly have thought it could be taken, except with great difficulty and many labours by great numbers of people. Our people found it well stocked with everything they needed.

Inside we found in prison fifty-three Christian slaves who had been there, they said, twenty-two years; they were released and brought before the King. They said that the Saracens had fled as early as the Saturday night and that they were saying to each other that "the swine had come". We found I know not how many Syrian Christians too, who were there subject to the Saracens. When they saw the Christians entering the town, they took crosses and carried them, and therefore had no need to defend themselves; after they had spoken to the King and the Legate they were allowed to keep their houses with their contents.

The King and the army struck camp and went to lodge in the city of Damietta. The King was the first to enter, on the day after the feast of Saint Barnabas the Apostle, and he had everything that was in the greatest mosque in the town, and all the others, taken away, and he turned it into a church dedicated in honour of Jesus Christ.

We feel sure we shall not leave the city before the feast of All Saints, because of the flooding of the river of Paradise which flows there and is called the Nile; for one can go neither to Alexandria nor Babylon* nor Cairo when it has spread over the land of Egypt, and they say that it will not go down before that time, and we must remain in Egypt. You must know that we know nothing of the Sultan of Babylon and the King has been

* The Roman fortress of Babylon some five miles south of Cairo.

told that other sultans would make war on him, and you must know too that never since God gave this city to us have we seen anyone near our army save Saracen Bedouins, who come sometimes within two leagues of the army; and when our cross-bowmen go to shoot at them, they flee. They come at night to seize the horses and cut off the heads of our people, and they say that the Sultan gives ten bezants for every Christian head they bring him. So the Saracens cut off the heads of men who have been hanged and dig up bodies that have been buried to get heads to take to the Sultan, so they say. A Bedouin who came quite alone was taken prisoner and he is still being kept here. They can commit these larcenies easily, for although the King has in Damietta the Queen his wife and part of his goods, in the palace and the fortified places which used to belong to the Sultan of Babylon, and the Legate has his lodging in the halls and fortified places of the leader who was killed in the battle, and each of the barons also has a large and beautiful house appropriate to his rank in the city of Damietta, yet the army of Christendom, and of the King and the Legate, is lodged outside the town. Because of these larcenies by the Bedouins, the Christians have begun to dig great ditches both deep and wide in their camp, but they are not yet finished.

This extraordinary success—it had formerly taken the companions of John of Brienne three years to get possession of Damietta—did not have the results that might have been anticipated. To begin with, the time spent in waiting for reinforcements allowed the Egyptian army to build up their forces again; then, instead of making for Alexandria and thus getting possession of the seaboard, the Crusaders—on the advice of Robert of Artois who exerted a baneful influence on the whole ex-pedition—marched on Cairo; they were held up for a time on the Bahr-el-Seguir, one of the branches of the Nile, where they were attacked with Greek fire by the Egyptian armies massed on the other bank.

Joinville:

The way in which the Greek fire worked was this: it rolled forward as big as a barrel of verjuice, and the tongue of fire that shot out of it was as thick as a stout sword. . . . It made such a noise as it came that it seemed like thunder; it was as if a dragon were flying through the air. It cast such a great light that one could see as clearly in the army as if it were day. . . . Every time our saintly King heard that they were throwing Greek fire at us, he rose from his bed and stretched his hands towards Our Lord and said weeping: "Fair Lord God, preserve my people." I truly believe that his prayers were of great help to us.

The army at last managed to cross the Nile, thanks to a ford pointed out by a Bedouin.

Joinville:

The King sent for all the barons to hold a council. Now they were all of one mind that they could not make a causeway to enable them to cross over to the Saracens' side, because however much our people stopped up on one side, the Saracens let out more on the other. Then the Constable, Imbert of Beaujeu, said to the King that a Bedouin had come who had told him that he would show him a good ford, if he were given five hundred bezants. The King said he would agree that this should be given him provided he truly did as he had promised. The Constable repeated this to the Bedouin and he said he would not show the ford if he were not given the money in advance. It was agreed that they would give it to him, and it was given.

The King decided that the Duke of Burgundy and the other oversea settlers who were in the army should supervise the army to see that no harm came to it; and that he himself and his three brothers would cross by the ford that the Bedouin was to show us. This was agreed and it was decided on the day of Shrovetide [February 8th, 1250]. . . . It had been laid down that the Templars would be the advance-guard and the Count of Artois would have the second battle-order after the Templars.

But these prudent dispositions were compromised by the rashness of the Count of Artois, Saint Louis' brother.
Robert of Artois is typical of the spirit of chivalry already in decline: full of foolhardy rashness, seeking for personal glory in action—everything that was to lead French chivalry to the disasters of the fourteenth and fifteenth centuries.

Joinville:

Now, as soon as the Count of Artois had crossed the river, he and his people flung themselves on the Turks, who fled before them. The Templars sent him word that he was causing them great affront by going before them when he should have gone after; and they begged him to let them pass in front, as it had been laid down by the King.

The Count of Artois did not dare reply to them because of my Lord Foucard of the Merle who was holding the bit of his horse; and this Foucard of the Merle, who was a very good knight, heard nothing of what the Templars were saying to the Count because he was deaf; and he cried: "Have at them! Have at them!"

When the Templars saw that, they thought they would be dishonoured if they let the Count of Artois go in front of them; so they vied with each other in spurring their horses, and pursued the Turks, who were fleeing before them, right across the town of Mansourah as far as the fields on the Babylon side. When they thought of turning back, the Turks threw beams and chunks of wood at them in the middle of the narrow streets.

There were killed the Count of Artois, the Lord of Coucy who was called Raoul, and so many other knights that there were thought to be three hundred. The Temple, so I am told, lost there two hundred and eighty armed men, all mounted. . . .

And the King arrived with all his battle-corps, with great shouts and a great noise of trumpets and kettledrums; and he halted on a high road. Never have I seen such a splendid knight, for he seemed taller than all his people, overtopping them from the shoulders up, a gilded helmet on his head, a German sword in his hand. . . .

While we were returning downstream on the bank between the stream and the river, we saw that the King had drawn near to the river, and that the Turks were driving the King's other battle-corps back, striking heavy blows with their maces and swords, and thrusting back upon the river all the other corps, with the King's corps.

The rout was then so great that many of our people thought of swimming back to the Duke of Burgundy's side.* But they were not able to do this for the horses were tired and the day had turned very hot; so while we were going downstream we saw that the river was covered with spears and swords, and horses and people

---

* The Duke of Burgundy was in command of the rear-guard which had not yet crossed the river.

who were drowning and dying. We came to a culvert which lay athwart the stream, and I suggested to the Constable that we should stay to guard it, "for if we leave it they will throw themselves on the King on this side, and if our people are attacked from both sides, they may well succumb".

So that is what we did. And it would be true to say that we should all have been lost from that moment, if the King had not risked his own life.

For the Lord of Courtenay and my Lord John of Saillenay told me that six Turks came up and seized the King's horse by the bridle and that they were taking him prisoner; and he freed himself from them single-handed, with great blows of his sword. And when the people saw the King's resistance they took courage and many of them stopped crossing the river and went to the King's help.

Heading straight for those of us who were guarding the culvert came the Count Peter of Brittany, who came direct from Mansourah, and had received a sword-wound in the face, so that the blood was pouring into his mouth.

He was on a stout-limbed, stocky horse; he had thrown his reins on the pommel of his saddle and was holding it with both hands, for fear lest his people who were behind him, and were hard upon him, should push him beyond the passage of the culvert. It rather seemed as if he had no high opinion of them; for when he spat the blood from his mouth, he said: "Ho there, by God's Head, have you seen these churls?"

In the rear of his battle-corps came the Count of Soissons and my Lord Peter of Neuville, whom they called Caier, and who had suffered many blows that day. When they had passed and the Turks saw we were guarding the bridge, they left them because they saw that we were looking in their direction.

I went to the Count of Soissons, whose first cousin I had married, and said to him: "Sire, I think you would do well to stay and guard this culvert; for if we leave the passage, those Turks whom you see here before you will rush over it; and thus the King will be attacked from behind as well as in front."

When the Constable heard that, he told me not to leave that place until he returned, and that he would go to seek for help.

So I stayed there on my pony, and there stayed with me the

Count of Soissons on the right and my Lord Peter of Neuville on the left. Then suddenly a Turk came from the direction of the King's battle-corps, which was behind us, and struck my Lord Peter of Neuville from behind with a mace so that he fell forward on the neck of his horse with the blow, and then the Turk dashed beyond the bridge and rushed to his own people. When the Turks saw that we would not leave the culvert, they crossed the stream and took up their position between the stream and the river, as we had done when we went upstream; and we then headed towards them in such a way that we were all ready to rush at them, whether they wanted to cross towards the King, or cross over the culvert.

In front of us there were two of the King's sergeants, William of Boon and John of Gamaches. And the Turks who had stationed themselves between the river and the stream led against them a horde of villeins on foot who threw clods of earth at them; they could never throw them at us.

Finally, they brought up a villein on foot who three times threw Greek fire at them. Once William of Boon caught the pot of Greek fire on the hand-guard of his sword; if it had set fire to anything on him, he would have been burnt.

The arrows that did not reach the sergeants all struck us. Now it happened that I found a padded jacket belonging to a Saracen; I turned the split side towards me and made a shield of the coat, which did me great service; for I was only wounded by their arrows in five places and my pony in fifteen. It chanced also that one of my burghers from Joinville brought me a banner with a spearhead; and every time that we saw they were harrying the sergeants, we rushed upon them and they fled.

The good Count of Soissons, as matters then stood, jested with me and said: "Seneschal, let this rabble yell; for by God's Coif (that was his favourite oath), we shall yet talk of this day's doing, in our ladies' chambers." . . .

At last the Christians gained the victory:

. . . In the evening, at sunset, the Constable led up the King's crossbowmen on foot and they lined up in front of us; and when the Saracens saw the crossbows being set up on their stands, they fled. And then the Constable said to me: "Seneschal, that is well.

Now take yourself to the King and do not leave him until he has gone into his tent."

As soon as I reached the King, my Lord John of Valéry came to him and said: "Sire, my Lord of Châtillon begs you to give him the rear-guard." The King did this very willingly and then set forth.

While we were going along, I made him take off his helmet and gave him my iron cap, so that he could get some air. Then brother Henry of Rosnay, Provost of the Hospital, who had crossed the river, came to him and kissed his hand in its gauntlet.

The King asked him if he had any news of his brother the Count of Artois; and he said to him that he had indeed news of him, for it was certain that his brother the Count of Artois was in Paradise.

"Come now, sire, take good comfort from it; for no greater honour ever befell a King of France than that which has happened to you; for to fight your enemies you have swum across a river, and routed and chased them from the battlefield, and taken their engines of war and their tents, in the place where you will sleep again this night."

The King replied that God should be worshipped in all that He had given him; and then great tears fell from his eyes.

But illness descended on the Christians.

Joinville:
After the two battles I have related, great sufferings began for the army; for after nine days, the bodies of our people who had been slain rose up to the surface of the water because their spleens were rotten, it was said, and they floated down to the bridge which was between our two camps, and could not pass because the bridge touched the water.

There was such a mass of them that the whole river was full of dead from one bank to the other, and as far as a small stone's throw beyond.

Because of this misfortune and because of the unhealthiness of the country, where never a drop of rain falls, we were seized with camp-fever [typhoid] with the result that the flesh of our legs quite withered up, and their skin turned earth-colour, blotched with black like an old boot; and in those of us who had that disease the flesh of their gums turned rotten; and none recovered from that disease but had to die of it. The sign of death was that, when the nose bled, death was certain.

A fortnight later the Turks, in order to starve us (at which many people marvelled) took several of their galleys upstream from our camp and had them dragged over land and put into the river flowing from Damietta, a good league below our camp. And those galleys brought famine to us; for no one dared come upstream to us from Damietta to bring us provisions, because of their galleys. We knew nothing of these things until a little ship belonging to the Count of Flanders, which escaped from them by force, told us of them; and they told us that the Sultan's galleys had taken at least eighty of our galleys which had come from Damietta, and killed all the people in them.

Because of this prices rose so much in the camp that, as soon as Easter came, an ox in the camp was worth eighty pounds and a sheep thirty pounds, and a pig thirty pounds, and an egg twelve deniers, and a hogshead of wine ten pounds.

Because of those wounds that I got on the day of Shrovetide, I fell victim to camp-fever in the mouth and legs, with a double tertian ague and such a heavy cold in the head that it poured from my head through my nostrils; and because of those illnesses I went to bed, ill, in mid-Lent, for which reason my priest sang Mass for me before my bed in my tent; and he had the disease I had. Now it chanced that in performing his sacrament he swooned. I had put on my tunic and when I saw he was going to fall, I leapt from my bed without putting on my shoes and took him in my arms and told him to perform his sacrament slowly and gently, and that I would not let him go until he had finished everything.

He came to himself and completed his consecration and managed to sing the whole Mass, and never sang it again.

The attempt to retreat was rendered dangerous by the rising of the Nile, more especially as the Saracens were blocking Damietta. It is described in the statement of Charles of Anjou at the proceedings for the canonisation of his brother, King Louis, in 1282:

It was then ordered that the boats should follow the bank where the retreat was taking place, for fear that the ships of the Saracens, who were holding the other bank, should divide and occupy both banks, thus harassing our people on the water and on land, from both sides at once; this was also ordered so that our people might be of help to each other, the boats serving as a rampart to those who were on land and they, in their turn, covering the descent of the boats along the bank that they were occupying. That was the reason why it was necessary for them both to wait for each other, and for the horsemen to take much longer than they needed to regain Damietta. Then the boats had not been able to take all the foot-soldiers, which increased the delay still more. And the very night that they left Mansourah, the King's condition grew worse: several times he had to be taken down from his horse, because of the diarrhoea which had him in its grip, in addition to his other infirmities. In the morning, which was the Wednesday after the octave of Easter [April 6th, 1250], they quietly and peaceably crossed the river Tanis. The King dismounted and stood leaning against his saddle; around him were his familiar knights, Geoffrey of Sargines, John Foinon, John of Valéry, Peter of Bauçay, Robert of Bazoches and Walter of Châtillon, who, seeing that his illness had grown worse and that he was exposing himself to peril by staying on land, began all together, and each one separately, to beg him to save his life by boarding a ship. He continued to refuse to abandon his people; King Charles, his brother, then Count of Anjou, said to him: "Sire, you do ill to resist the good advice that your friends give you, and to refuse to embark on a ship; for by waiting for you on land, the march of the army is delayed, not without danger, and you might be the cause of our loss." He said that, as he reported later, out of a desire to save the King, fearing so greatly to lose him, when he would gladly have given his whole inheritance and that of his children to have the King in Damietta. But the King, deeply upset, answered him with a wrathful look: "Count of Anjou, Count of Anjou! If I am a burden to you, rid yourself of me; but I will never rid myself of my people."

It was then that the King was taken prisoner with what remained of his army.

William of Saint Pathus:

None of the saintly King's household remained with him, save one, called Isambart, for they were all ill. So Isambart did the cooking for the saintly King, baking the bread, meat and flour that he brought from the Sultan's court. The King was so ill that his teeth chattered and were loosened, and his skin was pale and dull and he had diarrhoea and was so thin that the bones of his back were wonderfully sharp. Isambart had to carry the King whenever he wanted to relieve nature, and even to undress him and yet, as this Isambart, who was a mature and honest man, testifies on oath, he never saw the King irritated or impatient, nor grumbling to him about anything, but he bore and endured that disease with perfect patience and good temper. And he was always at his prayers.

Meanwhile, cut off in Damietta, there was a woman who was also to show heroism: Queen Margaret of Provence, wife of Saint Louis. She had left with him on his first Crusade and it was in Damietta, where three days later she gave birth to a child, that she learnt that the army of the Crusaders had been vanquished, the King taken prisoner and the town threatened.

Joinville:

Before she was brought to bed, she made everyone leave her room, except her old knight of eighty [a trusty old man who slept before her bed]; she knelt down before him and asked him a favour; and the knight promised it on oath; and she said to him: "I ask you, by the troth you have plighted me, that if the Saracens enter the town, you will cut off my head before they take me." And the knight answered: "Be sure that I will do it, for I had already quite decided that I would kill you before they took us."

The Queen had hardly given birth to her child when she learnt that the Italian merchants—Pisans, Genoans and others—who had followed the Crusaders there, were getting ready to leave Damietta: the town was to be abandoned, and with it the women, the old and the sick who had remained there. So the Queen summoned the chief merchants to her chamber (it was the very next morning after the birth of the little John Tristan) and asked them to take pity on her: "And if you will not do that, at least may you have pity on this weak creature lying here, and wait until I am up again."

But she was talking to merchants, to "realistic" men. "How can we do that? We shall die of hunger in this city!" *The Queen then suggested that they should requisition all the provisions in the city, which she herself would pay for, and distribute them. In consideration of this the Italians agreed to stay. The rationing made it possible to save Damietta, in exchange for which, later on, the King and his people were ransomed.*

In the meantime, the King was trying to negotiate conditions for the release of himself and his companions. A Crusader related:

When the King was taken by the Saracens, and many of his lords with him, he heard it said that some of the rich Christians who were taken with him were putting forward proposals for buying their release; the saintly King strictly forbade them, and upon very heavy penalty, to do this, for fear that it would prevent the release of the poor; for he said that, if this were done, the rich would be released and the poor, who had nothing to pay with, would remain in prison. "But leave entirely to me the question and business of our deliverance, for I do not want any of you to use your own wealth for your deliverance and I desire to be entirely responsible for paying the ransom of everyone with what I have."

The Saracens hoped to exchange the prisoners for the fortresses which were the key to the resistance of the Holy Land. They entered into negotiations with the barons:

Joinville:

"Gentlemen, the Sultan has sent us to you to know if you wish to be released?" The Count [Peter of Brittany, a companion of Joinville's] answered: "Yes." "And what would you give the Sultan for freeing you?" "Whatever we can reasonably manage," he said. "Would you give, for your deliverance, some of the castles of the barons of Outremer?" they asked. The Count replied that he had no power over these castles, because they were held from the Emperor of Germany, who was living at that time. Then they asked if we would surrender the castles of the Temple or the Hospital for our deliverance. And the Count answered that that could not be, that when governors of the castles were installed they were made to swear on the relics that they would surrender none of the castles to free the body of a man. Then they answered that it seemed to them that we had no great desire to be freed, and that they would depart and send us some who would torment us with their swords, as they had done with others. And they departed.

This discussion in fact took place after an appalling scene in which the Saracens made a group of prisoners file in front of them, asking each one: "Will you deny Christ?" *And then, related Joinville,* "those who would not deny were put on one side and had their heads cut off; and those who denied were put on the other side."

There were similar scenes when the Sultan's envoys conversed with the King:

Joinville:

The Sultan's counsellors tested the King in the same way as they had tested them [the barons] to find out if the King would promise to hand over to them some of the castles of the Temple or the Hospital, or the castles of other kings of the country. And God so willed that the King answered them in exactly the same way as we had answered. And they threatened him saying that, since he would not agree, they would put him to the torture. To these threats the King replied that he was their prisoner and they could do with him as they wished. When they saw that they could not overcome the good King by threats, they went back to him and asked him how much money he would be willing to give the Sultan, and in addition whether he would surrender Damietta to them. The King then answered that, if the Sultan agreed to accept from him a reasonable sum of money, he would ask the Queen to pay it for their release. And they said: "Why do you not wish to pledge yourself to this?" The King answered them that he did not know whether the Queen would wish to do it, because it was she who was mistress. . . .

The King then began to negotiate his deliverance and that of all the others: he promised to pay a certain sum of money, to surrender Damietta and to conclude a truce of ten years; and his two brothers, with some others, went to receive the Sultan's oath regarding this treaty.

When everything had been concluded on both sides, the King, his brothers and all the others were put into the ships to be taken down the river to Damietta. When they were already near this town, the Sultan made the King, his brothers and their suite, get out on to the bank and put them in a tent prepared for them, while the other captives remained on the river. But then, towards the third hour, such a violent quarrel arose among the Saracens that the guardians of the King and the princes were struck with amazement by it. They refused to answer the questions addressed to them; but it was clear from their gestures that the dissension was at its height and danger imminent. Then the King, turning to the Lord, had the Office of the Cross sung, together with that of the day, that of the Holy Ghost and that of Requiem, and certain other prayers that he thought suitable in the circumstances. Then some who had just slain the Sultan entered, and at least two hundred other men with them; their white tunics were still covered with blood; the King and the others firmly believed that they were going to be massacred. But on the contrary the assassins began to excuse themselves for the death of the Sultan, pleading two reasons: the first, doubtless false, was, they said, that they could not endure the lack of faith with which the Sultan wanted to treat the King and the Christians, for he had resolved, contrary to his oath and whether or not Damietta was surrendered to him, to kill the King and the prisoners, and meant to go about it in the following way; he would have had the King, his brothers and the barons tied to stakes set up before the walls of Damietta, and would have forced them by tortures to make the town surrender: if they had refused, they would have been put to death by the most refined tortures; if they had consented, they would none the less have been despatched in one way or another. And if proof of the homicidal plan were wanted, it was only necessary to recall that, after and in spite of his oath, the Sultan had had several captives killed, and had sent others away from Cairo, which he would not have done if he had really meant to set them free. But God had turned on him the death he had prepared for the Christians, just as once he caused Haman to be hanged on the gibbet prepared for Mordecai.

The second reason they gave for the murder was that the Sultan had deprived his father's servitors, who had fought with him, of their dignities, to give them to young people who had never fought.

And with them came an envoy from the Caliph of Baghdad. This man, greatly distressed at the death of the Sultan, insulted and rebuked the King, claiming that it was he who had delayed the payment of the residue of the ransom, and that that had been the true cause of the catastrophe.

And this envoy of the Caliph threatened the assassins with his master's wrath, which would rouse all Islam against them. So the assassins, fearing a war with those of their law, were in a hurry to get Damietta, which might serve them as a refuge, and the remainder of the ransom. . . .

The King replied that, for the moment, he had no money, but that with some delay he would procure some and pay, and would surrender Damietta, but that he wanted first to have a guarantee of his own release and that of the others, for fear lest he should be the loser both ways at the same time.

So as surety they offered him the choice between the following two methods: either to remain captive alone, all the others being set at liberty, or to depart alone, leaving all the others captive until such time as the ransom was paid and Damietta surrendered.

Without hesitation the King immediately replied before his brothers and the knights, that he chose to remain captive alone for them all. But his brothers and the knights answered that they would never agree to depart free, leaving their lord behind them in prison, and that the opposite course should be taken, leaving them captive for the King.

A great dispute arose between them and the King, so that the Saracens learnt through an interpreter of this contest of mutual charity, the lord desiring to remain a hostage for his knights and they for their lord. And then God touched the heart of those tyrants and, their hard hearts softening, they said that Louis should choose one of his brothers, who should act as hostage for the King and all the other Christians, until such time as Damietta and the rest of the ransom had been handed over, and who thereafter should be set free like the others.

When the King had chosen as hostage the Count of Anjou, the Saracens, thinking that he would have preferred the Count of Poitiers, whom he usually chose as a companion, wanted to keep this last Count, so that the King should make greater haste to carry out the agreement in order to have him back. And thus it was arranged.

And when they had arrived at Damietta, the King would not leave the ship until the money was paid and Damietta surrendered and until his brother, who had remained as a hostage, had been released.

The liberation finally took place:

At sunrise, Lord Geoffrey of Sargines went into the town and surrendered it to the emirs. They set the Sultan's standards on the towers of the town. The Saracen knights entered the town and began to drink wines and were soon all drunk; one of them came towards our galley and drew his sword, which was all bloody, and said that for his part he had killed six of our people. Before Damietta was surrendered, the Queen and all our people who were in Damietta, except for the sick, had been taken on board our ships. According to their oath the Saracens were to protect them; they killed them all. The King's engines of war which they were also to take care of, they smashed to pieces. And as for the salted meat, which they were to preserve since they do not eat pork, they did not preserve it, but piled up a layer of those war-engines, a layer of salted pork and a layer of dead people and set fire to it. The fire was so huge that it lasted all Friday, Saturday and Sunday. They were to have released the King and ourselves as soon as the sun rose; they held us until sunset; and we ate nothing that day, nor did the emirs either, but we spent the whole day disputing. One of the emirs said in the name of several others: "If you can believe me, I and all those who think as I do are going to kill the King and all the men who are here, and for the next forty years we shall hear no more of them, for their children are small and Damietta is ours, so that we may do this in all security." Another Saracen, who was called Sevreci and had been born in Mauritania, took the opposite view and spoke thus: "If we kill the King, after having killed the Sultan, it will be said that the Egyptians are the most wicked and most disloyal people in the world." And those who wanted to have us killed said: "It is true that we have done ill to kill the Sultan, for we have gone against the commandment of Mahomet, who commands us to keep our lord like the apple of our eye; but something else is written, by way of commandment, in the Book of Mahomet; listen to the other commandment which comes after." And he turned over a leaf of the book he was holding and showed them the other command of Mahomet, which ran thus: "To safeguard the faith, kill the enemy of the Law." "It is clear then that, if we have gone against the command of Mahomet in killing our lord, we shall do worse still if we do not kill the King, whatever promise we may have given him, for he is the greatest enemy of our Law." Thus our death was almost decided, and it chanced that one of the emirs who was on the side of our adversaries thought that they were going to kill us. So he embarked on the river and began to call out in Saracenic to those who were managing the galleys, and taking off his turban, he signalled to them with it. Thereupon they weighed our anchors and took us a good league back towards Babylon [Cairo]. At that we really thought we were lost and many tears were shed.

Nevertheless, in spite of Joinville's fears, the provisions of the treaty were finally observed, and the prisoners, in exchange for whom Damietta had been surrendered, were released. After this the King prepared to carry out the second part of the treaty: the payment of the ransom. For although he was now free, the King, far from nursing a grievance against the Saracens for their breaches of the treaty, insisted that the sums promised should be paid them with the most scrupulous exactitude.

When the payment had been made, the King's council, which made it, came to him and told him that the Saracens refused to release his brother until they had the money in front of them. Some of the council advised the King not to give the money until his brother had been handed over, and the King answered that he would give what he had promised and that they on their side could keep their promise as they thought best. Then Master Philip of Nemours told the King that they had kept back from the Saracens the contents of a set of scales with ten thousand pounds in it, and the King was greatly angered and said he desired that they should pay them the ten thousand pounds, for he had promised them to pay twelve hundred thousand pounds before he left the river. Then I pressed Master Philip's foot and told the King not to believe him, since he did not speak the truth, for the Saracens knew how to count better than anyone in the world. And Master Philip said that I was speaking the truth and that he had only said it for a jest. The King said he found it difficult to understand a jest of that kind: "And I order you," he said to Master Philip, "on your honour as my man, that if the ten

thousand pounds have not been paid you will have them paid
without fail."

As soon as the payment was made, the King, without anyone's
having besought him, told us that now he had fulfilled his oath,
and we were going to leave that place and embark on the ship that
was at sea. Then our galley got under way and we sailed for a
good league without saying a word to each other because of our
uneasiness at the fact that the Count of Poitiers was a prisoner.
Then Master Philip of Montfort came up in a galleon and called
to the King: "Sire, sire, speak to your brother, the Count of
Poitiers, who is on this ship." Then the King cried: "Lights,
lights!" And they lit up. Then indeed there was such great joy
amongst us that it could not have been greater.

*At last, on May 13th, 1250, Saint Louis reached Acre, where he
found his wife and children again. The question then was whether he
would remain in the Holy Land or whether he would listen to the
entreaties of his mother, Blanche of Castille, who had remained in
France as Regent, and return to the West. Joinville describes in detail
the war council that then took place. Saint Louis first spoke to his barons:*

Lords, the Queen my mother has begged leave to implore
me, with all her might, to go to France, for my realm is in great
peril; I have neither peace nor truce with the King of England.
Those of this land with whom I have spoken of it have told me
that, if I leave, this land is lost, for they will follow me to Acre,
since none will dare remain with so few people. I pray you therefore to consider this, and since it is a matter of great concern, I will
give you until eight days from today to answer me what you
think should be done.

*During the eight days, the barons consulted together; they charged
one of them, Guy Mauvoisin, to be their spokesman to the King; and
when the council proper was held, he spoke thus:*

Sire, your brothers and the barons who are here have considered your situation and have seen that you could not remain in
this country with honour for you and your realm; for of all the
knights who came with you, and of whom you led to Cyprus, two
thousand eight hundred, less than a hundred remain in this town.

They therefore counsel you to go to France and obtain troops and money with which you may speedily return to this country, to take vengeance on the enemies of God who kept you in prison.

Then the King asked each of the knights for his advice, particularly the Count of Jaffa, who held one of the frontier fortresses. This Count refrained from replying because, he said: "My castle is on the frontier, and if I counselled the King to stay, it would be thought it is for my own advantage."

Nevertheless, pressed to give his advice, the Count of Jaffa added that, if the King decided to continue the campaign for a year, "it would be a great honour". *Joinville, the fourteenth to give his advice, answered that he agreed with the Count of Jaffa; he was immediately taken to task:* "How could the King possibly continue the campaign with so few troops as he has?" *Joinville answered:*

It is said, Sire (I do not know if it is true), that the King has not yet spent his own money, but only that of the clergy; let him then spend his money and send to fetch knights from Morea and overseas; when it is known that the King is spending well and lavishly, knights will come to him from all quarters, and he will continue the campaign for a year if it please God, and during that time he will set free the poor prisoners who have been taken in God's service and his own, and who will never be freed if the King departs.

Silence fell in the assembly. "There was none there who had not some of his near relations in prison; and so," *says Joinville,* "no one chid me, but all began to weep." *The next to speak, Master William of Beaumont, Marshal of France, declared that the Seneschal had spoken very well. This enraged another Beaumont, his uncle who, says Joinville, greatly desired to return to France.*

He upbraided him very insultingly and said to him: "Filthy fellow, what do you mean? Sit down at once!" And the King had to intervene: "Master John, you do ill, let him speak." "Indeed, Sire, I will not." The Marshal had to hold his tongue, and after that none agreed with me [says Joinville] except the lord of Chatenay. Then the King ended the sitting: "Lords, I have heard you all carefully, and I will let you know what I have decided eight days from today." . . .

Then they set on me from all sides: the King will be mad, Master Joinville, if he sides with you against the whole council of the Kingdom of France. When the tables were laid, the King made me sit beside him to eat, as he always did when his brothers were not there. He did not speak to me once while the meal lasted, which was against his usual custom. I truly thought that he was angry with me, because I had said that he had not yet spent his own money and that he ought to spend it lavishly. While the King was saying his grace, I went to a barred window in an alcove near the head of the King's bed, and I leant my arms on the bars of the window and thought that, if the King returned to France, I would go to the Prince of Antioch, who thought of me as a relation, until such time as some other assistance reached the country, thanks to which the prisoners might be freed. . . . When I had got to this point, the King came and leant against my shoulders and put his two hands on my head. I thought it was Master Philip of Nemours, who had annoyed me very much that day because of the counsel I had given him, and I said: "Leave me alone, Master Philip"; but turning my head I felt the King's hand on my face and I knew it was the King from an emerald he wore on his finger, and he said to me: "Keep quiet now, for I have come to ask you how you dared to be so bold, you who are a young man, as to counsel me to remain, when all the important men, the wisest in France, counselled me to depart." "Sire," I said, "if I had some evil plan in my heart, I would in no wise counsel you to do so." "Do you say then," he asked, "that it would be an evil plan for me to depart, with God's help?" "Yes, Sire," I said. And he said to me: "If I stay, will you stay?" "I promise you yes, if I am able, either with my money or that of someone else." "Then be of good comfort," said he, "for I am very grateful to you for what you have counselled me, but do not say so to anyone all this week."

At the next session the King informed the barons what he had decided:

"The barons of this country say that, if I go away, the Kingdom of Jerusalem is lost, for none will dare to remain afterwards. I have therefore come to the conclusion that I will never abandon the Kingdom of Jerusalem that I came to protect and conquer; so my resolve remains as it has been hitherto. I therefore say to you barons who are here, and to all other knights who would like to stay with me: Come and speak fearlessly with me and I will give you so much that, if you do not want to stay, the fault will not be mine, but yours." There were many who heard that word and were astounded by it; and there were many who wept at it.

Saint Louis spent four years in the Holy Land and while he was there he restored the fortresses, calmed the dissensions formerly stirred up by the German Emperor, and renewed certain alliances, in particular those with the Assassins.

Joinville:

While the King was in Acre, messengers from the Old Man of the Mountain came to him. When the King returned from his Mass, he had them brought in to him. He made them sit down in such a way that in front there was an emir, well dressed and well equipped, and behind the emir a well-dressed young man who held three knives in his fist, the blade of each entering into the handle of the next; for if the King had refused to see the emir, he would have presented these three knives to him as an act of defiance. Behind him who held the knives, there was another who held a shroud wound round his arm, and he too would have presented this to the King to bury him in, if he had refused the request of the Old Man of the Mountain. . . .

The King asked them what they wanted. The envoys replied: that the Old Man of the Mountain should stop paying tribute to the Temple and the Hospital. The military orders were the only two forces that the Assassins feared; that was why they paid tribute to them. The King asked the envoys to come back and see him in the evening.

. . . When the emir returned, he found the King sitting with the Grand Master of the Hospital on one side and the Master of the Temple on the other. Then the King told the messengers to repeat what they had said to him in the morning and they said that they did not wish to repeat it except before those who in the morning had been with the King.

The two Masters then suggested to the King that they should each

come to see them separately, which they did; after which the messengers
were asked, very curtly, to return to the Old Man of the Mountain:

"We order you to return to your lord and to come back in a
fortnight from now, bringing to the King letters and presents
from your lord which the King will consider as payment and be
grateful to you for it." Within the fortnight the messengers of the
Old Man returned to Acre, bringing the King the Old Man's
shirt and a message from him to say that it was a token that, as
the shirt is closer to the body than any other garment, the Old
Man wanted in the same way to hold the King closer to his love
than any other king.

On another occasion the leader of the Assassins sent the King his ring
and a certain number of presents, including a crystal elephant and a set of
chessmen "inlaid with little flowers of amber".

Another well-known scene shows King Louis humbling, in the Holy
Land, the Grand Master of the Temple, the most dread authority oversea,
who had claimed the right to enter into treaties with the Sultan of
Damascus unknown to the King:

Joinville:

The King had the flaps of three of his tents raised and there
came there any common soldier who wished to; and the Master
of the Temple came there and all his knights, barefoot. . . . The
King made the Master of the Temple sit down in front of him and
the messenger from the Sultan, and he said to the Master: "Master,
you will say to the Sultan's messenger that you regret having made
truces with him without speaking to me of it; and because you
have said nothing to me of it, you will release him from all that
he has promised you, and return the whole treaty to him." The
Master took the treaties and gave them to the emir and said:
"I give you back the treaties that I was wrong to make and which
I regret." Then the King told the Master to rise and with him all
his brethren; and they did so. "Now, kneel down and ask pardon
for having gone against my will." The Master knelt down and
held out to the King the corner of his cloak and surrendered to
him everything he decided to take as a fine, according as he
should desire: "I rule," said the King first, "that Brother Hugh,
[Hugh of Jouy, Marshal of the Temple] who made these treaties

should be banished from the Kingdom of Jerusalem." Neither the Grand Master, who had been godfather of the Count of Alençon, the King's son, nor the Queen, nor anyone else could do anything to save Brother Hugh from leaving the Holy Land and the Kingdom of Jerusalem.

In order to appreciate what this public humiliation meant it must be remembered that in the thirteenth century the pride of the Templar was proverbial. But something important was at stake: the whole survival of the Holy Land depended on the unity that the presence of Saint Louis brought about between the Christians of Outremer, a unity which moreover did not survive him.

Saint Louis only left the Holy Land on April 24th, 1254, when he returned to France. But he had to take up arms again at the beginning of July 1270. He had been led to hope for the conversion of the Emir of Tunis. On July 18th he disembarked at Carthage and almost immediately the plague broke out in the army. Gravely ill with it, Saint Louis succumbed on August 25th, 1270, dying as he had lived.

Queen Margaret's confessor, William of Saint Pathus, has related the last moments of the saintly King:

On the Sunday before his death, brother Geoffrey of Beaulieu brought him the body of Jesus Christ and, when he had entered the bedchamber where the King lay ill, he saw him out of bed kneeling on the floor with his hands joined; and again on the night before the day of his death, while he was resting he sighed and said in a low voice: "O Jerusalem, O Jerusalem." And on the Monday, the day after Saint Bartholomew's day, the King raised his joined hands to heaven and said: "Fair Lord God, have mercy on those people who are here, and lead them to their country, that they may not fall into the hand of their enemies and be forced to deny your Holy Name." And a short while afterwards he said these words in Latin: "Father, I commend my spirit into your keeping." And when he had said that, he spoke no more. A little while after—it was soon after the hour of Vespers—he departed this life.

FROM ISLAM TO CHINA

✦✦

*I*N THE middle of the thirteenth century, the Crusades were to have the surprising side-effect of leading to direct contacts between the West and the Far East, as far as distant China and the city of Pekin, the residence of the Grand Khan of the Mongols.

In 1215 Jenghiz Khan, leader of the Mongols, seized Pekin. Less than ten years later, in 1223, a Mongolian expedition reached the banks of the Caspian and pillaged the Genoese warehouses established on the Black Sea. The Empire of the Khwarismian Turks then fell into the hands of these conquerors, who filled Islam with the terror that Islam itself had inspired in the world five hundred years earlier. Ibn-al-Athir relates that no one even dared to try and save himself from the "Tartar" horsemen, so that one day a single one of them seized a whole village, whose inhabitants remained paralysed by fear; and on another occasion, one of them met a group of seventeen Arabs and ordered them to tie themselves to each other with their hands behind their backs, and follow him; they were beginning to obey when one of them pulled himself together and slew the horseman.

Marco Polo, who lived in China for nearly twenty years, described the "Tartars" in the following words:

The Tartars drink mare's milk prepared in a way that makes it seem like white wine, and good to drink. They call it *koumiss*. Their garments are mostly of cloth of gold and silk, lined with rich skins like sable and ermine, and sumptuously adorned with squirrel and fox fur. And all their accoutrements are very beautiful and of great value. Their arms are bows and arrows and swords and axes; but they rely most on their bows, for they are excellent archers, the best that are known in the world. And on their backs they wear armour of leather that has been boiled and is very strong. They are good fighting men and very tough and valiant in battle. And they can endure more work than other people; for often, when it is necessary, they will go for a month, taking no meat with them, except the mare's milk they live on; and they will eat the flesh they hunt with the bow. And for their horses they have no need to carry either barley or straw or oats for they graze on the grass in the fields as they go, and are very obedient to their masters. And when it is needful, they will remain on horseback all night fully armed. And their horses go on grazing all the time. There are no people on earth who can so endure great pains and great discomfort, who have fewer wants to satisfy, and are better at conquering lands and kingdoms. And this can well be seen, for they are now lords of the greatest part of the world. They are very well commanded and I will tell you how.

You must know that, when any Tartar lord goes to war, he takes with him a hundred thousand men on horseback. He appoints a leader for every ten, and every hundred, and every thousand, and every ten thousand, so that he has only to command ten men and those ten men have only to command the other tens. And thus each one is only concerned with ten men; and by this means each one is responsible to his chief in so well ordered a manner that it is a marvel; for there are a great many men at the command of the master.

The most enlightened minds of the time realised what an advantage an alliance with the Mongols would be, in opposing the Moslem world; that was the reason why the first missionary attempts in the direction of the Far East began to be made at this time. In 1245, at the Council of Lyons, Innocent IV announced his project of sending messengers to the Mongols; on April 16th of the same year, the Franciscan brother John of Pian del Carpine set out accompanied by two other friars minor: Stephen of Hungary and Benoit of Poland.

The Empire of the Mongols at that time covered China, Persia and Korea; they had succeeded in imposing a sort of protectorate on Georgia, Armenia and on the Seldjuks of Asia Minor; they had inflicted some defeats on Russians and Bulgarians and had made incursions into Poland and Hungary. The death of Khan Ogodai, successor of Jenghiz Kahn in 1241, had necessitated the recall of the Tartar armies to Asia for the election of his successor, allowing Central Europe a little respite.

John of Pian del Carpine:

We went to see the King of Bohemia. As he was very friendly to us, he advised us to go by Poland and Russia, for he had relatives in Poland, who would help us to enter Russia. So after giving us two letters and a good escort, he ordered that our expenses should be borne by his vassals and his cities until we got to the Duke of Silesia, his nephew Boleslas. . . . He did likewise and we came to Conrad, Duke of Lenczy in whose house, by God's grace, Basil, Duke of Russia, had just at that moment arrived. Through him we were able to inform ourselves better concerning the Tartars: he had in fact sent them ambassadors who had already returned. So having learnt that one ought to give them presents, we bought some skins of beavers and other animals with the money which had been given us as alms for the expenses of our journey. Hearing of this, Duke Conrad, the Duchess of Cracovia, the Bishop and some knights gave us more of those furs. Then, at their request, Basil conducted us to his lands so that we might rest a little, and kept us for a few days at his expense.

John of Pian del Carpine had brought letters for the bishops of Russia from the Pope, exhorting them to return to the unity of the Church. But those to whom he was able to read them put off answering. And before long Duke Basil had them conducted to Kiev.

We went in danger of our lives because of the Lithuanians, who often make raids into the land of Russia, especially in the region through which we had to pass. . . . At Danilov [Ukraine] we fell so ill we nearly died; nevertheless, we had ourselves drawn by sleigh through the snow and the great cold. When we reached Kiev, we consulted the chief people of the place concerning our route. They replied that, if we took into the land of the Tartars the horses we had with us, they would all perish because of the depth of the snow, for they would not know how to find the grass under the snow as the Tartars' horses do, and we should not be able to find them anything to eat, for the Tartars have neither hay or fodder.

The whole thing was settled by a "bakhshish" handed to the governor so that when he was not there the horses, entrusted to the care of two servants, might be well looked after. On February 4th the missionaries reached Kanev on the Dnieper, the nearest town to the territory of the Tartars.

The first encounter was grim; an armed band spied the little troop of three brethren from a distance, at sunset, and fell upon them "horribiliter", says the text. A few small presents appeased them momentarily; but the next day they returned and the leader of the band, after interrogating them, decided to take them—always in return for gifts—to Kurencha. Kurencha was the residence of the "dux", with sixty thousand soldiers under his orders, who was responsible for the frontier dividing the territory conquered by the Mongols from that of the peoples of the West.

This was only the very first stage of the interminable route that was to bring the Christians first to Jenghiz' grandson, Batu, Khan of Kipchak, the Golden Horde, then to the Great Khan himself. To cross the immense plain of the land of the Cumans it took them more than five weeks (from Monday of the first week of Lent to the Wednesday of Holy Week). And yet, remarks John of Pian del Carpine, "We rode from morning till evening and often even by night, and changed horses three to four times a day". *One of the secrets of the power of the Mongols was in fact the posting stages where one could find a fresh horse at regular intervals.*

John of Pian del Carpine:

We had made great haste the whole way because our Tartars had told us that they were hurrying to take us to the ceremony arranged many years before for the election of the Emperor. That is why we rose early and went until night without eating; and sometimes we arrived so late that we did not eat in the evening, but what we ought to have eaten in the evening, they gave us in the morning. And as the horses were changed more often, we had no need to spare them and we rode fast and without respite, at as swift a pace as they could make.

In the course of the assembly of 1246, Guyuk, grandson of Jenghiz Khan, was elected to succeed Ogodai as Great Khan. John of Pian del Carpine described his own arrival there.

He ordered us to be given a tent and entertained at his expense, as he did for the Tartars; but we were treated better than the other envoys. . . . After we had stayed there five or six days, he sent us to his mother in the place where the solemn assembly was

meeting. When we got there we found a vast tent, all hung with
purple; it was so big that it looked to us as if it could hold more
than two thousand persons. . . . All the leaders were assembled
there, each with his men. The first day they all wore white
robes, the second red; then Guyuk entered the tent and on the
third day they all put on garments of blue-purple, and on the
fourth very beautiful "baldequins" [very rich stuff from Bagh-
dad]. . . . The armed guards stood at the entrances to the tent, and
the whole assembly displayed real barbarian luxury; those who
were mounted were, in my opinion, each carrying, what with
their bridles, breast-plate ornaments and saddles, at least twenty
gold marks' worth. The assembled chiefs were apparently
busying themselves with the election of the Emperor, and the
people, kept at a distance, looked on.

Towards midday they began to drink mare's milk. They drank
so much until the evening that it was prodigious to see. To us . . .
they gave beer made of barley, for we did not drink mare's milk.
And in that they thought they were doing us great honour: but
they insisted on our drinking, which we could not manage
because we were not used to it. We made them understand that
this upset us, and they stopped forcing us.

*There were there, come to take part in the election, envoys from
nearly all the Eastern nations: China, Manchuria, etc. . . . The Caliph
of Baghdad, the other Saracen sultans, and the King of Georgia had
each sent ambassadors. Duke Yaroslav of Russia had come in person;
with unfortunate results for him, for the poor man died in the course of
those solemn assemblies, probably poisoned. In all, our traveller puts
the number of the envoys at 4,000, all bearing gifts or tribute levied by
the Mongols on the subject populations—"more than 500 ox-drawn
wagons, filled with gold, silver, silken stuffs and precious furs".*

*Later on John of Pian del Carpine had an interview with Guyuk.
First he was carefully searched to make sure that he had no knife on him,
and he was asked to bring gifts, which the poor monk excused himself
from doing: "We could not as we had already given all we had."
In any case the interview proved abortive. Guyuk had decided to make
war on the West; the missionary's words had no more effect on him
than the Pope's letters.*

*As for the Empress-Mother, she received Brother John well and gave
the envoys presents of fur pelisses, which the Tartar servants immediately*

stole from them. Brother John had long since learnt to shut his eyes to such practices. The little troop then set off on the road back to the West and ended by finding again at Kiev those whom they had left there. The welcome they received made them realise that no one had expected to see them again alive; on the return journey across Russia, Poland and Bohemia they were met everywhere with marks of astonishment, demonstrations of joy and feasts and banquets which the poor men in any case greatly needed to regain their strength. John of Pian del Carpine brought back no positive result, but he had made a first approach to the terrible peoples of the Far East, and it was thanks to his narrative that henceforth some details were known about their life, customs and redoubtable power.

Consequently another mission was sent to the Mongols: that of the the Dominican, Ascelin of Lombardy, which proved unfruitful in spite of its length (three years and seven months). Shortly afterwards Saint Louis, when he was in Cyprus on the way to Egypt at the time of his first crusade, himself received an embassy from the Mongols. He at once resolved to reply by making further attempts to turn the Mongols into allies in the struggle against Islam.

John Sarrasin:

It happened at Christmas that one of the great princes of the Tartars, called Elteltay, who was a Christian, sent a messenger to the King of France, at Nicosia in Cyprus. The King sent Brother Andrew, of the order of Saint James, to bring this messenger before him, and they each talked in their own language. Brother Andrew told the King in French that the greatest prince of the Tartars had become Christian on the day of Epiphany and many Saracens among the great lords with him. He also said that Elteltay with his whole army would come to the help of the King of France and of Christendom against the Caliph of Baghdad and against the Saracens, for he intended to avenge the great humiliations and the great injuries that the Khwarismians and other Saracens had inflicted on Our Lord Jesus Christ and on Christendom. And he said that their lord also suggested that the King should cross to Egypt in the spring to fight the Sultan of Babylon, and said that the Tartars would at the same time go and make war in the territory of the Caliph of Baghdad. In this way they would be able to help each other.

The King of France thought of sending his messengers with them to their lord Elteltay, and to the sovereign lord of the Tartars, who was called Guyuk, to learn if these things were true. They said that to go as far as the place where Guyuk dwelt would be quite half a year's journey. But Elteltay their lord and the army of the Saracens were not far off, for they were in Persia; they had ravaged it completely and brought it under the power of the Tartars. They repeated that the Tartars were entirely at the disposal of the King and Christendom.

When the fortnight of Candlemas had come, the messenger of the Tartars and the King's messengers set off together, that is to say: Brother Andrew of Saint James [Andrew of Longjumeau] and one of his brethren, and master John Goderiche and another clerk from Poissy, and Herbert the cellarer, and Gerbert of Sens. And at mid-Lent the King had news of them, that they were marching with banners unfurled towards the master of the Tartars, through the land of the unbelievers, and that they had whatever they wanted because of the fear inspired by the messenger of the master of the Tartars.

After Andrew of Longjumeau, another Franciscan brother, William of Rubruck, set out in May 1253, this time by the Black Sea. In the month of June he landed in the Crimea, at Sudak. Hope had been kindled when news had come of the conversion of Sartaq, son of Batu, to Nestorian Christianity.

William of Rubruck, no doubt of Flemish origin, obviously had a less patient character than Brother John, his predecessor. The account that he composed for Saint Louis, on his return, is full of complaints of the weather, the road, the savage, brutal Tartars whom he could not endure, and against the merchants who gave him faulty information, etc.

William of Rubruck:

When we found ourselves among these barbarians, it seemed to me as though I had entered another epoch; they surrounded us with their horses after having made us wait for a long time in the shade of their wagons. The first question was: "Have you been among us before?" When they learnt that we had not, they began to ask us impudently for some of our provisions. We gave them some biscuit and some wine that we had brought with us. When they had drunk a flagon of wine, they asked for another, saying that one did not enter a house on one foot. We did not give it, making the excuse that we had not got much. Then they began to ask us where we came from and where we wanted to go. I told them that we had heard that Sartaq was a Christian and that I wanted to go to him because I had to take him your letters. Then they asked us what there was in our wagons, and whether it was gold, silver or precious garments that I was taking to Sartaq. I answered that Sartaq would see what we were bringing him when we got to him, and that it was not their business to ask that; but that they should have me taken to their chief and if he was willing to give me an escort as far as Sartaq, that he should do so; otherwise I would turn back. . . . So they agreed to this and had us conducted, but not without having made us wait a long time, demanding our bread for their children, and everything that they saw on our servants: knives, purses, gloves, belts, they marvelled at and wanted to take. I would not let them, saying that we still had a long way to go, and that we could not so soon deprive ourselves of the things we needed for such a long journey. Then they called me a liar; to speak truth, they took nothing from us by force, but they asked very insolently for everything they saw, and whatever one gave them was a waste, for they are ungrateful. They consider themselves the lords of the earth and that consequently no one ought to refuse them anything. . . . When they had taken themselves off, it seemed to me that I had escaped from the hands of demons. . . .

First encounter with a Mongol chief, Jagatai:

. . . One morning we met the wagons of Jagatai loaded with their houses: I thought I saw a great town advancing. I was also astonished at the vast droves of oxen, horses and sheep. . . . Then the boy who was leading us began to say that we must give something to Jagatai; he made us halt and went off to announce our arrival. . . . His interpreter came to us and when he learnt that it was our first visit, he at once asked for some of our provisions, which we gave him; next, he asked us for a garment to go and announce our arrival to his master; we said we could not do this. Then he asked us what we were taking to his master. We took a flagon of wine and filled a basket with biscuits and put on a tray apples and other fruit. But he was not pleased that we were not bringing some precious garments. So we went in with fear and reverence. The chief was on his bed, a little zither in his hand, his wife beside him; I really thought that she had had her nose cut away between her eyes, so as to look more like a monkey; she had absolutely nothing in the way of a nose and had anointed the place with some black ointment, and her eyebrows too; it was ghastly.

Brother William explained the symbols of the faith to the Mongol as best he could through an interpreter ("who had neither wit nor eloquence"). But he obtained nothing but a nod of the head; after which, the leader gave him two men as escort to take him to Sartaq.

In the course of the journey he met some Christians, Caucasians of the Greek rite. Their faith was very rudimentary, tainted with superstitions that Brother William tried to dissipate as well as he could. All the same it was a difficult expedition: they found nothing to buy, for their Greek money was refused: the barbarians were only interested in arms and precious garments.

When our servants offered them Byzantine coins they rubbed them between their fingers and held them up to their nostrils, to see from their smell whether they were of copper; and they gave us nothing to eat except pungent and foetid cow's milk. We were already beginning to be short of wine. The water was so muddied by the horses that it was not drinkable. If it had not been for the biscuits that we had, and the grace of God, we should no doubt be dead.

In addition there was the off-handedness and utter impudence of those they had just met ("they would have trampled over us to see what we had"), the heat, and, to raise Brother William's impatience to the uttermost, the incompetence of the interpreters:

What irritated me the most was that, when I wanted to say a few edifying words, my interpreter said to me: "Don't make me preach, for I don't know how to say words like that." And he spoke the truth, for I realised later, when I began to understand their language a little, that, when I said something, he translated all wrong, saying whatever came into his head; so seeing that it was dangerous to use him as an intermediary, I preferred to keep silent.

On the day of Saint Magdalen (July 22nd), they reached the banks of the Don ("it divides Asia from Europe, as the Nile divides Asia from Africa"); they crossed it, not without various setbacks, and then came the Volga before they at last arrived at the court of Sartaq.

I said to the interpreter Coiat, a Nestorian Mongol, that we had come to see his master, and I asked him to help us so that we could show him the letters we had brought. I apologised for the fact that, being a monk, possessing and receiving nothing, and carrying neither money nor any other precious thing, but only the books and ornaments for the Mass with which I served the Lord, I had brought no present either for him or his master. As I had given up my own possessions, I could not be the bearer of those of others. He then replied gently enough that I was right to act thus as I was a monk; in this way I was observing my rules, and he had no need of anything of mine; but if we needed anything of his, he would give it us. After a moment he asked us to pronounce a blessing on him, which we did, and he asked us who was the most powerful lord among the Franks. I said to him: The Emperor, at least if he governs his land in peace. "No," he answered, "the King of France." He had in fact heard tell of him from Lord Baldwin of Hainault. I even saw there a member of the Khan's household who had been in Cyprus and related all he had seen there. Then we returned to our encampment.

The next day I sent him a flagon of delicate wine, which had kept very well in spite of the length of the road, and a basketful of biscuits; this pleased him greatly and that evening he kept our servants with him.

The day after, he asked me to come to the court, bringing the King's letters and the books and adjuncts for the Mass with me, for his master desired to see them. This we did, loading one of the wagons with the books and the ornaments, and another with bread, wine and fruit. He wanted all the books and sacred vestments explained to him; and many Tartars, both Christians and Saracens, surrounded us on horseback. When he had seen these things, he asked us if we would give it all to his master. When I heard that, I was displeased and afraid, but I gave no sign of it and I answered: "We beg your master to condescend to receive this bread, this wine and this fruit, not as gifts for they are a small matter, but as a sign of greeting, that we may not present ourselves before him with empty hands. He will himself see the letters from our lord king, and he will know by them why we have come to him, and then we ourselves and all that is ours will be at his disposal. These vestments are in fact sacred things and none but priests are allowed to touch them. Then he told us to put them on to go to his master, which we did; I myself, clad in most precious vestments, bore against my breast the cushion which was very beautiful, and the Bible which you gave me, as well as the very beautiful psalter that the Queen gave me, in which were very beautiful pictures. My companion took the missal and the cross, and the clerk, clad in a surplice, took the censer: in this manner we went to his master, and they raised the felt curtain which hid the door, so that he might see us. . . . We entered chanting the Salve Regina. . . . Coiat handed him the censer with the incense which he looked at, taking it carefully in his hands; then he handed him the psalter, which he looked at for a long time, and so did his wife who was sitting beside him; then he took the Bible and he himself asked if the Gospel was there. I said to him: "And all the Holy Scriptures too." He took the cross in his hand and asked: "Is that the image of Christ?" I said it was. The Nestorians and the Armenians do not in fact show on their crosses the figure of Christ. One might think they feel uncomfortable at the Passion and blush for it. Then he ordered those present to stand back so that he could see our ornaments better. At that point I handed him our letters, with the translations in Arabic and Syrian. I had had them translated in Acre into the two tongues. . . . We left and took off our vestments; he took the bread, the wine and the fruit, and had the vestments and books taken back to our encampment. All that happened on the day of the feast of Saint Peter in chains (August 2nd).

Sartaq ordered them to go to the court of his father, Batu, who himself sent them to the Grand Khan Mongka at Karakorum, in North China. Brother William left very disappointed:

I do not know whether Sartaq believes in Christ or not. I know he does not want to be called Christian; he seems rather to laugh at the Christians. . . . He receives the Saracen merchants who travel through his lands rather better than the Christians. However, he has Nestorian priests about him, who sing him the office.

*So the journey continued, full of dangers and fatigues, as before.
As he went along, William corrected the geographical notions of
Isidore of Seville, which were accepted by the medieval world: for
instance, that the Caspian Sea opened into the ocean:* "What Isidore
says is not true, it does not touch the ocean at any point, but is
surrounded by land on all sides." *He adds that one must reckon four
months to travel all round it.*

*The court of Batu seemed to him like a town, covering three or four
leagues.*

*He was brought into the presence of the potentate with the same
ceremonial as John of Pian del Carpine a few years earlier:*

We were led into the middle of the tent. . . . He looked at us
attentively, as we looked at him; in stature I thought he resembled
Master John of Beaumont, whose soul may God preserve. At last
he commanded me to speak, and at that our guide ordered me to
bend my knees and speak. I bent one knee, as one does to a man,
but he signed to me to kneel down on both knees, which I did,
not wanting to fight over that. Then he commanded me to speak,
and I, thinking that I ought to pray to God because I had bent
both knees, began by a prayer, saying: "Lord, we pray God
from whom you come, and who has given you this worldly
wealth, that He will afterwards give you heavenly riches, because
those without these are useless." He listened with attention and I
added: "You must know for a certainty that you will not
have the riches of Heaven unless you are a Christian. For God says:
He who will believe and be baptised will be saved, but he who
will not believe will be damned." At these words he began to
smile, and the others began to applaud in mockery of us. My
interpreter fell silent and I had to exhort him not to be afraid.
When silence was re-established I said to him: "I came to your
son because we had heard that he was a Christian, and I brought
him letters from the King of France; he it is who sent me here to
you, you must know why." Then he made me rise and asked
your name, mine, that of my companions and of the interpreter,
and had it all written down. He told us he had known that you
had left your land with your army to make war. I said that it was
against the Saracens, who are desecrating the house of God and
Jerusalem. He asked me also if you had ever sent ambassadors to
him? To you, I said, never. Then he made us sit down and gave us

some of his milk to drink—for they think it important that one should drink koumiss with him, in his house.

They had still four months' journey to go to reach Mongka and, as it was then September, winter was not far off. At Batu's order the two monks were given the equipment they needed to brave those lands of snow and ice. This consisted of the same garments that the Mongols wore: a pelisse and stockings of sheepskin, boots lined with felt, fur hoods. Brother William tells of the interminable road, the camping in the evening round a meagre fire of dung that sometimes only half-cooked the meat; the wild asses they saw on the plain in the distance, the buffaloes, etc. He speaks of the customs and religion of the peoples whose lands they passed through, Tibet included. He was a shrewd observer, with the capacity for feeling equal astonishment at different kinds of writing, diverse beliefs, bizarre customs, or paper money.

There are Nestorians in fifteen towns of Cathay, and in that called Segin lives their bishop; outside there they are plain idolaters. The priests of the idols of those peoples wear wide yellow hoods. If one can believe what I heard tell, there are hermits too, who live a very austere life in the woods and the mountains. The Nestorians are very ignorant. Nevertheless, they say their offices and have sacred books in Syriac, which they do not understand, which means that they sing as do monks in our country who are ignorant of grammar; which results in great corruption. They are above all usurers and drunkards, and some, who live with the Tartars, like them have several wives.

. . . The ordinary money of Cathay is a card made of cotton [the word "paper" did not yet exist], of the width and length of a hand, on which are printed lines like those of the seal of Mongka. The Cathayans write with a brush like that of a painter, and a single sign comprises several letters expressing a single word. The Tibetans write like us, from left to right, and have characters just like ours. The people of Tangut write from right to left like Arabs.

The banknotes of the Mongols were in fact stamped with the Emperor's seal. Issued by the Mint of Pekin they were binding legal tender throughout the kingdom on pain of death: no one trifled with financial measures in the China of that time. The use of this "paper" money is

*attested from at least the reign of Ogodai, about 1236. Kubla-Khan
later inaugurated the system of inflation which finally, in the fourteenth
century, was to bring about the destruction of Mongolian power.*

Another kind of surprise awaited Rubruck at the end of the route:

A woman called Paquette, from Metz in Lorraine, who had
been taken prisoner in Hungary, came to find us and prepared the
best banquet she could for us. She belonged to the court of a
Christian lady; . . . she told us of the unheard-of privations she
had had to endure, before being attached to her court. But she was
at that time happy enough, for she had a young Russian husband,
who had made her the mother of three beautiful little children,
and who was a carpenter, which is a good trade among the Tartars.

Among other things she told us that at Karakorum there was a
goldsmith called William who came from Paris; his family name
is Boucher and that of his father, Laurence Boucher. She even
thinks he has a brother who lives on the Grand Pont and is called
Roger Boucher.

. . . As for the town of Karakorum, you must know that, with
the exception of the Palace of the Khan himself, it is not equal to
the burg of Saint-Denis, and the monastery of Saint-Denis is
twice as fine as the palace. There are in it two quarters, one of the
Saracens where the markets are situated and where the merchants
abound, because of the court which is not far away, and also
because of the great number of the ambassadors. The other quarter
is that of the Cathayans, who are all artisans. Outside these, one
sees large palaces that are inhabited by the secretaries of the court.
And there are twelve temples there consecrated to idols of
different nations, two mosques where the law of Mahomet is
observed, and a Christian church at the end of the town. The town
is surrounded by a wall of earth and it has four gates. At the east
side they sell millet and other grains, which are moreover very
rare; at the west end they sell sheep and goats; on the south, oxen
and wagons; on the north, horses.

*More astonishing seemed to him the palace of the Khan, and above
all the "automatic distributors" constructed by the Parisian goldsmith:*

Mongka has at Karakorum a great court below the walls of
the town, enclosed within a brick wall as priories of monks are

with us. There is there a palace where he gives a great banquet twice a year, at Easter when he passes that way, and in summer when he returns. This latter feast is the greater, because then all the notables who have gone two months' distance away from the court return to it, and the sovereign distributes to them garments and gifts and with his largesse displays all his magnificence. There are many houses there too, as long as barns, in which his provisions and treasures are kept. At the entrance to this great palace—for it would not be fitting to take skins full of milk or any other drink in there—Master William of Paris placed a great tree of silver, at the foot of which are four lions of silver each of which spouts through a pipe white mare's milk. In the tree are four pipes going right to the top of it, and from there they pour out their liquid through the throats of gilded serpents whose tails enlace the trunk of the tree. One of these channels pours out wine, another caracosmos or purified mare's milk, another boal or mead, another rice-beer. . . . This palace is like a church, with a nave in the middle and two side-aisles separated from the nave by two rows of pillars. There are three doors on the south side, and before the middle door, inside, is this tree. The Khan has his throne on a platform at the north end, so as to be seen by everyone, and two staircases lead up to it: one is used to take him up his food, and the other to come down. The space between the tree and these staircases is empty, for there stands the officer whose task is to hand the Khan the dishes he desires to eat, and the ambassadors who bring him gifts; and as for him, he sits on high, like a god. . . .

When he got back to Antioch, on June 29th, 1256, Rubruck did not fail, in his report to the King of France, to pass on all the observations he had been able to make at the court of Mongka, particularly on the relations between the Mongols and Islam.

I saw there at that time an ambassador of the Caliph of Baghdad, who had had himself carried to the court on a litter between two mules, and I was told he had made peace with the Tartars, the condition being that he would supply them with ten thousand horses in time of war. Others said on the contrary that Mongka would not make peace unless the Arabs destroyed their fortresses. The ambassador is said to have answered him: "When you have wrenched all the shoes from your horses' hoofs, we will demolish all our fortresses." I also saw ambassadors from the Sultan of India, who had brought with them eight leopards and two greyhounds: these had been trained to stand on the cruppers of the horses, as leopards do. When I enquired about this country of India, they pointed to the West. And these ambassadors journeyed back with me for about three weeks always going west. I also saw there ambassadors from the Sultan of Turkey; they brought precious gifts and told us (I heard them with my own ears) that their master lacked neither gold nor silver, but men; whence I concluded that he was asking for help in case of war.

The Khan's answer to the suggestions of alliance with the West, a reply that Rubruck was instructed to transmit to Saint Louis, was somewhat disquieting in tone:

We send you . . . by your afore-mentioned priests, the command of the eternal God that we would have you understand. And when you have received it and believed it, if you desire to obey us you will send us your ambassadors and notify us in this way whether you wish to live in peace or in war with us. When through the power of the eternal God the whole world shall be united in joy and peace, from the East to the West, then it will be revealed what we can do, if you have heard and understood the command of the eternal God. If you resist it, saying: "Our land is far off, our mountains are high and many in number, our sea is wide", and if, encouraged by this thought, you were to declare war on us, the eternal God knows that we know what we can do, He makes easy what is difficult, and brings near what is far off.

William of Rubruck's conclusions concerning the chances of an agreement between China and the Western world are not hopeful; for him the victories of the Mongols were essentially due to the fact that their people were content with an extremely low standard of living, and subject to an iron discipline. The most he does is to give information for future missions to the Far East:

I will tell you in confidence that if your peasants—I am not speaking of the kings or the knights—were willing to walk as do the kings of the Tartars, and be satisfied with the sustenance of those potentates, they would become masters of the world.

It seems to me useless for a religious like myself, or for preaching friars, to go henceforward to Tartary. But if the Pope, who is the head of all the Christians, were willing to send a bishop there in a suitable manner, and to answer all the letters that the Khan has already sent three times to the French (the first to Pope Innocent IV of happy memory, and the second, to you; the third time, by the intermediary of David, who deceived you, and finally, by me), he could say to the Khan everything he wished, and carry out everything contained in his letters. The Khan listens readily to everything an ambassador says, and always asks if he has nothing to add; but it is important that the ambassador should have a good interpreter, and even several, and money to spend. . . .

These first contacts bore fruit and occasioned attempts at evangelisation towards the end of the thirteenth century. In the meantime, Argoun, the Mongol King of Persia, had made advances to Christendom that had remained without result, and even sent to the Pope and the Kings of the West an ambassador, the Chaldaean bishop of Turkish origin called Rabban Sauma. Philip the Fair, who was then King of France, was too taken up with his own ambitions to listen with an attentive ear to the envoy of the Mongols. Pope Nicolas IV tried through him to renew the links with the Church of Chaldaea and sent to Baghdad the Dominican Ricold of Monte-Croix; a small convent of Dominicans was established at Maraghah, and a hierarchy sketched out, since one of the preaching friars was appointed bishop of the region in 1318. In 1289, Argoun renewed his proposals for an alliance, addressing to Philip the Fair a letter which is now in the Archives Nationales of France; it is a magnificent document written on a scroll of stamped, official paper.

In this letter the King proposed that they should launch an attack against Jerusalem, which might take place two years later. This was a startling project if one thinks that precisely two years later, in 1291, Acre was taken by the Mameluks of the Sultan al Ashraf, and that its fall marked the disappearance of the Kingdom of the Holy Land and the massacre of the Christians who lived there. As Argoun had died in the meantime, the hopes begun by the Mongolian alliance were short-lived.

THE END OF THE LATIN KINGDOM
OF THE EAST

✝✝✝

*I*T WAS a Turkish Mameluk, the Sultan Baibars, who dealt Frankish Syria the final blows. He had first distinguished himself, at the head of the Mameluk guard, when Saint Louis' brother, Robert of Artois, rashly pursued the Turks through Mansourah and was there slain. A few months later Baibars took part in the conspiracy that led to the slaughter of Saladin's last descendant, the Sultan Turan-shah, under the terrified eyes of the Frankish prisoners. Joinville related the scene, which he witnessed.

Turanshah had had built "a tower of planks of fir, enclosed round with painted cloth"; when the Mameluk guard attacked him as he was leaving a banquet he had given them, his first thought was to take shelter there:

Joinville:

The Sultan, who was young and fleet of foot, fled into the tower that he had had made, with three of those who had eaten with him. They called out to him to come down; he asked that they should first guarantee his safety. They replied that they would make him come down by force and that he was not in Damietta, and they threw at him Greek fire, which caught the tower that was made of fir-planks and cotton fabric. The tower burst rapidly into flames, so that I never saw such a beautiful, soaring blaze. When the Sultan saw it he came down with all speed and fled towards the river along the path which I mentioned to you earlier ... [The Mameluks] had broken up the whole surface of the road with their swords and, as the Sultan was passing on his way to the river, one of them drove his spear into his ribs and the Sultan fled towards the river trailing the spear. And they all came down and even plunged into the water and slew him in the river quite near our galley where we were.

A series of assassinations—among others that of the Sultan Qutuz whose lieutenant he was, and then of his Damascan successor—brought the whole Moslem world under the authority of Baibars. René Grousset called him a Turk from Russia "who had in his veins a little of the blood that produced Ivan the Terrible and Peter the Great". And the Arab historians spare no detail to describe the man:

Ibn al-Furad:

The Sultan never gave his officers a moment's rest; he levied heavy taxes on the peoples; his vizier introduced great administrative measures; under his rule most of the rich people perished in torment; he had a particular aversion to Christians and Jews. One day when he needed money he had all the Christians from Cairo and Old Cairo brought to him, their patriarch at their head, and ordered that they should be thrown into a great ditch that he had had dug for the purpose, and where a fire had been lit. The Christians, appalled, offered money to ransom themselves, and were set free. Cudgels were used to collect taxes; a great many Christians turned Moslem; many others expired under torture.

When Baibars left for his expedition in Asia Minor, he levied a special tax on the inhabitants of Damascus to pay for the cost of the war: this measure provoked indignation. The Imam Mohieddin, a very pious man venerated throughout the country, came to remonstrate with him. Baibars listened to him with much respect and said, to mollify him: "Permit it, O my master, this one time more. As soon as this war is ended, I will abolish the tax and we will be friends." These words calmed people's minds; Baibars was victorious; but on his return he sent this order to the head of the Syrian Council: "We will not dismount, we will not take our foot from the stirrup, until Damascus has paid two hundred thousand pieces of silver, its province three hundred thousand, its towns and villages another three hundred thousand, and southern Syria a million pieces of silver." This excessive harshness changed the joy of the Syrians into sadness; the people longed for the death of the Sultan; all went to complain to the Imam Mohi-eddin; and the tax was not yet levied when the Sultan died.

Some relate this event thus. Baibars was passionately fond of *koumiss*, which he drank with all the more pleasure because he abstained entirely from wine and all other spirituous liquors. On his return from Asia Minor, finding himself at Damascus, he one day assembled his emirs to drink some of this *koumiss* with them. He enjoyed himself so excessively that he drank too much and was seized with fever. It was then Thursday [June 17th]; on the following Saturday, since his fever was increasing, someone, in the absence of a doctor, gave him a potion to soothe him; the malady at once grew worse and it was not long before he breathed his last.

Faced with this cruel warrior, who knew neither pity nor scruple, the last descendants of the Crusaders showed themselves unbelievably inadequate. The inhabitants of what had been the Kingdom of Jerusalem spent their last days in a frenzy of pleasure, to which they gave free rein during the coronation of Henry II of Cyprus (1286):

Gerard of Montreal:

They kept holiday for fifteen days in a place in Acre called the Inn of the Hospital of Saint-John, where there was a very large palace. And it was the finest festival that had been known for a hundred years, with rejoicings and tourneys. They imitated the Round Table and the Queen of Feminia, that is to say knights dressed as ladies jousted together. Then they imitated nuns who jousted with monks; and they imitated Lancelot, Tristan and Palamides, with many other delectable and pleasant games.

But the young man who was crowned in the midst of these extravagant tourneys was an epileptic. . . .

Meanwhile, Baibars, in less than three years (1265–68), had forced the finest fortresses of Frankish Syria to capitulate one after the other: Caesarea, Arsuf, Safed, Jaffa, Beaufort. Then he attacked Antioch. A letter which he wrote to the Count of Tripoli, Bohemond IV, leaves no doubt as to the savagery with which that war of extermination was waged:

Baibars:

You will remember our last expedition against Tripoli . . . how we swept the churches from the face of the earth, how wheels turned where once the houses stood, how on the sea-shore there rose piles of corpses that looked like peninsulas, how men were killed and children reduced to slavery, how free people became slaves, how trees were cut down leaving only enough wood for our machines. . . . how we pillaged your riches and those of your subjects, including the women, children and beasts of burden; how those of our soldiers who had no family suddenly found themselves with wives and children, how the poor man became rich, the servant was waited upon and the pedestrian found a mount. . . .

And he goes on to enumerate the episodes of the recent siege of Antioch:

Ah! if you had seen your knights trampled under the hooves of the horses, your town of Antioch given over to ruthless pillage and become the prey of everyone, your treasures distributed by the hundredweight, the ladies who lived there sold at the rate of a gold piece for four! If you had seen the churches and the crosses overthrown, the leaves of the sacred Gospels scattered, the sepulchres of the patriarchs trampled on. If you had seen your enemy the Moslem walking on the tabernacle and the altar, immolating the monk, the deacon, the priest, the patriarch! If you had seen your palaces given over to the flames, the dead consumed by the fire of this world before that of the other, your castles and their dependences annihilated, the Church of Saint-Paul in ruins from top to bottom! . . .

After Antioch it was Tripoli's turn to succumb, besieged in 1289 by the armies of Baibars' successor, the Sultan Qalawun, with atrocious butchery:

Abu'l Feda:

The inhabitants fled towards the port, but very few were able to embark. The majority of the men were slain, the women and children reduced to slavery. When the slaughter was ended, the town was razed to the ground. Near the town was an islet, where there stood a church of Saint Thomas. An enormous crowd had taken refuge there. The Moslems galloped into the sea on horseback or swam to the islet. All the men who were there had their throats cut. Some time after I went to that islet and found it full of putrefying corpses; it was impossible to stay there because of the stench.

The Latin Kingdom was reduced to a single fortress, that of Acre. A truce was concluded with the Sultan, guaranteeing it a temporary survival. But this was stupidly broken by a troop of Italian Crusaders who had just disembarked:

Gerard of Montreal:

As some people remained in Acre, the truce which the King had concluded with the Sultan was well observed by both parties, and the poor villeins [Saracen peasants] went back to Acre, carrying their goods to sell as they used to. It chanced one day, by the machination of the enemy from hell, who delights to perform evil deeds among good people, that those Crusaders who had come to help the city of Acre, as a good work for the sake of their souls, instead destroyed it, for they rode one day through the lands belonging to the city, and put to the sword all the poor villeins, Saracens from the countryside of Acre, who were carrying their goods, wheat and other things, to sell.

They also slew many Syrians who were bearded and belonged to the Greek religion, and because of their beards they slew them, taking them for Saracens. This was an evil deed and was the reason why Acre was taken by the Saracens, as you shall hear.

This massacre was the cause of the fall of the last Christian city in the East. In reprisal for it the Sultan al Ashraf embarked on the siege of Acre, which was the death knell of Frankish Syria.

Abu'l Mahasin:

The siege of Acre began on Thursday [early in April]. Warriors from every country fought there. Such was the enthusiasm of the Moslems that the numbers of volunteers far surpassed that of the regular troops. Many machines were set up against the town; a few came from those which had already been taken from the Franks; some were so large that they hurled stones weighing a hundredweight and even more. The Moslems made breaches in different places.

The besieging army comprised 66,000 mounted men and 160,000 foot-soldiers, whilst amongst the besieged there were 14,000 foot-soldiers and only 800 knights; the city contained in all some 35,000 inhabitants.

The vicissitudes of the siege were related by an eye-witness, known as the Templar of Tyre:

The Sultan had his tents and pavilions set up very close to one another. They stretched from the Toron as far as Samaria, so that the whole plain was covered with tents, and the Sultan's tent, which is called *dehliz*, was on an eminence, where there was a beautiful tower with gardens and vines from the Temple. . . . For eight days he remained before Acre without doing anything . . . and at the end of those eight days they set up and established the range of their engines, which cast stones weighing a hundredweight.

The Sultan had at his command powerful "artillery"; four great perriers, one aimed at each of the principal towers of the town. They began by beleaguering the one called the Accursed Tower.

They had their mounted men all armed, and their horses in housings, all round the city from one end to the other. . . . And finally they came to the ditch below the walls, and all those on horseback brought a log, each one on the neck of his horse, and threw them down behind the shields, and the pile became like a wall, against which an engine could do nothing.

During the siege, the King of Cyprus came to the help of the town. On the night of his arrival, the besieged lit great fires as a token of joy. But he only remained in the place three days; having seen the desperate state of the besieged, he dreaded sharing their dangers and withdrew.

He had sent two messengers to the Sultan who, according to the chroniclers, awaited them "in a little pavilion", and asked: "Have you brought me the keys of the town?" The messengers tried to extract other conditions from him, but the Sultan would hear nothing: "Be off with you then, I have nothing more to say."

One day our people decided in council to make a sortie on foot and horseback from every part of the town and set fire to the pyre. . . . And the Master of the Temple, a Provençal who was

Viscount of the Port of Acre, gave orders to set fire to the pyre of the Sultan's great engine; and they went out that night and got as far as the pyre; and he whose task it was to throw the fire threw it timorously so that it fell short and burst into flames on the ground. All the Saracens who were there were all killed, both those on horseback and those on foot. And our people, brethren and temporal knights, went so far forward among the pavilions that their horses got their legs tangled in the cords of the tents and stumbled, and the Saracens killed them; and in this way we lost that night eighteen mounted men; but we seized several Saracen shields and bucklers and trumpets and kettledrums. On our way back we came across many Saracens ambushed, all of whom we killed, for the moon shone like day and so we could see them easily. . . .

So the siege continued.

On the side of the King's Tower, the Saracens filled little canvas sacks with sand, and every mounted man carried a sack on the neck of his beast and threw it to the Saracens who were there; and when night came these Saracens took the sacks and spread them on the stones and made it all level like a pavement, and the next day, Wednesday, at Vespers they walked over the sacks and took the said tower.

When the tower had been taken as I have told you, the people were greatly afraid and the majority put their wives and children on board ship. The next day, Thursday, the weather was very bad and the sea so rough that the wives and children who had embarked on the ships could not bear it, so they disembarked again and returned to their homes.

And when the Friday came, before it was day, a great kettle-drum sounded very loud, and at the sound of that kettledrum, which made a very loud and horrible noise, the Saracens attacked the city of Acre on all sides. And the place where they entered first was that Accursed Tower that they had taken; and I will tell you of the way in which they came.

They came on foot, in countless numbers; and first came those who carried great tall shields, then those who threw Greek fire, and after those who shot darts and feathered arrows so thickly that it seemed as though rain was falling from the sky.

They seemed to strike on a wall of stone, and those who threw the Greek fire threw it so often and so thickly that one could hardly see for the dense smoke; and in the midst of the smoke the archers let fly masses of feathered arrows which wounded our people and our animals cruelly. . . . And when the Saracens had remained there for a while, they raised their shields and advanced a little, and when we buffeted their shields, they quickly lowered their shields and halted; and the fire-throwing and the arrows never ceased, and that hand-to-hand struggle continued until tierce.

Abu'l Mahasin

On Friday, at daybreak, when all was ready for a general assault, the Sultan mounted his horse with his troops; and we heard the sound of a drum mingled with horrible cries. The attack began just before the sun rose. Soon the Christians fled and the Moslems entered sword in hand. It was then towards the third hour of the day. The Christians rushed towards the port; the Moslems pursued them, killing and taking prisoners; very few escaped. The town was given over to pillage; all the inhabitants were massacred or reduced to slavery. In the middle of Acre rose four towers belonging to the Templars, the Hospitallers and the German or Teutonic knights. The Christian warriors made ready to defend themselves there. However, on the next day, Saturday, when Moslem soldiers and volunteers assaulted the house of the Templars and one of their towers, they offered of their own accord to surrender; their request was granted; the Sultan promised them safety; a flag was given to them as a protection and they planted it on top of the tower. But when the gates were opened, the Moslems, jostling their way in, prepared to pillage the tower and violate the women who had taken refuge there. Then the Templars closed the gates again and, falling on the Moslems who were in the tower, massacred them. . . .

The Templar of Tyre

The Sultan was greatly angered but gave no sign of it and sent to them once more to say that he well understood his men had died through their own folly and because of the outrage they had committed, and that he bore the Christians no grudge and they might come out safely in all confidence. The Marshal of the

Temple, a fair and prudent man ... believed the Sultan and came out towards him; but some of the brethren, who were wounded, remained in the tower. As soon as the Sultan got hold of the Marshal and the people of the Temple, he cut off the heads of all the brethren and all the men. ...

This barbarous act, in contempt of a given word, led to the third and last episode of the struggle:

... When the brethren who were inside the tower, and were not so ill that they could not help themselves, heard that the Marshal and the others had had their heads battered, they prepared to defend themselves. At that the Saracens prepared to mine the tower, and mined it and supported it with props, and those inside the tower surrendered, and the Saracens entered the tower in such numbers that the props which supported it gave way; and the stones collapsed and both the brethren of the Temple and the Saracens who were within died; and even in its fall the tower fell into the road and crushed more than two thousand Turks on horseback.

And thus was taken the city of Acre, on Friday the 18th of May, and the house of the Temple ten days after, in the way in which I have recounted.

CHRONICLERS AND HISTORIANS
QUOTED

FOR the various works in which these sources have been published, the reader is referred to the bibliographies in the three volumes of Steven Runciman's *A History of the Crusades*, Cambridge University Press, 1951–54. The most important collection of the sources is the *Recueil des Historiens des Croisades*, published by the Académie des Inscriptions et Belles Lettres, Paris, 1814–1906, where the texts of the Latin, Greek, Arabic and other oriental writers are given in a French translation as well as in their original tongue. It is these translations which were mainly used in the compilation of the French version of the present volume.

Fuller information concerning the chronicles and their authors can be found in Appendix I in each of the three volumes of Runciman's *History*.

ABD EL-LATIF, 1162–1231, wrote an *Autobiography* and other works. He was greatly reputed for his learning and his skill as a doctor.

ABU'L FEDA. A descendant of Saladin, who was present at the taking of the Castle of Margat, and in 1289 at the taking of Tripoli. He died in 1331. His *Moslem Annals* are merely a summary of the work of earlier historians, but were very popular.

ABU'L MAHASIN. An Arab chronicler of the fifteenth century.

ABU SHAMA, born in Damascus in 1203, he completed in 1251 his *Book of the Two Gardens*, a history of the reigns of Nur ed-Din and Saladin.

ALBERT OF AIX (Aachen) wrote in Latin, some time about the year 1130, the fullest contemporary account of the First Crusade, based largely on the eye-witness testimonies of returning soldiers and pilgrims. Although he did not himself visit the East, his history, at least for the years 1100–19, is regarded as very reliable. Nothing is otherwise known of him.

AMBROISE, a Norman who went on the Third Crusade, and afterwards wrote both a poem in old French, *L'Estoire de la Guerre Sainte* and, in Latin, the *Itinerarium Regis Ricardi*, an account of Richard Cœur-de-Lion's expedition on the Third Crusade.

ANNA COMNENA, the favourite daughter of the Byzantine Emperor, Alexius (1083–1118), and author of his biography, the *Alexiad*. This, the only important Greek account of the First Crusade, was written about forty years after the events of it.

Anonymi Gesta Francorum. The anonymous author of this, the most popular of contemporary accounts of the First Crusade, was an ordinary soldier in Bohemond's army. He wrote his history in the form of a diary during the expedition. It first appeared in 1101. Several later chroniclers republished it in altered versions.

ANONYMOUS OF MAINZ-DARMSTADT. This unknown author wrote a Hebrew chronicle called the *Memorial*.

BAUDRI OF BOURGUEIL, Archbishop of Dol, re-wrote the *Anonymi Gesta Francorum* in about 1110, under the title *Historia Jerosolimitana*.

BEHA ED-DIN IBN SHEDAD, wrote a *Life of Saladin*, whose friend and follower he was.

EDRISI, (or Idrisi), author of *Geography*.

ERNOUL, a squire of Balian d'Ibelin, whose eye-witness accounts of events, particularly those of May 1st, 1187, are contained in the *Chronique d'Ernoul et de Bernard le Trésorier*, an old French chronicle continuing the *History* of William of Tyre. Ernoul may even have written this French chronicle himself, and it may have formed part of a longer work by him, now lost.

Estoire d'Eracles, an old French translation and continuation of William of Tyre's *History*, made in the middle of the thirteenth century, with various alterations. The 'Eracles' of the title is the Byzantine Emperor Heraclius, who has no connection with the text.

FULCHER OF CHARTRES, the most reliable of the Latin chroniclers of the First Crusade, in which he took part, first with Stephen of Blois and later as chaplain to Baldwin of Boulogne. He wrote his *Gesta Francorum Iherusalem Peregrinantium* between 1101 and 1127.

GERARD OF MONTREAL, put together, about 1325, the various chronicles, covering the years 1131–1309, which make up the compilation known as the *Gestes des Chiprois*.

Gestes des Chiprois. This chronicle consisted of three parts. The first is a *Chronique de Terre Sainte*, from 1131 to 1222. The second, written about 1245, in French, by an Italian, Philip de Novara, is a history of the wars of the Ibelins, to whom he was devoted. The third section, covering the period 1249–1309, was by an author known as the Templar of Tyre, who was present at the final fall of Acre. He was not in fact a Templar himself, but acted as secretary to the Grand Master of the Temple, William of Beaujeu.

GUIBERT OF NOGENT, a monk who in about the year 1109 rewrote the *Anonymi Gesta Francorum* in a more critical tone, incorporating other testimonies, under the title *Historia Hierosolymitana*. He died in 1124.

History of the Patriarchs of Alexandria, an anonymous Arabic history, ending about the year 1260.

IBN ABI TAYYI, an Arab historian, born at Aleppo, whose work only survives in quotations.

IBN AL-ATHIR, 1160–1233, the greatest Arab historian of the thirteenth century, wrote a history of the Moslem world, the *Sum of World History*.

IBN AL-FURAD, 1335–1405, Arab historian. Wrote his *Chronicle* at the end of the fourteenth century.

IBN JUBAYR, born in Spain, went on pilgrimage to Mecca in 1183 and wrote his *Travels* in Arabic.

IMAD ED-DIN, 1125–1201, served first under Nur ed-Din and from 1173 onwards was secretary to Saladin. His account of Saladin's wars is the best authority for the latter's life.

JOHN ELEEMOSYNA, or Elemosina, a friar minor, wrote in 1136 *Chronicon seu Liber Romane Ystorie plurime*.

JOINVILLE, JOHN, Sieur of, 1224–1317, Seneschal of Champagne, accompanied Louis IX on his first Crusade and wrote his *Historie de Saint Louis*.

JOHN SARRASIN (or Sarrazin) a thirteenth-century troubadour.

MAQRISI, Arab historian of the fifteenth century, author of *Histoire des Sultans Mamelouks*.

Novgorod Chronicle, an account by a Russian pilgrim or merchant of Mongol affairs, with some interest in Byzantine matters.

ODO (EUDES) OF DEUIL, chaplain of Louis VII, whom he accompanied on his crusade as far as Attalia.Wrote the history of the Second Crusade in his *De Ludovici VII profectione in Orientum.*

ORDERIC VITALIS, a Norman. His *Historia Ecclesiastica* ends in 1138.

PHILIP OF NOVARA, see *Gestes des Chiprois.*

PIAN DEL CARPINE, JOHN, a Franciscan friar sent by the pope on an embassy to the Mongols, wrote a *Historia Mongalorum.*

RAYMOND OF AGUILERS, took part in the First Crusade as chaplain to Count Raymond of Toulouse. Wrote his *Historia Francorum qui ceperunt Jerusalem* during the siege of Antioch and completed it in 1099.

ROBERT OF CLARY, *c.* 1170–*c.* 1216, a crusader whose *Conquête de Constantinople*, in old French, is an eye-witness account.

SALOMON BAR SIMEON, author of a *Relation*, in Hebrew.

TEMPLAR OF TYRE, see *Gestes des Chiprois.*

USAMA IBN MUNQIDH, wrote his *Autobiography.*

VILLEHARDOUIN, GEOFFREY OF. A knight who took part in the Fourth Crusade and wrote, about 1209, *La Conquête de Constantinople.*

VITRY, JAMES OF. A Cardinal whose *Epistolae* and his *History of Jerusalem* are important sources of information on the Fifth Crusade.

WILLIAM OF RUBRUCK, a preaching friar sent by Saint Louis on an embassy to the Mongols, wrote an account of it in his *Itinerarium.*

WILLIAM OF ST. PATHUS, Confessor of Queen Margaret of Provence, wrote a *Vie de Saint Louis* based on the accounts of witnesses during the proceedings for the canonisation of the King.

WILLIAM OF TYRE, *c.* 1130–*c.* 1184. Born in the East, educated in France, he returned to Palestine about 1160 and was successively appointed Chancellor of the Kingdom and Archbishop of Tyre. He was also tutor to Baldin IV in his childhood. One of the most important medieval historians, his great work is the *Historia Rerum in Partibus Transmarinis Gestarum.*

INDEX

CAPRICORN TITLES

1. *Dewey,* ART AS EXPERIENCE. $1.45.
2. *Rilke,* NOTEBOOKS OF MALTE LAURIDS BRIGGE. $1.25.
3. *Adler,* WHAT LIFE SHOULD MEAN TO YOU. $1.25.
4. *Bell,* ART. $1.25.
5. *Whitehead,* MODES OF THOUGHT. $1.15.
7. *Olmstead,* SLAVE STATES. $1.45.
8. *Malone,* AUTO. OF THOS. JEFFERSON. $.95.
9. *Matthews,* THE FUGGER NEWSLETTERS. $1.25.
10. *Hough,* DARK SUN (D. H. LAWRENCE). $1.25.
11. *Hawkes,* COLERIDGE'S WRITINGS ON SHAKESPEARE. $1.35.
12. *Shaw,* ADVENTURES OF THE BLACK GIRL. $.95.
13. *Whitehead,* SYMBOLISM. $.95.
14. *Golding,* LORD OF THE FLIES. $1.25.
15. *Chekhov,* ST. PETER'S DAY. $1.25.
16. *Nashe,* UNFORTUNATE TRAVELLER. $1.15.
18. *Coates,* EATER OF DARKNESS. $1.15.
19. *Bryce,* THE AMERICAN COMMONWEALTH, 2 Vols.'$2.90.
20. *Moore,* CONFESSIONS OF A YOUNG MAN. $1.25.
21. *Tolstoy,* LAST DIARIES. $1.35.
22. *Wain,* LIVING IN THE PRESENT. $1.25.
23. *Lovejoy,* ESSAYS IN THE HISTORY OF IDEAS. $1.65.
24. *diPrima,* VARIOUS FABLES FROM VARIOUS PLACES. $1.15.
25. *Symonds,* THE REVIVAL OF LEARNING. $1.45.
26. *White,* THE BESTIARY. $1.65.
27. *Chesterton,* THE MAN WHO WAS THURSDAY. $1.35.
28. *Dewey,* QUEST FOR CERTAINTY. $1.45.
29. *Wood & Edmonds,* MILITARY HISTORY OF THE CIVIL WAR. $1.35.
30. POETRY OF BORIS PASTERNAK. $1.25.
31. *Helper & Fitzhugh,* ANTE-BELLUM. $1.45.
32. *Valency,* PALACE OF PLEASURE. $1.45.
34. FREMANTLE DIARY: THE SOUTH AT WAR. $1.35.
35. FOUR MODERN FRENCH COMEDIES. $1.35.
36. *Torrey,* LES PHILOSOPHIES. $1.65.
37. *Ault,* ELIZABETHAN LYRICS. $1.75.
38. *Symonds,* AGE OF THE DESPOTS. $1.65.
39. *White,* MISTRESS MASHAM'S REPOSE. $1.45.
40. *Gilbert,* THE LETTERS OF MACHIAVELLI. $1.65.
41. *Still,* THE WEST. $1.65.
42. *Myers,* HISTORY OF BIGOTRY IN THE UNITED STATES. $1.65.
43. *Armstrong,* GRAY WOLF. $1.45.